The "How To" Series For Men

How to Keep a Wife

Product manual and trouble-shooting guide

Jim Hatton, Ph. D.

ISBN-10: 1944154019

ISBN-13: 978-1-944154-01-1

Contents

For Rachael, whom I would like to keep.

Introduction

So you chased her until she caught you. The wedding was a smash and you've gotten into your life together. But you're starting to realize that this relationship is harder than most of the ones you've had before. Why is that? Should you go back to your bachelor life? Try to recall an early comic in the Calvin & Hobbs series. Calvin was in the living room with his father and questioned his Dad in an off-hand way. "Dad," he said, "Why do you live here in this house with Mom and me, instead of in a bachelor apartment with several scantily-clad women?" The Dad's puzzled look said it all.

OK men; clear your minds of the visual. There is a reason we make that choice. There <u>must</u> be. Some people say it comes out of a wish to be domesticated, to give up the "wild hunt" for a saner (and safer) family existence. Perhaps this is true, but men "of a certain generation" are frustrated. We've grown up working hard, trying to be successful, providing for our families, being dutiful sons, and thinking we're doing the right thing. We've also grown up with the notion that men are pigs. Even Time magazine reminds us of this on occasion. What's the truth? Are we heroes or livestock?

Men know the answer to this question. We must be heroes, just misunderstood ones. However, the men-as-pigs perception continues. This might be due to misunderstanding by women of men's motivations and behaviors, and from men's misunderstanding of women. This invites a comparison, albeit a biased one. Men <u>know</u> they don't understand women. For men, a woman is both a delightful foray into mystery and fantasy, and a maddening dervish of moods and confusion. We're confused and we admit it. Many women act as if they understand the inner workings of men, and they see men as "hairy women choosing to misbehave." The secret is that women don't understand men, but they don't <u>know</u> that they don't understand men. I've heard it suggested that women don't really want to understand men, they just want men to act like women. This might be true, but men want to please their wives, and understanding is crucial to that goal. Our part is that we don't understand how women think, or what they want, well enough to present ourselves so that they can respect and be happy with us. After all, what do we want from women besides for them to think well of us?

You can find lots of advice about how to find the right person both to marry and with whom to settle down. Men rarely ask for dating advice - most of the self-help books on this subject are written for women. Much less has been written about how to keep a good woman once you've found one, something in which men are often much more interested. That's what this comes to: learning how women are different from us, so you can make the good life you want with your Angel.

This book is devoted to helping men use their immense problem-solving skills to negotiate their relationships, but it takes license with political correctness. In that pursuit, we need to understand our own mistaken assumptions regarding women and communicating with them. With any luck, this will help men understand women better, and help them value themselves more as good people and not as failed evolutionary experiments. It should allow men to give women what they want, allowing men to get what they want from women. The companion book "Men – The Missing Manual" helps women find similar enlightenment about men; just because we bring home the bacon doesn't mean we ARE the bacon.

A warning to readers: I make many gross generalizations here for example and instruction. Since no generalization is true in every case (including this one), and since every person is different, be cautious in your application of these ideas. Any of these might not apply to you or your wife. I remind readers of this at several points in the book, but I felt it prudent to include a generalized (pun intended) warning here. Stereotypes are just gross generalizations, leftovers from historical conditions and cultural biases. They focus on differences between men and women and gloss over similarities. It might be the case that men and women are more alike than different in most psychological and sociological realms. However it's those differences when we expect to find similarities that often cause the confusion and problems. For example while we all have a head, two arms and two legs, it's good we don't look alike.

I also use the terms "men" and "women" in a stereotyped way. It might be more correct to refer to "masculine" and "feminine." While no less stereotyped, this might point out that roles can be gender-reversed. For example, imagine a marriage where the husband is a therapist and the wife is a professional wrestler. He might practice more connection and communication (traditional feminine traits) at work while she practices more competition and comparison (traditional masculine traits) at her job. This might change when they get home even if they don't trade clothing (or even if they do!).

Jokes based on stereotypes may be funny for several reasons. They reflect at least a kernel of truth or historical precedent; they often speak the socially awkward or politically incorrect position; and they stress differences instead of similarities. With any luck, these jokes and stereotypes will introduce a problem area from which we can distill a more specific route to understanding your particular relationship. At least we'll have fun trying.

When I first conceived of this book, I discussed several thoughts concerning its direction with my own lovely wife Rachael. I wanted to direct this at Baby Boomers, since they have been through "sliding down the razor blade of life" as Tom Lehrer[1] says. They have figured out how to manage their careers, families of origin and friendships, but might still be confused about how to please their mates. Yet I realized from my 20 years of practicing therapy with my clients that women are still a mystery to men at most ages. On one particular walk with our dogs, Rachael said, "it sounds as if you're aiming to help men figure out how to keep their wives!" The title stuck.

This book for men about women is written in a problem-oriented format. It's somewhat like a trouble-shooting guide to your wife. This is how we think, sometimes to our detriment. We find the problem, search our logic and experience for solutions to that problem, and sort out which one might best fit the problem. Each chapter explains certain concepts about areas of potential difficulties and ends with one or more example problems you might find. At the end of the book is a test to help decide which of you were paying attention and who fell asleep during class...

PART ONE - The General Case

1 - How do I know what my wife wants?

What Women Want a Man to be when they first start dating:

1. Handsome

2. Charming

3. Financially successful

4. A caring listener

5. Witty

6. In good shape

7. A stylish dresser

8. An appreciator of finer things

9. Full of thoughtful surprises

10. An imaginative, romantic lover

What Women Want a Man to be when they are age 32:

1. Nice looking (hair on his head)

2. Courteous when he opens car doors, holds chairs

3. Rich enough for a nice dinner

4. Willing to listen more than talks

5. Willing to laugh at my jokes

6. Able to carry bags of groceries with ease

7. An owner of at least one tie

8. Appreciative of a good home-cooked meal

9. *Able to remember birthdays and anniversaries*
10. *One who seeks romance at least once a week*

What Women Want a Man to be when they are age 42:
1. *Not too ugly*
2. *Someone who won't drive off until I'm in the car*
3. *Someone works steady, but splurges on dinner out occasionally*
4. *One who nods his head when I'm talking*
5. *Someone who usually remembers the punch lines of jokes*
6. *In good enough shape to rearrange the furniture*
7. *Someone who wears a shirt that covers his stomach*
8. *Someone who knows not to buy champagne with screw-top lids*
9. *Someone who remembers to put the toilet seat down*
10. *Someone who shaves most weekends*

What Women look for in a Man when they are age 52:
1. *Keeps his hair in nose and ears trimmed*
2. *Doesn't belch or scratch in public*
3. *Doesn't borrow money too often*
4. *Doesn't nod off to sleep when I'm venting*
5. *Doesn't retell the same joke too many times*
6. *Is in good enough shape to get off couch on weekends*
7. *Usually wears matching socks and fresh underwear*
8. *Appreciates a good TV dinner*
9. *Remembers my name on occasion*
10. *Shaves some weekends*

What Women look for in a Man when they are age 62:
1. *Doesn't scare small children*
2. *Remembers where bathroom is*
3. *Doesn't require much money for upkeep*
4. *Only snores lightly when asleep*
5. *Remembers why he's laughing*
6. *Is in good enough shape to stand up by himself*
7. *Usually wears some clothes*
8. *Likes soft foods*

9. Remembers where he left his teeth
10. Remembers that it's the weekend

What Women wish for in a Man when they are age 72:
1. Breathing, best if on his own
2. Doesn't miss the toilet too often

Unknown

What if you can't figure out what women want?

If you're a man, you've occasionally asked yourself, "What the heck do women (or perhaps this woman) want? And what do they want from me?" Hopefully the list above answered your questions. If not, then read on. You might have failed to figure this out in several arenas. A love interest might have rejected you ("You're the nicest guy I know, but..."). You might have bought her the wrong birthday gift ("No, it's a great blender, but I was hoping for something more sparkly") or failed to please her by your effort in taking out the trash ("Yes, you took out the kitchen trash, but you forgot the one in the guest room!"). In the movie "What Women Want," the male protagonist discovers he has the ability to hear the thoughts of the women around him. In the world of his advertising business, he uses this newfound ability to understand their silent attention to him. He also hears some of the private pains and agonies of his female co-workers. It finally leads him to lose his love interest when he tells to her he has also been stealing her professional ideas by reading her mind. Perfect use by a man of a competitive advantage, right?

Right, but wrong – it's a good competitive advantage, but that's not what women want. The movie might present an engaging romantic comedy, but it also presents a disservice to men and women (just not the one you might think!). It's not that it paints men to be jerks, competitive at all costs and being quite thoughtless. It also suggests women think like men, and that they merely want different things while having the same motivations. If only this were true! A lot of needless confusion would be eliminated. The main character's mind

9

reading takes place in the business world where most people are direct and competitive. Another problem is that the thoughts of the women are presented how a man would think or speak. These thoughts are direct, unambiguous and focused. Many women think this way in the work world, but only some of the time elsewhere.

Even worse, the title indicates the movie addresses what women want, not how women think. Women want some of the same things we do, but they also want things about which we don't care, and others we don't even acknowledge or understand. The thinking process women often use to get those things, and the assumptions make about men, are as foreign to us as a teacher speaking another language. Not that it matters - you still must pass the quizzes!

<u>Before you assume anything about your wife, remember that the word is spelled ASS-U-ME</u>

If you're like most men, you might think to yourself, "Henry Higgins in My Fair Lady was right! Why can't a woman be more like a man?"[2] Perhaps all you could muster at certain moments of interaction is "Huh?" Men are obvious to other men, and we often think that this makes us obvious to women. Guess what? Men are not obvious to women, leading women to make erroneous assumptions about us. Women aren't obvious to men either, leading us to make poor assumptions about women. It's worse if we dismiss them out of hand as Henry Higgins did, saying "women are just men with too many emotions and not enough logic!"

The hard lesson here is that women think, but their starting assumptions and their thinking processes both differ from ours - go figure! These are so different that we can't draw useful conclusions about them. Hard as it is, men need to learn to ask questions, in particular about things such as someone's motivations. This might be as difficult as asking for directions, and we know how men are at that. We also know how many times we end up lost because of our morbid fear of being judged to be incompetent or "less than" when we ask. Not asking means you have to assume, and as the saying goes, if you assume you make an "ass out of u and me."

Don't you ever try to understand women. Women understand women and that is why they hate each other.

www.Someecards.com

The above might seem like pithy advice but it doesn't help you in your quest to troubleshoot your wife. The similarities between men and women are much greater than are our differences. John Gray does a wonderful job pointing out the differences between men and women in his "Mars and Venus" series. However, some people have criticized his approach as being too centered on the differences. Yes, we have them, in spades. Many problems in relationships arise because we see all these similarities and then take them for granted. We get caught off-guard when a difference pops up.

When men assume a similarity exists between men and women but we find a difference, we are disappointed, shocked, and sometimes left in a state of denial. We find the situation does not match our expectation. For example, suppose you assume she wants the honest answer when she asks, "what are you thinking?" You can figure out the honest answer, and it might be, "I was thinking about the Big Game coming up." Do you think you'll be met with a disappointed look? Right. What she more likely wants is for you to get out of your head and stop thinking, and instead attend to her. How were we so off base? Didn't we use our logic and our years of experience in predicting that? We did, so the only possible explanation is that the resulting behavior must be irrational. Oh, wait - we might also have to question our starting hypotheses.

Suppose you opened the front door to your home and stepped off your porch, expecting to have the worms or snails on your damp sidewalk squish beneath your shoe. Instead you found yourself in a torrent of rushing water. You might conclude that a flood of cataclysmic proportions has hit your home and that you need to brace yourself for a struggle of survival. Then you realize you tossed back a few too many Black Jacks the night before and in the moment forgot where you were. Your conclusion might then be that you were still on vacation aboard the yacht and that you'd stepped off the deck into the passing ocean waves. The usefulness of your conclusions depends on the accuracy of your starting assumptions (oh wait, there aren't normally fish on the sidewalk).

This analogy holds for men understanding women. We assume women value things similarly to us, need similar things, and interpret things similarly. Here we will arrive at errant conclusions. While challenging our starting assumptions at this point in life might be unfamiliar, it is something men can do. We're trainable and we can learn new tricks, old dogs or not. If we want to be happy husbands with satisfied wives, it's something we must do.

What do we mean when we say, "want?"

In getting back to our original question, we can start with our assumptions about what women want. It is natural to assume women want what men do. We also have to ask ourselves "what do we mean by the word 'want'?" Maybe a better question is "what motivates women?" In general, we find people are motivated by one of two things, either pursuing a reward or escaping a punishment. Men view certain things as rewarding, like sex, money, power and sex. OK, in truth money isn't all that important. Respect is also an important motivator for men, as are accomplishment, productivity, and success among others ("winning," recently overused to the point of becoming a verbal jab, is the usual validation of masculine power). Men compete in sports, in business, and in communication.

It's probably correct to say that men want (or are motivated) to succeed. We want to win at something. Practice at this also makes us more accustomed to losing. For men, losing is simply what happens while not winning, and we learn traits like honor and sportsmanship in competition. Well, that's the theory anyway. Sometimes men forget there are at least two kinds of competition, one for sport and one for survival. We could forget we are competing for sport and not for survival, and that losing is just part of having fun. In that case we might end up looking like the enraged Little League dad threatening to gouge out the eyes of his son's coach with the brim of a ball cap when his kid doesn't get enough playing time. That's survival, not sport.

How many times has a woman complained "it feels like you're competing with me" or "you always have to be right!"? Have you ever heard a man complain about this? Certainly not on the ball field or at work, where competition is expected. If you have heard this from a woman, it might be because her values differ between men and women. There are places where women want to succeed and business is one of them. In those arenas, women are called upon to act from their masculine side. Men and women can each be masculine or feminine, either some or all of the time. Women seem to have an easier time switching between their masculine and feminine sides than men do. Being on the "other side" is taxing (unless of course, you were born that way).

Most often, women do not want to compete, especially not with men. Competition is terrifying for women because the thought of losing is so scary. For many women, losing is the same as failure, a catastrophe, not just "another one in the L-column." On the other hand, have you ever watched a girl-fight? Scan Facebook some time. It's a reminder that for women, competing is required for survival. When women compete it's not often for sport. They are often more cutthroat than men because they are not limited by things like honor, and they are rarely testing their off-field sporting mettle. This suggests two good reasons not to compete with your mate: one is that they hate to lose, and we hate to not win; the other is that women will compete as if it means survival and "hugging it out" won't satisfy her. Women generally seek to connect instead of to compete, most often by talking (see Chapter 2). When a man competes with a woman, she might think it represents the end of any connection. For men to compete at something else means they are less likely to compete with their mates. Grab yourself a football and head outside if you want to help yourself to not compete with her. Remember: keeping your wife happy means connecting with her, not competing with her.

In relationships, women want to feel safe

Believe it or not, one of the most important things for many women is safety, in a relationship or in life. That means safe in every way, including in physical and emotional ways. Alison Armstrong is fond of asking men "when was the last time you thought about your physical safety?"[3] Perhaps it was back in High School, or during military service. If you ask a woman that same question, she will likely look at her watch, as it will have been minutes or hours ago. Men take safety lightly, almost making it seem irrelevant, but women are concerned about their safety all the time.

To help her feel safe might mean that you put in outdoor lighting, have a security alarm, or just have pepper spray in her purse. It might mean being safe financially, knowing the household financial situation (she can be your best financial ally if she knows the whole story). It might also mean helping her feel safe from herself or from her impulses, meaning you don't always bend to her every whim. Compromise, yes, but don't be a pushover. It might mean feeling safe to be open and vulnerable with you, which can lead to the paradox of her wanting to tell you her troubles but not wanting you to fix them for her. Safety also means being connected to others, since social connectedness has been women's traditional pathway to survival (Facebook seems to be an exception to this rule).

Women also want to feel loved and desired

To extend that idea, many things that a woman does are because of how they make her feel (safe, happy, connected, validated, etc.). Among those feelings that she cherishes most after safety are feeling loved and desired (we will come back to this later in Chapter 7). Since each woman is unique, different things will make different women feel loved and desired, but telling a woman you love her, while important, is rarely enough. You tell her every day and it still doesn't seem like enough, right? Find out from the particular woman in your life what makes her feel loved; this is crucial.

You won't be able to read her mind on this, and assuming you know will only get you into trouble. Be direct about asking her this. Here's a sample question you might use: "What thing that I do makes you feel the most cared about?" She might say "I feel loved when you hold my hand," or "I feel loved when you make me a priority, like coming home from work early (or on time)." She might tell you something completely unexpected, like it makes her feel loved when you take out the trash for her (if she says, "I feel loved when you wax off all your body hair," RUN!). Asking her what things make her feel loved might be one thing that make her feel loved too (are you paying attention to how this works?). We like to know the rules in order to follow them. Here's how we can find out some of the rules – ask! Then do the thing she tells you will make her feel loved. It's a tiny investment that leads to a big payoff – a satisfied wife.

Many of the other things that motivate women involve achieving other feelings. Some say that the primary reason women do things is because of how that thing makes them feel. In relationships, that often translates into "women want men to help them have those certain feelings". Besides feeling safe and loved, women are motivated to feel cherished by the man in their life and to feel organized or "settled" in their homes (this phrase means that everything in the environment is now in its optimal place, or that the man of the house has no hope of ever finding it again without his wife's direction). Women want to feel connected to others, especially their mate (this connection is an integral part of feeling safe) and, oh yes, to feel attractive and desired. We'll visit each of these more in coming chapters.

Men want to feel respected and admired (who ever thinks about safety?)

Most men want to feel competent, respected and admired. As it was for Caesar's Roman Legions, feeling respected might be more important to us than being liked or loved. How do we get respect? Some of us feel respected when our wives tell us we did a good job. You're reading this because you want to know how to keep your wife, and feeling respected is how we get the emotional "juice" to keep up the efforts of keeping her happy. Sometimes we need our wife to show an interest in our sports or hobbies, things that make us feel competent. For some of us, even success in video games is a measure of competence unless that impedes real-life competence; hearing a positive reaction to "I beat my personal best level!" can feel as good to us as receiving flowers can to her.

We men have to tell women about this because they won't think that's important. After all, "it's just a game!" However anywhere we prove our worth we get to feel competent and valuable. This allows us to feel strong enough to protect her and to provide for her. Hail the current champion of Grand Theft Auto! It would not be as important to most women because it doesn't result in her feeling safer or more loved. Feeling competent is as important to men as feeling loved is to women. By telling her which things make you feel competent and productive, she can help you feel empowered enough to help her feel as safe and special as she desires. Yes, a tit for tat.

What men do if they can't make a woman happy (or give her what she wants)

It's unfortunate how many men make the mistake of thinking they can make their female partners happy. It seems reasonable to men, doesn't it? Just tell us how to make you happy, we'll do it, and then you'll be happy, right? It's not possible in most cases, even though it's what we're compelled to do. Because women fear "losing" so much, the state of "having" something she could lose can make women feel vulnerable. This is especially true of losing certain good feelings, the currency by which women are motivated. To lose certain feelings, like being loved and being happy, is so catastrophic that sometimes women would rather not risk having them. To a woman, saying that something makes her happy in fact puts her in a vulnerable position. Alison Armstrong says, "If a woman feels happy, it's as if she is naked."[4] Of course, that sounds just fine to us, but let's try to understand that Alison means the woman feels vulnerable. Many women also fear that if she told the man in her life what would make her happy, he would simply stop trying in other areas. So asking a woman what makes her happy is a non-starter in most cases.

It might seem like a Catch-22: having our mate feel happy is what makes men feel "good enough", but it makes women feel more vulnerable. In fact, even having men feel "good enough" can be scary to women. Men will then often shift gears from "trying-to-win" mode to "trying-not-to-lose" mode. If a man can't make her happy, he will shift over to trying to not upset her. This includes avoiding conflict and staying "off the radar" to preserve the peace.

Connection-oriented women then interpret these actions as the man becoming more distant and less connected – the proverbial downward spiral! To wrap this up, if you want to make her happy, don't ask what makes her happy. Stick with inquiries about safety, feeling loved and feeling appreciated, as these are much better bets.

We all want to be appreciated

The most common thing men and women want is appreciation. The specific way each of us feel appreciated can be very different. We each have a different "currency" of appreciation, and getting the wrong currency of appreciation can be as meaningless as getting the wrong paper currency for an item you're selling. This would be like getting paid in yen instead of dollars when you sell your old Honda on Craigslist. For example, a boss might value the currency of praise and thus go about telling his employees that they are doing a great job. She might not do this often, hoping the scarcity of praise will make it more valuable. However to the workers who need to feed their kids, *praise* might pale in comparison to a *raise* as appreciation.

Similarly, in some cultures a hearty belch shows appreciation for a good meal, while in other cultures it might be received as an insult to the host. Learning the currency of appreciation that our mate values means we can pass along the feelings we intended. Appreciation, well received in the correct currency, helps women feel valued and therefore safe; it gives men motivation to continue and compete by making us feel successful. Either way, appreciation makes it worthwhile doing that certain thing. We could all use a little more appreciation; we could all give a little more of it too. You might need to teach your wife how to give you appreciation (or approval, different from appreciation but also important). You could start by telling her what you want to hear and letting her know why it's important to you. When she approves of you, be prepared to give back in her currency of appreciation.

Lessons

1. Don't assume you know what she wants (you make an ass of u and me).

2. Women may want to feel safe first, before anything else is possible.

3. Women do things because of how they make women feel. Ask her what things make her feel safe and loved. Don't try asking what makes her happy.

4. Men do things in order to feel competent or productive, or to win at something. Tell her what things make you feel competent. Remind her that this helps you provide safety for her.

5. Learn her currency of appreciation (a thank-you, a foot rub, a flowers...) and use it. Then tell her what your currency of appreciation is.

Example Problem: "I work very hard at my job. But no matter how hard I work, my wife never seems satisfied with me – how can I get respect for all I do?"

Rodney works hard at his technology-driven startup company. As one of the early employees, he knows his stock options package means that if the company does well he will do well too. He left a more stable but less lucrative job to come here and now sees this period as "investing time in his future." But this means working some 12-hour days, often coming home exhausted. Joan is a High School teacher. She regularly points out to Rodney that she works a full-time job, manages the house, and takes care of their last child still at home (age 17). The household responsibilities are distributed in a traditional way. At this point in their lives she expected him to take more responsibilities at home. She also expected him to spend more leisure time with her, and she often voices her displeasure with the current state of things.

Rodney may indeed toil to provide for his wife and family. Because his job is out of sight for Joan, it might appear to her as another example of him competing (in the business world) at the expense of connecting (spending more time with her). Joan needs to be more connected, and she may interpret Rodney's actions as if another woman had performed them. In this case, his dedication to work would mean that his priority was not about his family or his relationship, but rather about work. She would feel less important to him than she wants to be. John needs to make time to connect with Joan, either during his day (by a short phone call or a text message), or right after arriving home from work (by asking her to tell him about her day), or even better, both. This will help her feel more connected to him, and then she will be more receptive to listening to his needs from her. He might also ask her what chore he could do for her that day (often asking this will result in a specific request, but as often it will bring "nothing right now, but you're a dear for asking"). He could ask her what he could do that would make her feel loved. Rodney then needs to remind her that his way of helping her feel safe is to provide financial security for her, and that he can be the best protector/provider if he knows that she appreciates his efforts. He can remind her they are both working for the good of the relationship (a third entity bigger than, and different from, either individual). Their respective roles in this joint effort are different.

2 - What if I am told, "you don't understand"

when my wife talks?

*I left three notes scattered around the apartment for my girlfriend. One said, "Will",
another said "You" and the third said "Me". That should keep her busy while I watch
football...*

*A wife and a husband sit in the room and enjoy a bottle of wine. Suddenly the wife
says, "I love you."Husband asks in surprise, "Is that you or wine talking?"The wife, without
missing a beat, replies, "This is me. I'm talking to the wine."*

Women talk to connect and to create intimacy

While these examples might seem harsh, they convey that men have at
least some awareness of the differences in the way men and women talk. Yes,
these differences can be leveraged, but that's not quite the effect we're after
here. To understand the assumptions that lead to these differences can help us
out of some confusing situations. One assumption is that women talk much

more than men do. For example, my aunt was always the talker in her family. Whether on the phone or in person she seemed to ask questions and always give others their speaking time, but filled up most of the empty spaces with "chatter." She admitted this herself. On one occasion during lunch at their house, without warning my long-suffering uncle developed a quizzical look on his face. "Are you OK?" I asked him. "I think I just heard a burst of silence!" he reported, as if the Higgs boson was the second most important discovery of the day. Not to be outdone, my aunt retorted, "Oh, bother. If it wasn't for me nothing would get said around here!" She may have proven his point, but she illustrated something as important about men and women talking. We talk differently.

In "You Just Don't Understand," Deborah Tannen points out several studies showing men talk as much as women do, and in certain cases, even more.[5] This may surprise most men. It's always seemed that talking was the social activity of women while doing was the social activity of men. Yet women talk for different reasons, at different times, and in different styles than do men. Tannen calls these styles "rapport-talk" for women and "report-talk" for men.[6] Women talk primarily to connect with others and to create relationships. This establishes "rapport" which turns out to be the key to social safety in women's lives. This is akin to private talking, where comfort, intimacy and similarity are valued.

Women ask questions hoping to get validation of their own opinions or values form the answer ("Don't you think ... ?" As with any question starting with these three words, the single good answer is "Yes, of course!"). It also lets women know they will have a social network to provide support in case their primary support (their mate, or their family of origin) fails them. This might also help us understand why "mean girls" who exclude others from social networks are reviled from childhood on up in age; a girl or woman left out of a social network will feel unsupported, vulnerable, and rejected in a profound way. In the animal kingdom we see a similar thing in horses excluded from the herd – they know they are being left alone to die.

A man might respond to the statements above with "Wow, I never knew it was that important for women to connect through talking!" He might also reflect on his own experience and respond with "It's just talk – it shouldn't be so serious!" This is in part because men talk for a different reason, mainly to relay information when in a public setting. This style of talk is less often connected to emotional content (unless we are reporting on the latest victories of our favorite team, or our latest exploits in the dating world). A lot of our reactions to things like connecting, inclusion, independence and status are linked to primitive fears and drives. These allow us to navigate many things on autopilot, without having to engage our brains.

This is important in another arena, one familiar to men having been in a long-term relationship with a woman. When a woman talks to a man about her day, or about her family, or about her friends, it might sound to him like she is just complaining. This is the case when he tries to offer suggestions regarding how the problems she is describing might be addressed. She tells him her troubles, he responds with answers or solutions, but then there's a galactic disconnect. She's disappointed, frustrated that she "can't talk to him" because what she wanted was just to tell her story and have her feelings about it be validated by him. It seems he was listening to the facts of the story, not to the implied feelings she was communicating. The facts presented a problem, and he rose to the occasion to provide a solution. John Gray calls this disconnect "men speaking male and women speaking female[21]". When a woman is telling a story and trying to have her feelings validated, it might sound to a man as if she were "just complaining."

If this were another guy he <u>would</u> be complaining, and a response like "quityourbitchin'" would suffice. Perhaps you'd try to show your superior grasp of the situation he's in by offering advice or trying to solve his dilemma for him. You'd most likely err if you tried this approach with a woman. To respond in a way she appreciates, you must learn to listen to the feelings she is intimating, and not to the facts of the story. You must resist the urge to fix her problem and change your "job" from giving advice to listening for her feelings. As foreign as this sounds, the facts are not the important parts of this discussion. Of course, she could help this along if she could let you know ahead of time what she was hoping to get back as a result of her communication. Until she learns this preparative assist, you might need to ask her what response she wants at the start of her story. It might be good practice to explain this recurrent conflict to her in advance, at a time of low tension and emotion. You can emphasize that overriding your natural inclination to solve her trouble will be strange for you and it will require practice.

Men talk to establish independence and to exchange information

Men talk for different reasons than do women. We talk to exchange information, to negotiate status (to compete) in a perceived hierarchy, and to establish independence. "Just the facts, ma'am," as Joe Friday said, "just the facts." This competitive style is similar to public speaking, where the hierarchy between the speaker and the audience is evident. Men use challenges and insults to relate to one another ("Good morning you old fart!" or "Did you check with your teenagers about whether it's OK for you to hang out with us men tonight?"). Most women are aghast to hear how men speak to one another (in what we consider to be friendly terms). Men also ask questions with information in mind ("Where did my power drill go when you cleaned up the garage?" or "Did you decide what color you want to paint the kitchen?"). When men talk to other men about the challenges of life, they trade stories and emphasize differences rather than similarities ("Well, let me tell you about MY experiences with that!"). This is part of negotiating status with other men and proving our independence.

What about men and women together?

This is where things get interesting (or dicey). If women talk to emphasize similarities and men talk to emphasize differences, you get conversations like this:

Her: "I had a really rough day at work today. None of the other gals even seemed to notice I was upset."
Him: "Well I had lunch with the president of the company, and he told me I was doing a great job!"
Her: "Did you hear what I was saying? I had a really bad day!"
Him: "Oh, I'm sorry to hear that. I was just trying to tell you that I

didn't. What's for dinner?" (You might think this is an extreme example of an obtuse man, but it actually happened).

After this encounter, he likely felt fine and thought they exchanged the important information, while she likely felt invalidated and even stunned at the lack of empathy he showed. She was trying to get him to relate to her pain to create rapport. He was trying to show he was different from her, hoping his report of work success might make her feel more financially secure. Of course, you can guess at the outcome of that conversation - a setup for her to feel annoyed by him and for him to be surprised by her annoyance.

If you are trying to get information and she is trying to relate feelings, you might get this interaction:

Him: "Did you remember to get to the bank today as I asked?"
Her: "My day was so disrupted! I had a lot to do already in the morning, and when my lunch hour started, my friend Janice came in and started to cry because of her hateful husband. It took my whole lunchtime to calm her down. I didn't get to eat and I felt overwhelmed all afternoon!
Him: "But did you get to the bank?"
Her: "No! How can you even think I had time for that?"

The fact of her getting to the bank (or not) was on his mind with his question, and he might have walked away thinking, "Why can't she just answer my question?" It might have frustrated him that the errand important to him didn't get accomplished. She might have wanted to receive comfort or empathy from him for her stressful day. It was obvious from her description she didn't have the time to deal with the lower-priority errand. This is a setup for each of them to walk away hurt and frustrated.

<u>Men aren't invested in the answer to a question like "do you like this?",</u> <u>they just want honesty; women want to feel validated</u>

When men use questions to gain information, they are not invested in the answers themselves, except in the truth of the answer. If a man asks, "Do you want to go out for a pizza," he doesn't care whether his buddy says "Sure!" or "You know, I'd rather go out for a burger." If a woman, expecting validation for her opinion, asks a girlfriend the same questions, the expected answer is simply "Yes, that would be lovely." This is because she's already decided that is what she wants to do even before she asks the question, and just wants her friend to agree. However, if a <u>man</u> asks that question of a woman listening with feminine ears, she will think he wants validation and she will answer either "Yes, that's fine" or "If that's what you want." If he sees through what he perceives as a non-truthful answer, he might reply with "No, do you really want to go out for a pizza?", insisting on having her go against her primitive drive to provide validation. At that point, she's stuck, and she hasn't even gotten to decide what she's going to wear to the pizza place.

On the other hand, let's say she was the one offering the inquiry. She asks him if he wants to go out for pizza, expecting to get validated; he gives his best honest answer of "No, I'd rather have a burger" and she's immediately hurt by the lack of validation. How could he be so thoughtless? And he might think "Don't you want me to be honest?!" The feminine answer is "No" but she would never say that. We have to learn to inquire about how we are asking or replying – I often ask my wife "are you asking like a girl or like a guy?" It's become a humorous query in our house, but it solves many dilemmas and removes some assumptions. This is important for masculine/feminine interactions regardless of gender (sometimes a sensitive man can use his feminine side, or an assertive woman can use her masculine side, and the differences will be as great). It might sound like this:

Me: "Do you want to go to the new testosterone-laden adventure movie with me? It starts in 30 minutes."

Her: "Are you asking like a guy or like a girl?"

Me: "Well, I really want your honest opinion about this one. Even though I'd like to see it, I'd rather see something you like. If you're not interested in this, I can go to that movie later with the guys. So I guess I'm asking like a guy."

Her: "Now you're sending me mixed messages, because you told me you really DO want to see it, so it sounds like you're asking like a girl. If you really want my opinion, then no, I'm not very interested in that particular movie.

I wouldn't mind seeing a romantic comedy, but it would take me too long to get ready. It would be easier if we just find one on Netflix and stay at home. Or we could play a game. Or maybe go to the beach. How does that sound?"

    Me (befuddled): "Uh, well, ok. Is that what you want to do?"

    Her: "Are you asking like a guy or like a girl?"

    Me: "Uh, I'm not sure any more. A guy, I think. I really want to know what you want to do."

    Her: "OK, then, yes, that's what I'd like to do. One of those. You pick."

    Me: "Um, rats."

See how well it works?

Women confide because sharing is connecting; men don't confide because they will lose status or their competitive edge, or because they want to protect their spouse from negatives

When women talk with men in order to connect, the subject or point of the story is not as important to her as are the words used to create a relationship. This can have painful consequences for men busily listening for the useful piece of information (it must be buried in there somewhere). Women see the details of a story as just as important to the rapport as the spices are to a main dish – they flavor everything, and without them, the story is bland. We get overwhelmed with the details and will often ask, "Can you just tell me the bottom line?" This feels disconnecting to the woman but it feels like a simple request for information to a man.

When a man comes home from work and his wife says, "Gina's husband told her you didn't get the raise you expected two weeks ago. Why didn't you tell me?" he's likely to defend himself first. In doing so, he's likely to protect her from the negative event (procreate, protect and provide – it's what men do. This is in the "protect" category). "I knew it wouldn't affect us financially, and I just thought it would be bad news and ruin your day." "But you kept it from me," she might retort, showing how not sharing resulted in her feeling left out, disconnected and thus unsupported.

If he actually came home and said, "I didn't get the raise I expected," that's the piece of information he wants to give her. He's already assessed that anything more would be superfluous (or worse, might obscure the facts of the case). When she asks, "When you talked to the boss, what did he say? Did anyone else get the raise? How did you feel about it?" he is likely to get annoyed. She might even think that his annoyance is due to the retelling of the event being painful. More likely it is due to his having to include information he sees as having no added value. To her, it provides a richer connection with her guy.

Men see questions and challenges as part of interacting; women find they convey loss of respect and loss of connection

When men talk to other men, they challenge each other's points of view, conclusions and values as a way of showing interest and competing. "You don't actually <u>believe</u> that, do you?" would be taken in stride. We think of this as "spirited debate," while women listening think of this as "conflict." Men struggle to be one-up, or to avoid being one-down. Women are struggling to be equal in their conversations. When men and women converse on a subject, she will tend to be "polite" and not interrupt or challenge (unless she is angry), and this might lead her to talk less in a mixed-gender conversation. It might also make him sound like he's lecturing; as he's jockeying for status and showing he knows his material, he's also waiting for the challenge he just knows is right around the corner.

"Don't lecture me Frank – I'm capable of being part of this discussion."
"I wasn't lecturing you dear; I was just telling you" (or these days, "I'm just sayin'").

If he contests her opinion or her statements, she might end up feeling less than or one down in status to him. Likely she will also feel discounted by him. This is particularly based on her interpreting his contest as breaking the connection.

Him: "I really like that new crossover Buick put out."

28

Her (emphasizing similarity): "I do too!"

Him (contesting): "I never heard you mention it before. Do you know enough about it to have an opinion?"

Her (hurt and discounted): "No, I guess not. Never mind."

In a similar way, men tease each other to promote camaraderie. "Are you still driving that old rattle-trap?" "Yeah, but it's a chick-magnet!" "Only for the type of chicks you find in a barnyard!" Men make errors when they try to tease women in a similar manner. If a man teases a woman without a great deal of trust and understanding being established first, she will interpret that as a rejection, or at least a break of connection. This alone makes it very important to speak to women differently than the way you speak to men. Before you can tease, contest or challenge a woman's statements, you must have established a great deal of trust, understanding and even ground rules. These are required so the woman will understand that your communications are not designed to break the connection.

The problem with opinions

My father used to say, "Everyone is entitled to their opinions as long as they agree with mine." He also used to say, "Of course this family is a democracy – you all get one vote and I get ten," so take these comments with a grain of salt. Opinions are everywhere and most people have them. We are used to recognizing opinions in the media as being something with which we either strongly agree with or strongly disagree. We sometimes forget that medical opinions and legal opinions are just that, opinions and not facts. However, opinions are very different coming from men or women.

When a woman states an opinion, it can be something she has thought long and hard about, or it can be simply the current state of her preferences. "I don't think I like this" can be translated into man-speak as "I've tried this now, I'm unsure about what I think of it, and I hope that by talking out loud about it I will come to a firmer conclusion." In this case, she's trying on an opinion to see if it fits by talking as if it were long considered. She's stating the situation in the here-and-now, available for change based on further input.

This often flummoxes men. Men form opinions by putting together all the information he has at the moment, the research he might have done on the subject, and the values and lessons his life history has taught him. It's the best of what he is regarding that topic. He expects that someone else will understand that and respect it as such. Other men understand even if they disagree:

Him: "I think our congressman is doing a pretty good job."

He (stunned that his friend admits to such a profound character flaw): "That's because of your liberal bias."

Him (not surprised by the rebuke made by his grievously ignorant friend): "No it's because I know the facts, and I don't give in to hysterical conservative judgments like some people I know."

He (reminded that this topic is normally off-limits): "I get that this is your considered opinion, I just don't consider it much of an opinion."

Even in the midst of verbal sparring, each one understands that the positions of the other are entrenched and thought through. When a woman asks a man his opinion, he will tell her with some measure of pride about his "considered opinion." She, on the other hand, will collect the opinions of others as multiple inputs in forming a course of action. She will not feel beholden to agree with anyone's opinion nor to follow his advice. If she then she follows a course of action different from his implications, he may interpret this as a sign of disrespect.

Her: "I bought the pink bicycle from Target today!"

Him: "You did? When you asked me what I thought about it, I told you I thought that a sturdier one would help you become a better rider, and that you should wait to make a decision."

Her: "I know, and I thought that was great feedback, but the pink one was so cute, and it has a basket on the handlebars!"

Him (Grumbling under his breath): "Why do you even ask me what I think?"

He will likely conclude that she feels his opinion was valueless, resulting in him feeling hurt, angry and dismayed. She might be surprised by his reaction.

For her, his input was just one more piece of information about the moment at hand. She wanted to honor him by including his input, but she also wanted to get the item that made her feel the best. This might not be the one that was "the most logical choice." After all, it was pink.

A short comment on nagging

Why do women nag men? When a woman requests something from a man, different things happen inside each of them. He receives the message "can you take care of this for me?", usually answering it with "Yes, dear". It then is prioritized against the other things on his to-do list. If he thinks it can wait until after he finishes his current task of sorting the coins in his 5-gallon change jar, he will put it off. He figures since she delegated the task to him, it is now <u>his</u> job and he can decide when it should get done.

For her, a desired feeling is often associated with that task. This feeling is possibly safety, completeness, cleanness, order, or that at least now she can check it off her list. She figures since she delegated the job in the first place, she is still responsible for making sure that the job gets done. If she sees the job isn't getting done, she might assume he didn't understand that she really needs that job done. She might also assume that he wasn't paying attention because his mind was on something else. She is not necessarily being impatient, but rather she is waiting for that feeling she so desires. So she asks him again, hoping to make sure he hears this time, and that he better understands she really wants it done. He is put off by her second request, as he has already prioritized that job and its turn in the cue of tasks has not come up yet. He also starts to feel she doesn't trust him to get it done.

The third time she asks (because by now she <u>really</u> wants that feeling) the word "nagging" occurs to him. Or worse, he ascribes the term to her as a person instead of to the behavior, as in "my wife is a nag". He starts to feel that she doesn't believe he will do the task and that she doesn't think he is capable. He might not understand that to her, it's as if she told him "I'm thirsty, can you get me a glass of water". While he's finishing with his coins, she's still thirsty. She starts to feel he doesn't care about her because if he did, he would take care of this task and therefore her desired feeling.

When your wife asks you to take care of a task a second or a third time and if it's gotten to the point of "nagging", make sure you ask her how it will make her feel for you to do that for her. Then tell her what your idea of priorities is and ask if she can wait for her task to get done. That way she knows what to expect and that you really are noting her request.

<u>Lessons</u>

1. Men and women talk differently, and for different purposes.

2. Pay attention to the different ways you use language to compete with other guys. Notice how important it is for you to be one-up and how badly you feel when you're one-down.

3. Practice asking, "are you speaking like a girl or like a boy?" to help reduce assumptions.

4. Remember not to tease, contest or question women unless you have a lot of trust built up with her. She will otherwise see this as competition and loss of connection.

5. When you give a woman your opinion about something, don't be too invested in how she uses it. For her, it might just be one more piece of information about the moment.

6. If she's nagging (or better, when she asks you to do something), ask her how it will make her feel for you to do it. Then let her know how it fits into your list of priorities.

Example Problem - "My wife tells me we don't talk enough, but when I try to her talk to her about politics or business, she gets more distant. What gives?"

Eddie and Rebecca have what appears to be a terrific marriage. They each have careers, raise their two kids together, spend time with friends and often attend social events. When Rebecca asked to spend more time talking, it surprised him but he agreed. Eddie has a pet interest in politics. He is also a successful businessman. In trying to accommodate Rebecca's request, he began to talk about the upcoming elections. He invited her feedback on his opinions, but then challenged them when her opinions differed from his. When Rebecca got frustrated, he was taken aback. What Eddie didn't understand was that Rebecca's request was really for more time connecting, not debating or being lectured to. She was asking for more time talking in order to connect and share emotionally. This usually implies speaking about each other, about the relationship or about other intimate subjects. Talking about an abstract concept often seems to women to be equal to watching TV together or attending a concert. The focus appears to be on something else rather than on each other. Likely, Rebecca was requesting time with Eddie to focus on each another instead of on something else.

Example Problem – "It seems like every time I give my wife an honest answer to one of her questions, I hurt her feelings. She doesn't seem to want the truth. Do I have to lie to her instead?"

Bill is a software engineer in the large corporation, and Tonya is a schoolteacher in the local district. They have been married for over 20 years. During that time, Tonya has learned a lot about the different ways Bill expresses his opinion. He is direct and meticulous in his speaking, which suits him as an engineer. Bill has seen a pattern over time of Tonya getting upset when she asks a question and he offers an opinion. This occurs when she asks questions that, to Bill, seem to be about his preferences. For instance, "Would you like to..." or "Do you want to..." or "Do you like..." questions always lead him to get himself into trouble. Since Bill values exactness and honesty, he assumes that Tonya must value those traits too, so he tries to be honest and exact in his answers. This came to a head when she asked him, "Do you like this new outfit I'm wearing?" He answered honestly, "No. I like the one you had on yesterday better". Tonya burst into tears. While Tonya valued honesty to a great degree, in

33

cases like this, she was not looking for a purely honest opinion. She was looking for validation. What she really wanted was for Bill to express his approval of her. A negative answer, no matter how honest, appeared to her to be disapproval.

This kind of situation presents a great opportunity for a man to learn how to ask a question in response to a question. When the woman in your life asks a question like this, you can ask her, "Are you asking like a boy or like a girl?" Doing this a few times will establish this as a meaningful question with your partner. She can let you know whether she is seeking an honest answer from you or whether she is seeking your approval. If she's "asking like a girl," make sure that you know the acceptable answer is "Yes!" Remember, you are not lying to her; you are giving her your approval.

3 - What if my wife and I value different things around the house?

Q: What's the difference between a woman and a dog?
A: Your dog gets upset if you DO decide to decorate.

What if we disagree about value of something?

Men and women have differences about what makes for a livable space. We men don't care if there is art on the wall or rugs on the floor (isn't that why there's carpet?). When we approach a space we are most concerned with how functional it is. If it's functional it doesn't matter much if it's dusty or if there are a few papers lying about. The only reasons we might change it are if a woman is coming over, if we are going to sell the place, or if we just want to screw with the dog (can't you just picture Dutch when he comes barreling into a familiar room, only to apply the brakes at the last minute on a newly-polished hardwood floor, failing to avoid the repositioned sofa? Bastard!).

When Bob and his wife got married, she moved into his house. Well, it's their house now, but it was the house in which he had been living for 6 years.

The house was too big for a single guy, but Bob bought it as an investment before the housing crash. It was a work in progress. He was still installing flooring, some of the windows were undressed, and the rooms he never entered were devoid of furniture. Bob's male visitors would often tell him, "Nice place!" However, his female visitors would ask him, "How come it's not finished yet?" The male visitors were talking about the structure of the house itself, while the female visitors were responding to the way Bob decorated it.

Bob's wife had a wonderful eye for decor. With his input, they picked out window coverings, eventually put art on the walls, and furnished the rooms they were using. Eventually they moved the older furniture into the rooms they used less. Bob thought, "I never needed all this stuff before. Why do we need it now?" He was thinking like a man and asking the wrong question. He was focusing on the function of the items rather than their form or the feel of the environment. That's often how it is for men - we attend to the way a situation functions. Women pay more attention to the "form" or the feel of the space, and don't always prioritize the function. To understand why he was now buying new furniture, he had to be asking, "How does this room make me feel when I walk in?" If he was honest, he might have answered, "I feel nothing in here because there is nothing in here" or even "I can't remember the last time I was in this room."

Women do many things because of how those make them feel

Women do many things for practical reasons. They can be goal-directed about household and family chores, business ventures and healthcare, among others. However, a woman does many things because of how they make her feel. She puts flowers on the dining room table because it makes her feel happy to see them. She spends time on her hair and makeup because it makes her feel pretty. She talks to her friends because that makes her feel connected. She reads because it makes her feel intellectually stimulated and she does very many things because they make her feel safe.

Men do few things because of how they make him feel, sex and conquest aside. Men do many things because of the reward they expect to get as a result of doing them. A man goes to work expecting to get paid. A man plays sports because he expects to win and therefore gain status. For many men, that's why they date as well - to "win." That's a big reason men get married - to win in the eyes of society, to gain a bride and therefore gain status. The things we do to keep a wife after we "win" one (to keep on winning) will require us to learn that women don't do things as often to win as they do to feel good.

This includes the items with which she surrounds herself

This difference between the reasons men and women do things often applies to the items they buy. A woman buys decorations because of how they make her feel. A man buys tools because they are a means to gaining competence. Here's a real-life example: I bought a bicycle because it had better components than the 20-year old road bike I was retiring, and it gave me the ability to ride where I wanted to ride. My wife chose her bike because it was pink and it had a handlebar basket. This is a classic case of women attending to form and men attending to function. Here, however, form is more than just the shape of an object. It includes all of those attributes (shape, color, style, smell and even texture) that can affect how a woman feels. If a woman enjoys the way she feels around a certain object, she will want it, and perhaps even buy it. This is true even if it has no apparent functional value. Like the thing that's on the flush box of your visitor-accessible toilet. What is that thing anyway? It might just sit on the table or countertop and look pretty. The object sitting there looking pretty will be enough to make the woman feel happy, pretty, or some similar positive feeling. It also serves to give men hours of wonderment.

Whereas a man might neither want nor buy objects without functional value, women often do this. Women often desire these kinds of objects as gifts. A female colleague of mine used to call objects like this "shiny." She had to explain to her husband what "shiny" meant because it meant something different to her than it did him. His view of "shiny" was "something that shines." Her view of "shiny" was "something that sparkles, looks expensive, looks impressive, makes me feel excited, or shines." In fact she was after a feeling, something he could not provide for her. She wanted something that made her feel "special." Her description of the word "shiny" was the best way she could explain to her husband what an object that would make her feel "special" would look like to him.

This concept is important for men for gift giving. To impress a woman with a gift, make sure you know how that gift will make her feel. If you just consider its function, you'll be missing 90% of its value to her. Perplexed men will often ask their wives, "but what do you do with it?" This points out the difference in how we view things. A man will not see much value in an object if he can't "do something with it." The value of that same object to a woman is based on more than what she can do with it. If you give a woman a gift that makes her feel pretty, special, safe or happy, she will appreciate it more than she will a gift of just functional value. The classic example of this used to be jewelry; these days it's more likely to be an iPhone.

One other area where this disparity applies is in terms of clothing. Men buy their clothing with primarily utilitarian values in mind. He may ask himself, "When will I wear this?" He may even ask himself, "Do I already have one of these?" Those kinds of questions go into a man's decision process when considering buying apparel. This is why men's closets often have only a few pairs of shoes: dress brown, dress black, casual and sports (and flip-flops, for those living in suitable environments). We view shoes as functional items that protect our soles and perhaps hide our knurled troll-feet from outside observers. A woman looks at apparel differently. While those considerations are important, she will also consider how she feels when looking at or wearing a given item, and this is especially true for shoes. Shoes are sometimes an accessory, sometimes their own fashion statement, and always reflect "how they feel" that day.

This is one reason it's so important to a woman to try on an item before buying it. When a man tries on a shirt or pants, he is only trying them on to see if they fit his body well. When a woman tries on an item, she is also trying it on to find out if it fits her personality and mood well. That means she wants to know how it makes her feel. In fact, trying on items is often enough for her to feel a certain way. This is a big reason the clothing shopping is such an enjoyable experience to women (here's a little secret: women often dance/ sit/walk in the dressing room as appropriate for the article of clothing to experience the feel). Listen up men: going clothing shopping for women often makes them feel as good (even buying nothing) as watching the football game does for men. It's an enjoyable sport, and it helps them express a mood. The next time she asks you to go clothing shopping with her, remember that she may not be trying to buy something. She may just go for the sport. Imagine how you would like her to respond if you asked her, "do you mind if I watch the game today?"

Clothing may make a woman feel pretty or happy even when she's not wearing it. Just looking into her closet and viewing her clothing options may remind her at that moment of how she feels with each piece of clothing. She may not even have to put them on to feel that way! Looking at her array of hanging tops, she may gain all the feelings she would have if she individually tried on each of them. When she views all her shoes she may acquire all of the feelings she might have wearing each item. Plus, looking in her lingerie drawer may remind her of how pretty and sexy she feels wearing each of them. Men don't have that kind of emotional connection to their clothing. Of course, we might have a strong connection with certain items of <u>her</u> clothing (no, not like that. I mean...never mind).

<u>Men see the function of a thing and don't notice how it makes them feel</u>

A man also notices what is there and what is functional outside the home. He might appreciate other houses in his neighborhood based on the size of the house, size of the yard, the presence of a swimming pool and the quality of the view. He may appreciate a car or truck based on how fast it goes or how much it can carry. He may look at his own yard and evaluate whether the trees shade the desired area, whether the pathways are efficient, and whether the barbecue is close enough to the entertainment area. These evaluations are all about the reward (status, value) that he might gain by having these items. He might not understand how these elements make him feel.

This isn't that they make him feel nothing, nor is it because he's not in touch with his feelings. Most likely, it's that feelings are not the currency that matters to men. Men's currency is function over form. It's important to remember that this is not true for women. Often women's currency is form over function. Neither of these values is right; we are just different. For example, that knick-knack on the shelf does not need a function; your chain saw does not have to be pretty.

Women notice what is missing

A woman may constantly scan the environment to see how it makes her feel. She has an emotional connection with her environment that leads her to have what Alison Armstrong calls a "diffuse awareness." This means she's aware of many things in her environment at same time. Men focus on one thing at a time. This is, in part, the reason men don't want to discuss something like in-laws or travel plans when we're watching the game; we do best if we're focusing on one thing. Women often assume we must be like them, we must have a diffuse awareness as well, and therefore we must also do best if we are multi-tasking. Because women are also tuned into their feelings, and the environment makes her feel a certain way, a woman will notice when something is wrong in the environment much more readily than a man.

More specifically, a woman will notice when something in the environment is <u>missing</u>. Men see what is there while women see what is missing. In terms of decor, when a woman looks at a room, she will often pay attention to how an additional piece of furniture or decoration would enhance the room. This may be an end table, a throw pillow on the sofa or a knick-knack on a shelf. If one of her children is missing, a woman is much more likely to notice the absence of screaming, crying or demands than a man is (he will notice eventually, most likely around halftime, when he's getting up to refill his drink or relieve himself and notices the unfamiliar quiet in the house).

A man sees what is there, including other women!

A man will be more likely than a woman to notice where he can sit or put down his drink. He will notice how the room functions and how it serves him. This is why a "bachelor pad" may contain just a few items of function and little resembling decoration. It might also contain items that are old and worn; to men these are still functional ("yes, I can see that the sofa is worn and ripped - I just put a blanket on it and it still works fine!"). It's also why, when a woman enters a home, she can immediately tell if another woman lives there. To her, there are signs of "a woman's touch." She will notice how the environment makes her feel, and not just whether it functions.

There are many extensions of this dichotomy outside the home. Men see what is there, including in the external environment. Sometimes this even includes other women! Some people suggest that men are very visual, turning their heads as a reflex towards attractive women with no conscious control. This might well be true. All women know men are visual creatures. When men see something they think is intriguing or beautiful, they feel excitement. When men are excited, they are more interested in connecting and relating.

Because physical attraction between people is more important to men than to women, and because men are so visual, on first glance (literally) men view women as art. Seeing an attractive woman well dressed or attractively underdressed leads men to feel excited and happy. Here's the big surprise for women: for men in a relationship, most of the time it ends right there. A man rarely continues on with any thought about whether he wants to be with that woman, talk to her, have sex with her or marry her. They are just appreciating the beauty of the art.

However, women often feel threatened by this "appreciation" by their men, because they would only notice another man if something were missing for them, meaning if they were dissatisfied. Fabio himself could walk down the beach with his golden locks flowing and the woman on your arm wouldn't notice unless there was something missing in her relationship. OK, that's a slight exaggeration - she might want his signature on her paperback romance novel. Men, if you notice a womanly form while you're out with your main squeeze, be subtle about your response. If she sees you looking, she might well be hurt, wondering if you're thinking something is missing and that she's not sufficient for you. Make sure you're aware of how she sees things (like the environment and you), and then let her know you like looking at her better than anything else.

Even football.

As Steve Jobs would have said, there's one more thing. Each of you will have your strengths and your abilities, and each of you will have your preferences and desires. As you're explaining y<u>our</u> preferences to your wife, make sure you express gratitude for getting your preferences met more often than you express distress at having them not met. After all, this positive reinforcement of the behaviors is what you want to see in your wife (helping you get your preferences met). This makes her happier to meet them with you. We model negative reinforcement a lot with kids (punishing them when they do something wrong) and at work (getting criticized when something isn't done well enough, but barely acknowledged when something is done well). In this respect marriage should be different.

<u>Lessons</u>

1. Women do things because of how it makes them feel.

2. A woman may values physical objects mostly for the same reason (because of how they make her feel).

3. When you give her a gift, try to understand how it will make her feel first.

4. Men value function in an activity or an object, using a very different currency than do women.

5. Men see what is there while women notice what is missing.

6. Express gratitude more often than distress.

Example Problem – "I'm going crazy with all the knick-knacks that my wife buys for the house. We don't need any more stuff, and our older stuff is still fine. Why does she keep buying and changing the household items?"

Brian and Rosemary were two years into their marriage. It was the second marriage for each of them. Both had lived on their own for several years since their first marriages ended. When they married, Rosemary moved into the condo that Brian purchased after his divorce. Since she was moving into his space, he felt it was only fair to let her decorate the place, to give it "her touch." After two years of decorating, he was becoming exasperated. He was convinced that the things he had been living with should still be fine for the two of them. She was beginning to think that she had married a tightwad. He resisted letting her spend money on even little things at that point.

It became clear to Brian that Rosemary did not feel at home in his place. This had nothing to do with her desire to be there or her level of appreciation for it. It was just that his environment did not make her feel the way she wanted to feel. She was not choosing decor items at random, but because they would make her feel more at home. She agreed with his assessment that their old furniture still served the desired functions. However the fact that some of it was left over from Brian's first marriage made Rosemary feel like a guest in her own home. She wanted to feel she was an equal to Brian and therefore safe in this new marriage. To do that she needed to be surrounded with items that made her feel that way. Once Brian understood she was not rejecting his values, nor was she disagreeing with the way he lived before she moved in, he was much happier to let her decorate the place as she wanted. "If putting a few knick-knacks around the place makes her feel like she belongs there, why should I resist?"

44

4 - How do I know when to support her and when to offer solutions?

A man was sitting alone in his office one night when a genie popped up out of his ashtray and said, "And what will your third wish be?"

The man looked at the genie and said, "Huh? How can I be getting a third wish when I haven't had a first or second wish yet?"

"You have had two wishes already," the genie said, "but your second wish was for me to put everything back the way it was before you made your first wish. Thus, you remember nothing, because everything is the way it was before you made any wishes. You have one wish left."

"Okay," said the man, "I don't believe this, but what the heck. I wish I were irresistible to women."

"Funny," said the genie as it granted his wish and disappeared forever. "That was your first wish, too."

This might be a simple reminder to be careful what you wish for. As an example, imagine having every woman you know venting on your shoulder because they thought you were the Best Listener? I suppose just what kind of "irresistible" we're talking about might matter as well.

What if you try to comfort your wife and she blames you for not listening?

A woman friend used to tell me about growing up with three sisters. "The only place we could have privacy in the house was the bathroom," she would say. "The sisters crowded into the bathroom at the same time and we took turns using the facilities. The main reason for being in there was to talk to each other in private, without our parents or brothers listening. One of us would take a turn talking, telling the others about our problems with our parents, and our boyfriends and at school. We would just listen and agree with each other. We wouldn't ask questions or offer solutions or even feedback. Then, without needing to be asked, another one of us would take her turn talking about her problems. This would go on until each of us had our chance to relate our own story, getting to feel validated and accepted by the others. By that time, it had often been over an hour, and we were very done using the facilities! No one ever offered solutions, and we never had to ask each other what was going on with them because they would just talk." You thought they went to the bathroom in pairs.

This story is both amusing and illustrative on several levels. First, it happened in the bathroom. If a man goes into a bathroom, he must pretend there are no other men in there. If he uses the urinal, the other man next to him ceases to exist; if he uses the stall, everyone outside that stall ceases to exist. Even if he knows the other person, he deflects the attention back to the outside world. Perhaps he might borrow a phrase from the Fonz, saying "Now we're meeting in my office!" He would never discuss anything with another man in the bathroom, especially not anything "private" like problems or feelings. Second, a man would never just listen without trying to provide a solution to a friend's problem. These women wanted to talk and be heard and were pleased not to have any feedback that would disrupt their flow of words. Third, no man would ever be in the bathroom for an hour without at least a newspaper to read, or better still, his iPad.

Women want to be comforted when they are in distress and feeling heard comforts them

Not all families crowd into the bathroom for private time, but this is a great example of "girl talk". As Deborah Tannen states in "You Just Don't Understand", women talk for "rapport." By sharing stories, they build connection and therefore increase their sense of safety, connectedness and validity. One key element in the story, though, is contained in the phrase "the others would listen..." It's important to know what's meant by the word "listen".

Men and women listen in very different ways. If you ever overhear a woman on the phone talking to her girlfriend, sister or mother, pay attention to what's happening. You may hear the woman on your end of phone saying things like "uh-uh", "really?", "what you mean?" and "that's terrible!" This might go on for many minutes, with the other woman doing most of the talking while yours is responding. These brief responses are enough to let the other woman know that she is being listened to (this is called active listening). At some point, the conversation may shift and the woman on your end of the phone will do most of the talking. You won't be able to hear the other woman making similar utterances, but no doubt they are there.

This differs from man speak in several important ways. First, if you're on the phone with another man and he's telling you a story, it's likely you will listen patiently while making no sounds at all. You might think it's a sign of respect you're not interrupting him. He is telling you for a different reason, of course. He just wants to relay information. Tannen calls this kind of talking "report talk." Men talk to report information. So if he's on the other end of the phone telling you information, you wouldn't risk missing some of the information by commenting. To a woman, not responding is taken as a sign of not listening. This is especially true when the woman is reporting something distressing. At that moment, she not only wants to be sure you are hearing, understanding and validating her, but she also takes comfort from that interaction. Not responding (at least to let her know you're listening) will not make her feel comforted, and will probably increase her distress.

Since men are used to listening for information, the time for his reply

47

will come when he perceives that there is no more information flowing. This is like listening to the play-by-play announcer of a football game. If he's talking to another man, that time is signaled by having the first man stop talking. This silence is an implied request for input or a solution to the problem. Sometimes the request is more direct, as in "I just don't know what to do" or even "what would you do in a case like this?" However when a man is listening to a woman, the perceived flow of information may stop even while she is still talking. This might occur when she repeats herself to discuss the feedback from others or the actions of uninvolved parties. This is more like listening to the color commentator of the football game (Dandy Don, we still salute you, but Howard always had the basic facts). The problem is that for many women, the color guy, not by the play-by-play caller, relates the important part of their story. The facts are often not as important as their feelings about those facts.

This looks like support and understanding from others for her feelings

As you listen to the two women on the phone, you'll notice another element missing that is common in male conversations. Woman will rarely (compared to men) question or challenge a story relayed by a female friend. This kind of challenge would be common for men who are negotiating status, offering interpretations or seeking clarification:

Man: "I can't believe that I have to miss the poker game tonight! My wife scheduled something else we have to do. I'm pretty bummed that..."

Friend: "Wait. Is it possible she forgot we have this game every year on this date?"

Man: "Yeah she remembered, but she thought it wasn't a big deal just because we do it every year. Anyway, I'm bummed I won't get to see Johnny after his surgery, so give him a 'what's up' for me. And then whup his ass in Hold 'Em."

If this interaction were between a man and a woman, the interruption would seem to the woman that you are breaking the connection and choosing not to comfort her. When a man interrupts a woman, challenges assumptions, or asks for clarification, he is still no doubt seeking to be helpful. He is offering value in his currency, not in hers; she's likely to feel disconnected from him. As a result, she does not receive helpfulness, but rather she receives invalidation, disconnection and more discomfort. More than likely, she is not trying to report information nor focus on the facts. She is telling this story to relay her feelings, she is looking for support for her feelings:

Woman: "I really hate my boss! Nothing I ever do is good enough for her, and I never feel respected enough for what I do. After all I run the whole office, take care of her work calendar AND her social one, and I never hear any kind of compliment for my efforts. I don't know why anyone..."

Man: "If you hate it that much, why don't you just quit? You could probably do better on the outside."

Woman: "But you're not listening! I was telling you how frustrated I am! And besides, I really like the people I work with, just not the boss. I would miss all my friends if I quit."

When a woman asks a man to listen, or tries to tell him a story, it's common he will misunderstand her motivation. Listening like a man will cause him to listen for the "facts of the case" and to interpret them to find a solution. "Speaking like a woman" means to her she is using the story as a way of conveying an emotion. She either wants to share that emotion (if it's a positive one) or receive comfort from you (if it's a negative one). If men break that connection by offering a challenge or a solution, she will receive it as invalidating and unsupportive.

This is really tough for men! Our reflex to offer solutions is so strong that listening for the emotion takes lots of practice. To illustrate how this looks, let's try the conversation above one more time with a well-trained husband on hand:

Woman: "I really hate my boss! Nothing I ever do is good enough for her, and I never feel respected enough for what I do. After all I run the whole office, take care of her work calendar AND her social one, and I never hear any kind of compliment for my efforts. I don't know why anyone would ever choose to be treated like that. It's like being a servant to a tyrant."

Man: (Thinking: 'If you hate it that much, why don't you just quit? You could do better on the outside') instead says: "It sounds like don't feel appreciated for all you do."

Woman: "You're right! I <u>don't</u> feel appreciated. I'm sure you wouldn't feel that either in this situation. I mean, how would you feel if you got treated like that?"

Man: (Thinking: 'I'd either tell her I deserve better treatment or I'd just quit and look for another job') instead says (realizing this is not a real question but rather a request for validation): "I'm sure anyone would feel that way in this situation."

Woman: "That's what I think! How come the boss doesn't get it? She ought to know how it feels to be overworked and under-valued!"

Man: (Thinking rationally: 'You can't tell what she's thinking or feeling. Maybe she's had a different experience from you') instead says: "Yeah, that's pretty tough."

Woman: "I'm glad you understand. It's tiring to be at work all day, and it's so good to come home."

Isn't that the result you wanted? It's not about arguing whether her feelings are rational or how to solve her problem. What she's wanting is to have her feelings heard and validated. Practice this a lot - it will be hard at first

50

(maybe always).

But how is this different from complaining?

This might sound a lot like complaining to the untrained ear (or even to the trained ear). OK, it is complaining. Many of us were raised with the admonition "Don't complain." There was no getting sympathy for it's own sake, especially if the problem had a solution. However, it turns out there are at least two versions of complaining. Instrumental complaints are goal oriented, meaning they are requests for change (you complain that the temperature is too low so it can be raised; you complain that the octopus is undercooked so the waiter will take it back and sear it at least until it stops moving). Expressive complaints let the speaker get acknowledgement and sympathy (if you call a friend to complain that your child just failed his English As A First Language exam, you're probably not looking for teaching advice as much as sympathy for having a dumb kid).

There may also be a difference in complaint goals between men and women, which might explain why men favor the instrumental brand and women prefer the expressive. According to Deborah Tannen, women complain in an expressive way in order to bond, something that men usually don't do.

If your wife is complaining, try to determine if the complaint is instrumental or expressive; if you're not sure, then assume it's expressive until she asks you, "What do you think I should do?" Don't tell her why she shouldn't feel that way, or that the situation is not as bad as she says it is. She's probably looking for sympathy and validation. Don't give solutions. If your ability to tolerate the complaint gets stretched, express as much sympathy as you can and then redirect her to the task at hand. "I do understand how unappreciated you feel at work, and you do a lot there for your boss, but I hope you know how appreciated you are here at home, especially when you help me do things like prepare dinner." This might become important depending on the degree of her complaints and your level of tolerance. But remember, she's usually looking to you for a comforting connection, not a solution.

51

<u>Men think this means she wants to be rescued from her distress</u>

When we speak with other men about a problem, we each assume we are there to work together on a problem to find solution. The "report talk" is there to provide the information necessary. Challenging assumptions is something we do to direct each other toward a solution. Even when the problem is laden with emotion, like a man telling his friend that he is not getting along with his wife, the friend will assume the man desires a solution to his problem. His aim in helping his friend find a solution is to provide relief from the distress. It seems logical to most men that when a woman presents a problem of her own, she must be seeking relief from her distress. This starts two powerful dynamics. First, men attend to problems as dogs attend to squirrels. They're always vigilant for problems to solve and quick to find a solution. It's what they do, and they pride themselves on their abilities to do so. Solving a problem is a chance for a man to feel competent, and he's not likely to miss this opportunity!

Second, if a woman presents this problem, it's also the man's opportunity to be the hero. It may be cliché, but most would-be heroes are suckers for a damsel in distress. At least sometimes presenting a problem to a man will not only elicit his urge to solve it, it will also elicit his urge to rescue. This additional dynamic, compounded with the first one, sometimes leads to significant frustration on both their parts. While he is busy paying attention to the details so he can collect enough information to plan the best possible solution to her problem, she is convinced he is actively listening and therefore she is getting what she desires. However, as soon as he has what he thinks is enough information, he changes gears. Even in the softest possible way, if he offers advice or solutions, she will not only conclude that he isn't comforting her, but also that he doesn't want to hear her anymore.

This appears to be the complete opposite of what she thought she was receiving a few minutes earlier. How distressing! We men want to "help" or "rescue" by slaying the dragon while she wants to be helped by thoughtfully considering the difficulty <u>without</u> slaying the dragon (I know. Picture this in the middle ages: "Yes, Maid Marion, I truly empathize that yon dragon is breathing fire down thy neck and is threatening to eat thee. I'm sure even the bravest of knights wouldst quake in their boots were they in thy position. The distress unto thee merits my every reflection. I'll pour us some tea now - wouldst thou ask the dragon if he is so inclined as well, that I might thus fully attend to the continuation of thy woe?")

Helping implies a "one-up, one-down" relationship to men

There is another problem with this kind of interaction between men and women. Talking between women to receive comfort and support also emphasizes similarity and equality between the two. That is the nature of connectedness. Most talk between men, who are competing and negotiating for status, is hierarchical in nature, and emphasizes dissimilarity. This is especially true in asking for help. When a man asks another man for help, he is accepting the "one-down" position compared to the helper's "one-up" position. Asking for help lowers our status compared to our friend. This is one reason men don't like asking for instructions or directions! Asking for help diminishes our sense of independence, reduces our competitive position and diminishes our status.

However, when someone asks us for help they are putting us into the "one-up" position. Men see this as an opportunity to gain status. We're likely to milk this as much as we can, offering as much help to a woman as possible, coming up with multiple scenarios and solutions to cover all the bases. Each time we do this, though, we get further from the comfort and empathy for which the woman might look. We want to be "one-up" and women who speak with us are looking to be equal, so each of us will end up feeling frustrated that we are not getting what we want. If we really want to be helpful to women in situations like this, it's important that we recognize what kind of help they want. Here "help" is not a solution as much as it is listening and empathizing.

These days we will hear women talking in "one-up, one-down" ways, especially in the business world. This is an area where women do best when they can access their masculine thinking. For instance, I know a young woman who is trying to go into business with her mother. The daughter is business-oriented and seeks to be a doer; she gets frustrated when she gives her mother "one little job" and her mother is slow to act on it. Meanwhile, her mother is busy networking with friends, and emphasizing social interactions. Her mother has never been in business and is used to more stereotypical female ways of thinking. This business partnership would work well if the women understood that their approaches to business were as different from one another as if they were a man and a woman.

The daughter would often complain about the business in instrumental ways, hoping that her mother would make different arrangements to make a change. The mother would complain to the daughter in expressive ways, complaining that the internet was slow on some days, or that certain clients didn't call her back in time. In business, women express both the masculine and the feminine. It is important to understand that these differences in speaking, interacting, being productive, and negotiating status apply to many types of partnerships, not only to traditional ones.

Lessons

1. When in distress, women want comfort and understanding of their feelings (unless the toilet is overflowing. Then they want action).

2. While it is natural for men to offer solutions to the problems they hear about, often the "solution" to a woman's problem will be emotional support and not action.

3. Men look at getting help as being in a "one-down" position, but women look at getting help as enhancing connectedness.

4. When your wife presents a problem to you, ask her before she starts if you can help best by listening or by providing a solution. Let her be your guide.

Example Problem – "My wife is always presenting me with problems about her workplace, but she never takes the advice I give her. I'm a business consultant, so this is right up my alley. Why won't she take my suggestions?"

Duncan was a very successful organizational psychologist who consulted with many large corporations in his city about matters of management style and employee relations. He prided himself on understanding what kinds of forces made people the most productive in the most efficient at their jobs. His wife Kelly was a biochemist at a large biotech firm. She spent her days in the lab, primarily running experiments at the bench with other scientists. Sometimes she would come home having spent the day having her productivity interrupted by tempestuous colleagues. She would express her frustrations to Duncan as a series of complaints about those men and her disrupted schedule. As a man, he thought he understood men in general and male scientists in particular fairly well. He gave her suggestions about how to handle the different personalities that she might encounter in the lab.

A very tolerant woman by nature, Kelly would often respond with a sad smile, saying "thanks, honey" but walked away feeling misunderstood. Duncan observed over time that many of the issues they had discussed came up over and over again, so he concluded that Kelly was not taking action on his advice. Unfortunately for Duncan, he misunderstood what kind of response for which Kelly was looking. She wanted his problem-solving skills to be focused on her emotions, and not on her environment at work; she was using expressive complaining rather than instrumental complaining. She wanted him to "help solve her problem by listening." Once he learned what she was really after, Duncan could listen to her frustration without trying to solve the lab's personnel problems. He would acknowledge her feelings with comments like "wow, that must've been hard" and "I hear you on that one." With this change in Duncan's listening behavior, more often than not Kelly concluded their conversation walking away saying, "thanks honey!" The difference in her tone of voice let Duncan know she got what she needed from him.

5 - What if I realize there are things about my wife

I don't know?

There were three guys talking in the pub. Two of them are talking about the amount of control they have over their wives while the third remains quiet.

After a while one of the first two turns to the third and says, "Well, what about you, what sort of control do you have over your wife?"

The third fellow says, "I'll tell you. Just the other night my wife came to me on her hands and knees."

The first two guys were amazed. "What happened then?" they asked. "She said, 'get out from under the bed and fight like a man'."

How well do you know your wife?

This third fellow might have known his wife pretty well even if he didn't let his friends know what he knew. Most guys think they know their wives pretty well even if they admit they don't understand them (yes there's a difference). At least until they see a pattern in their disagreements, or until she asks him to take one of those quizzes from Cosmo called something like "How well do you really know your spouse?" After submitting to your wife's request that you take it while she's watching (you knew that was a bad move, but didn't know just how to get out of it), you find out you don't know her favorite movie, her least favorite type of dog or her mother's middle name. So you get a score of 5 on the quiz. Out of 50.

Recovery is still possible - you could stop right there and tell her, "Boy, you'd better take time to tell me all about yourself!" At least she'd be happy to tell you things about her, even while steaming that you must not have been interested before. More likely, as a guy you'll walk away saying something like, "well, at least I know what kind of sex you like." Sadly, you probably don't know that either - not if she's been trying to keep you happy all this time. Or you might end up thinking to yourself, "boy, I guess I don't know a lot of things about my wife - maybe I should find out!"

What if you realize there's a lot about your wife you don't know?

This is another place where it's important to repeat the admonition about using generalizations to describe people. The first portion of this book explained things about women in general. You're likely reading this book because you want to understand one woman (or a few women, if you include daughters, mothers and in-laws) in specific. Some of these generalizations may not apply to that one woman. So, rather than have you make assumptions about your wife based on what many other women do or think, it's important to spend time getting to know your wife. You may already think you know her; you've probably been married to her for a while. It might seem to you she's spent a lot of time telling you about herself, which might be true. In fact, many of the things you know about her are true. There are probably also things about her you never thought to ask, never knew you should ask, or about which you have made assumptions. You might begin this chapter by scanning the headings first and reading through those sections you know have already presented conflict (or at least discussion) in your marriage. You can always read the other parts of this chapter later.

Your wife as a person

Unless you have been friends since childhood, you undoubtedly knew little or nothing about your now wife before you met her. When you began dating or otherwise getting to know each other, you may have asked her a lot of questions about herself or allowed her to tell you about herself. You might have learned about what kind of music she liked, whether she got sick on roller coasters, and that she liked sushi. These were important for your dating activities. At what point did you learn everything there was to know about your wife? Probably never. The things she might value the most may be what she thinks and what she feels (and when she feels them). These you have to pay special attention to because those things are so straightforward as to be non-issues for men. Women seem to give these words much different importance than we do.

This is true because people grow and change, and as legend has it, women grow and change more than men. Given your wife has grown and changed since you married her, you probably don't know as much about her as you used to. Why not let her continue to tell you about herself and pay attention to what these truths tell you about her as a person? Or, if there are things you don't understand, ask her about them. Be careful to let her know your questions about her are honest questions and are not scoldings (an honest question might be "I really don't understand - what things lead you to that conclusion?" A scolding dressed up as a question might be "What were you thinking??").

What is your wife's history?

When you are dating, you probably told each other about where you grew up, what your family environment was like, what things you liked to do as a child and perhaps about your friends and school. She might even have told you she had a possum in her back yard she named Harry and that she tried to introduce Harry to the family dog thinking they would be good friends (of course they were - they ran off together looking like they were playing, right?). These things are all part of your wife's history. However, she lived for many years before you met her, and there's no way she could have told you everything about her earlier life, all her thoughts and feelings about various parts of her history.

I have heard women say, "I'm nothing like my family," but that doesn't tell you whether she wishes she were more like her family or if she was happy to distinguish herself from them. Once you meet her family, you might realize she was right, and it's a darned good thing (or you might realize there was a lot more in common than she realized). These things impacted her sense of herself, her expectations and assumptions, her tastes in other people and things, the strengths she brings to your marriage and the needs she has of you. Many of these latter two (strengths and needs) may be hidden from conscious view, even to her, but might indicate what forces create her specific behaviors.

How has your wife changed since you met her?

Even though the answer to this question might seem clear, it's worth taking a second look. If you met your wife when she was young or if you've known her for more than a few years, your wife has likely changed a great deal. Women do that; they call it growth and they consider it to be a good thing. Why do they do that? It's one of the mysteries of the universe - we pick someone we like and with whom we want to make a life, and then once we're committed, they change. Although sometimes men feel they struggle to keep up with their ever-changing wife, there is a big upside to this evolution. Each time you notice that your wife has changed, evolved or developed new traits, you have new things to appreciate and get to know. For those men excited about meeting someone new, here's your opportunity! It's like having a new wife but better because most of her is the same person you fell in love with originally. How have her activities changed since you met her? What interests has she developed? How have her friendships changed (perhaps from superficial, school age friendships into more mature, mutually nurturing ones)? How has her relationship with you changed? Perhaps she has turned from a willing follower, being smitten by your charm and brilliance at first meeting you, into an understanding co-leader and voting member of this corporation you call a marriage. A friend told me the main way his wife had changed was that she used to ask him to stay home to be with her; now she's always asking him to stay home with the kids so she can go out.

<u>Who is your wife at home?</u>

Most men have little idea of how their wives spend their day except for what their wives tell them. Here's an interesting challenge. Sit down with your wife, with a calendar page divided up into hours, and have her tell you what she did from the time you left her (or she left you) until you reunited later that day. Go through each hour and ask her what were her activities, thoughts and feelings during that hour. She might have a hard time recalling all the details because some of her day was automatic for her. You might be surprised about all the different things she did, all the different things she thought about, and the vast array of feelings she experienced during that time. If she was multi-tasking, she might well have had more thoughts and awareness in one hour than you did all day. One husband learned that his wife watched the Disney channel in the morning while she did the crossword puzzle, imagined replanting the flowerbeds and searched online for books about traveling to Brazil. All before 8am. On a Saturday. Dig for the details.

If she tells you, "after you left for work, I first took Johnny to school," ask her about the details of the drive and whatever conversation the two of them had. Ask her about the traffic, or any interesting things they might have seen along the way. Ask her about what she listened to on the radio on the way home. You will probably surprise her (and very likely please her) if you ask her these kinds of details, and it will give you a very different look into who your wife is at home. Part of knowing your wife at home will be observing her when you are both there. This might be before work, after work, or when you're together on weekends. Watch what things she does, and how she does those things, even for one day. If you see something unfamiliar, ask her about it. This is not very different from what you did when you were first dating. It's a matter of letting go of assumptions you might have made about her. It's amazing how many times men unconsciously believe their wives cease to exist during the day, magically reappearing when the husbands get back home. Yes, they have their own lives, and they're every bit as interesting to them as ours are to us.

Who is your wife at work?

These days many families contain two working spouses regardless of whether there are children in the family. Your wife might be the CEO of a major corporation. She might be an attorney in a large firm or a pole dancer - they both make good money. She might be a teacher or work in school administration. She might have the most difficult job of all, being a mom. She might already be prone to telling you about her day if you are prone to listening. Whenever she tells you the facts, events, situations and interactions of her day, ask her some variation of the following question: "How did you feel about that?" This is a level of understanding your wife may rarely hear you pursue and one for which many women wish. Does she feel competent or doubtful? Was she pleased or hurt? Was she eager to have a certain encounter, or did she say sit with anticipatory dread?

If you've been married for any length of time, she might have gotten used to just reporting the facts (often this is all men value). Because the work environment is still dominated by masculine thinking and communicating, your wife often has to leave her feminine side behind when she goes to work. Women flip between their feminine and masculine sides with more ease, and more often, than do men. If you ask her how she felt about certain things, it will encourage her to leave that masculine style at work and to return to her feminine self at home. It will also show you an entire dimension of your wife's being about which you may be unaware.

Who is your wife in the marriage?

Your wife is a married woman. It's part of her self-definition, just as being a married man is part of yours. How does she present that part of her self to the world? Is she still proud of her engagement ring and her wedding band? Does she speak about you as "my husband", reinforcing public recognition of the relationship? Or are you "my other child"? How does she interact with you within your marriage? For most couples there is not only a division of labor (chores and responsibilities), but also an unspoken agreement about the different situations in which one person takes the lead and the other person follows. Initiation of sex is a common one of these; others include suggesting ideas, planning vacations, organizing activities, chasing the naked children still dripping from the bath down the hall, etc. When is your wife the leader, and when is she the follower? Are you equal co-partners or does your relationship appear to be more of a hierarchy?

There are certain times you might be more comfortable letting your wife lead. Common examples of this include when caring for the kids, interacting with social groups and maintaining the household (just make sure she leaves the garage to you). Does she see herself as a leader here? And is she comfortable with that role? Knowing who your wife is in the marriage is not just a matter of how you see her, but also of how she sees herself.

What is your wife's relationship with your family members?

Most of us grow up with just one family to which we compare the concept of "normal." Even though we might be conscious of differences among families (seeing how our friends interact with their families), we still make a tacit assumption that when we get married, our spouse will fit in with our family (or our idea of family). For instance, if your family is loud, thick-skinned and forever joking around, you might expect your wife will participate in this behavior, or at least tolerate it in good humor. Suppose her definition of normal (coming from the family she grew up in) was one of quiet and tempered mutual respect, or a tendency to take things that were said as serious comments. If your family instead presumed any comments might be sarcasm or witticism, she might not fit in at all to the humor of your family. A nice book on Appreciating Humor might be perfect for a Christmas gift for her.

How does your wife get along with your family? How does she feel about the interactions she has with them? Does she feel supported by you when issues involving your family come up? There are many great in-law jokes, primarily because there are so many in-law stereotypes. Most of those stereotypes came about because of a kernel of truth (the overbearing wife's father or the over-protective husband's mother do exist in some families). It's important to know the side of your wife that interfaces with the kernels of truth represented by your family.

You might not fit in with the dynamics of her family. This gives her the opportunity to reciprocate next Christmas with a nice book on Communicating in Dulcet Tones. You might have a sister-in-law who is too demanding of your wife's time (because that interaction was normal in the family in which she and her sister grew up). You might have a father-in-law who makes jokes about your wife's competence, sense of humor or creativity. You might have a mother-in-law who is critical and judgmental of your wife's position in the marriage. If she accepts these dynamics and you are offended by them, they can not only strain your relationship but lead to resentments directed at you by your in-laws. You might have to look harder to find a nice book on Managing the Outlaws. Or perhaps one on Moving to the Australian Outback.

What are your wife's dreams and aspirations?

Everyone old enough to imagine a future has dreams or aspirations; this includes your wife. They say women worry about their future until they get married; men never worry about their future until they have a wife. Marriage allows women not only to focus on their present and not worry about their future, but also to focus on their wishes for the future instead of their worries about it. By dreams, I don't mean the dreams where she's walking on a sandy beach and is swept away by a dark-haired muscular man on a white horse.

What are your wife's wishes for the future? Does she dream of continuing her education? Does she have aspirations for more important positions at work, or more fulfilling employment? Does she dream of running her own business? Perhaps she dreams about having children, or about the day the current children move out of the house. Does she dream of moving to a farm or moving to the city? Does she dream about traveling with you or just growing old together (if so, what does that look like to her)? Does she dream about having more friends, or being a big influence on society? Each of her dreams will tell you about something quite important to her and it will tell you something important about her. Often those dreams are rooted in expectations and values at your wife's core, and understanding these dreams will help you resolve differences that otherwise seem "irreconcilable."

What are your wife's wants and needs from you?

To your wife, your relationship with her is the potential fulfillment of many of her wants and needs. Her Superman, that's you; well, minus the blue tights. That's what drew her to you in the first place. She might not have known exactly what those wants and needs were. They might have comprised things like the need for security, a need to be needed, a desire for closeness and intimacy (at least as she defined these two, whether physical, emotional, or some other kind of closeness), a need to feel respected by you, and a need to respect you. Over time, her needs and wants have likely become more diverse and more identifiable. Who does she want you to be with her? How does she want to feel when she's around you? What does she appreciate that you are already doing, and what did she wish you would do that you are not yet doing?

Men are often afraid to ask their wives questions like these because they fear their wives have an unmet agenda for them. As if there is also a silent emotional version of the Honey-Do list, a "Honey-Be" list with nearly impossible things at the top. Don't worry. Your wife may have unmet wants and needs from you, but most of the time she does not want to change you as a person. What she wants is to change the way she feels around you, and you can influence that. The amazing thing that most men don't realize is you may not need to change your character, and some strategic changes in your behavior might make a world of difference *if only you knew what they were*. The secret is this: your wife may know what those things are, and she may be dying to tell you (or perhaps to discover them with you). Take the risk and invite her to try.

Lessons

1. Get to know your wife all over again, the same way you did when you were first dating. Ask her about herself.

2. Pay attention to knowing your wife in any of the different realms of

her life. Each of these brings out a different side of her.

3. Remember to let your wife know these questions are truly a search for your understanding. They are not meant to be implied criticisms or scoldings. Be sure to explain the difference.

4. When your wife answers your questions, do your best to listen to the information provided. Don't take her comments personally; remember, this information is about her, not about you.

5. Your wife is <u>always</u> changing! Understand that the new wife you discover this year will be new again next year. Expect change, learn to embrace it and let it fascinate you.

Example Problem - "I've been married for 13 years, and now my wife is starting to say and do unfamiliar things, like wanting things she's never wanted and changing her priorities. It's like I hardly know her any more. What gives?"

Wilbur (his real name) and Kathy were both scientists, married straight out of graduate school. Both had successful careers in jobs related to their fields of study and others in the workplace viewed them each as having wisdom and authority. Since they decided against having kids, they enjoyed each other's company at home, going out with friends, and an active life that included hiking and camping. After about 10 years of this pattern in their marriage, Kathy started to express an interest in crafts and writing, things that gave her a lot of pleasure but rarely included Will. Will tried his hand at each of these, found them amusing but not rewarding, and discontinued his efforts in those areas. While he appreciated that his wife was doing things she enjoyed, he felt a little left out of her solo activities. But mostly he was befuddled by the change he perceived in his wife going from a scientist to an artist. He felt left out by her artistic interests and resented her new activities. He became more irritable with her and somewhat more distant.

Will eventually asked Kathy about her dreams for her life and for their relationship. Kathy explained she was happy with their relationship, but she needed to be challenged in a way science couldn't meet. Kathy also wanted to challenge herself. She went into science in the first place because she was good in school, particularly in math and science, and people encouraged her. That her father and mother were both in related fields gave her reason to respect the sciences and the choice seemed natural. She felt bored and unchallenged in her job, which was in a field related to science but was rather routine in nature. Her artistic hobbies allowed her to be challenged in a different way, limited only by her creativity. When she explained this part to Will, he understood his wife had not changed from one personality type to another, but rather had just changed the way in which she satisfied her cravings for challenge. Without asking her, he might never have known. In fact, he wondered if there were non-science things that might provide challenges for him as well.

6 - What if there are things about me my wife doesn't know?

A man charged with domestic assault and battery insisted at his trial he had pushed his wife "just a little bit". When he was pressured yet again by the prosecuting attorney to illustrate just how hard, the defendant approached the prosecutor, slapped him in the face, grabbed him firmly by the lapels and flung him over the table.

He then faced judge and jury and calmly declared, "I would say it was about one-tenth that hard."

What if you realize your wife doesn't know enough about you?

Explaining yourself to your wife will hopefully not feel like being in a courtroom, unless your wife is an attorney or a judge. In that case you might need more than this book, such as references on stating the facts in a civil case.

What do I mean when I say "explaining yourself to your wife"? Well, I don't mean get defensive (never a good idea) or offer excuses, and I don't mean, as an old friend used to tell me, "justify your existence!" I mean teaching her about you. When you were first dating, you told her a lot about yourself (here

69

I'm thinking about the wonderfulness of how you do things, what you do, and what you <u>will</u> do that she would discover). She asked a lot of questions about you (no doubt you answered these questions referencing that same wonderfulness). It's time to repeat that with a slightly different emphasis. To teach her about you as a person is one of the most important things you can do with her, for her, and to include her. When she feels she understands you better, she will feel more connected to you and she will be more of the woman you want her to be. Even the act of trying to explain yourself to her will likely impress her as you'll be getting closer to sharing your thoughts and feelings with her.

The act of teaching her about you is a form of connection. Plus (as an added benefit to you), you get to be in the role of the expert; no one knows more about you than you! The trick is to bypass the wonderfulness and get to the thought process, such as how you come to certain conclusions and decide what's important on any given day. You'll also want to tell her about your doubts and uncertainties (vulnerabilities make you more human, but don't overdo this one) and your feelings about certain moments. For this last point, remember feelings are always a single word, like "happy" or "mystified"; if it takes more than a single word it's probably a thought.

How to teach your wife about you

How do you teach your wife about you as a man and as a person? She's already learned quite a few things just by living with you and observing you. For example, she knows many of the facts and figures about your life, like how often you miss the clothes hamper with your dirty laundry. She knows some of what you like and what you don't like because you've told her (especially about not liking chick-flicks, and she persists - go figure). She knows some of your habits and routines. She knows the brilliance of your thinking and the corniness of your jokes. She may even know a few things about your feelings, like when you're hurt, angry or excited. There are more things you can tell her about you that can enhance your connection to her. The problem is that these can be somewhat scary to tell.

We are finally leaving the era during which men were told, "To connect with women you need to get in touch with your feminine side." This was a nonstarter for many men because it sounded like they had to be less manly. Not true. No need to start eating edamame and yogurt, reading romance novels, taking bubble baths or going to yoga (unless you actually like yoga). However, to be more connected with the woman in your life you may need to be more vulnerable, something that feels risky to most men and natural to many women.

The first time I heard this phrase as a teenager, I had the image in my head of a dog lying on his back with his throat exposed, exposing his jugular for a ritual bloodletting. Yeah, sign me up! This might be extreme, but many men feel it's risky being vulnerable in any sense. It is a risk for women too, but women seem to know that the benefit of taking this risk (emotional intimacy) is well worth the cost. Men have a harder time with that idea, in part because we raise men with the idea that vulnerability reduces one's competitive edge. This is true on the playing field, in the locker room, even in the workplace. At home, being vulnerable is a requirement for having an emotionally intimate connection. Yes, it's a risk. You might perceive the situation as one that risks rejection, criticism, humiliation, embarrassment or shame. These are powerful reasons that men use to avoid taking that risk, but that avoidance isolates the real core person you are from someone with whom you want to connect.

How do you take that risk on purpose? The ways of doing this are infinite and vary greatly from person to person. A common response to this question from women (and many relationship therapists) is for men to share their feelings about different things. This is great advice in theory; the problem is that men do not have immediate access to their feelings about things as do women. We do have immediate access to some feelings though. Our caveman brains are adept at evaluating a new situation within seconds and answering the question, "Do I kill it, eat it or mate with it?" For most things, however, we need time to think. Neurologically we are not wired to have immediate emotional awareness of our reactions (other than the adrenaline-fueled fight or flight response).

If you can't quite tolerate discussing your feelings (or can't figure them out), try telling your wife about one of the random thoughts you had during the day. Most people have thoughts that fly into and out of their heads, and many of the these thoughts are bizarre, confusing, and sometimes embarrassing. They are almost always meaningless, the random bits of brain static that go on while your processing something else. Try taking the risk of telling her one of these random thoughts. An example of this might be "I was sitting at my desk at work, and it flashed through my mind that it would be horrible to get my pen lodged in my ear accidentally." Telling her this might seem trivial, but you would be taking the risk that she might find you strange, humiliate you or reject you.

Another example of a risk you could take is to tell your wife one of your private worries. This might be a worry about money, family, your future or any number of things. It might be a worry that the Cubs might actually win the World Series some day, leading to anarchy and chaos. You might preface this by letting her know that you don't want to explain this worry, just to let her know that you have it sometimes. You might tell her it will be important for you to check on the baseball scores from time to time to keep an eye on any impending doom. Not fully explaining the depths of the worry, but just that it occurs, might mitigate some of the risk of being vulnerable. If your wife is at all aware of sports, she will know immediately that this is one of those irrational fears about things that almost never come true, and she might empathize with how much this silly fear bothers you. You would definitely be sharing your vulnerable side with her, and you would be telling her a little about you as a person and as a man. Being vulnerable does not diminish your manliness one iota. Neither does having a silly worry like this one.

Telling your wife about your wants and needs

Everyone has wants and needs; you have them too. You might be used to listening for the wants and needs of others if you have a family. It sounds like this: "HONEY!! Can you bring me my towel? I forgot it when I got into the shower!" Here we're talking about more basic, essential wants and needs. Things like wanting to stay in shape, needing more acknowledgement for things you do, or wanting finally to put a child-proof lock on the bedroom door. If you haven't told her what your wants and needs are, you left her to guess what they are based on your actions and the things you have told her. Remember, this process is about teaching your wife who you are, and not just who you have let her see.

What do you want from her? This might include wanting her to be loyal to you, to put up with your cranky moods, to laugh at your jokes, even the mother-in-law ones. Try to remember that the mother-in-law in question, the foil of your best jokes, is your wonderful wife's mother. What do you want from yourself? This might include wanting to be more financially comfortable or respected at work, or wanting to have more time to pursue hobbies like playing World Of Warcraft or skydiving. What do you want from family? This might include wanting to spend more time with your children (playing WOW with them), wanting more respect from your in-laws (idea - stop telling them the mother-in-law jokes) or wanting more love and approval from your grandchildren (bribes like taking them on a trip to the store work here; if the grandkids are teens, getting them out of the house and away from their parents works well too).

Your needs are very important and they differ from your wants in that needs are essential for life and happiness. You may need time for exercise and physical activity (yes, your life does depend on that). You may need time to spend with your male friends (your happiness depends on your social integration). Your need for sleep, solitude, spontaneity, intellectual challenge and adventure may all differ from those of your wife. Share these with her. She may not realize the degree to which your needs dictate your behavior and influence who you are.

Don't forget to include in this list your desire to make your wife happy. For many men, this one is tops. We might forget to show it (while we're busy attending to all the other urgencies of our lives), but take the time to remind her of that. Most men know that their life is better when their wife is happy, in part because her happiness removes a potential black cloud from over our heads. We also take pride in knowing that our wives are happy with us, and that feeling of pride can fuel us to excel in so many other areas. Having a happy wife gives us "go-juice".

Who are you in the marriage/relationship?

You may have thought about this question superficially, and you may have adopted the title role of husband or boyfriend. What does that role mean to you? Are you the main breadwinner, working hard to provide and coming home in the evening to relieve your wife from some of her child rearing duties? Or are you the one who stays at home while your wife attends to the corporate world? Are you the decision-maker and leader of the family? Or are you a follower? Or better yet, are you an equal partner in your decision-making? If you consider yourself an equal partner, how do decisions get made when each of you is equally passionate on opposite sides of an idea? While most men consider carefully how they contribute to the household and family, often men forget to consider how they feed and nurture their marriage. Like a garden, this relationship will wither and die if it's not tended and nurtured. It's a living thing that demands attention, much like having another child. How do you nurture your marriage? What do you do to show value for this third entity you call your relationship (not you, not your wife, but a hybrid of the two)?

Who are you are at work?

If you're like most men, regardless of whether your wife also works you might tell her some of the more notable activities and conversations you have been a part of at work. However, if you're like most men, you may not relate what was going on inside of you during those times, or your internal process. For instance, your boss was describing to the entire team that the big contract renewal was looming. You would have become annoyed at his repeated reminders while everyone was already working at warp speed, except that your allergic reaction to the new laundry detergent you bought on sale, even though your wife suggested you buy the detergent you always use, gave you such crotch-rot that you were completely distracted from the boss's droning on and on. These are the internal processes at work.

By telling your wife about your workday you tell her the kinds of forces and stresses work exposes you to, but it doesn't do very much to tell her about who you are at work. How did it impact you when you are trying to finish an important project by a certain deadline, but one person comes into your office to ask a favor while another one is on the phone making another request of your time? Did you feel stressed and overwhelmed, or were you thinking it was good to be indispensable and needed? Or were you trying to suppress the image of slamming the door in the interloper's face? Work is a very important part of both a man's day and his self-definition; telling your wife about that side of you might be like shining a light on the dark side of the moon. It might be a side of you she rarely sees.

Who are you at home?

Most men have a relatively defined home life. Monday night football might be as important to you as a manicure is to her; each of these is pleasurable to one of you and perhaps not understandable to the other. If puttering around the house makes you feel productive, tell her that. She may view the tasks of home repair and home improvement differently than you do. Tell her exactly what relaxing at home (or being active/productive at home) means to you. If you enjoy entertaining others at your home, your appreciation for that activity might differ from hers. Let her know what you get from it. If you are involved in the local school, community or other organizations, share with your wife what these activities mean to you. Don't assume that they will mean the same things to her, because they probably won't. As much as it might seem "obvious" to you, it won't be "obvious" to her; tell her.

Who are you historically?

When you were dating, you shared a lot about your childhood, formative years, and perhaps even work and dating history with your then wife-to-be. Being married and or having a family may have triggered other thoughts about who you were before you met her. These thoughts represent a side of you she does not yet know. How does interacting with her remind you of interacting with your mother or your father when you were a child? For example, do you ask her permission to play with the other boys, or do you bring home for her inspection the "grossest thing ever to be found in our yard"?

What patterns are you seeing in your marriage now that might repeat those from earlier dating relationships? What things did you traditionally love or hate to do that you still feel the same way about now? Even if you've been married for over 30 years, your thinking changes daily. Filling in your wife on some of these new thoughts and awarenesses, even about ancient history, will be to her as if she were meeting a new version of the man she's already grown to love. However, if you're already very accomplished at telling her your thoughts and she's taken the extraordinary step of asking you to keep some of those thoughts private, you might consider heeding her suggestion.

Lessons

1. Teaching your wife about yourself means taking the risk of being emotionally intimate with her. This might be scary, but it will definitely enhance your connection.

2. Tell your wife about yourself in all the different realms of your life. Each will display a different side of you to her.

3. Remember that telling her about yourself will feel like a risk because you will face potential embarrassment or rejection. It's this risk that allows you to be vulnerable, and its vulnerability that allows you to be intimate.

4. If these risks seem too great at first, preface your comments with a statement about how important it is for you to share this information without judgment. She will no doubt try her best.

Example problem - "I recently read on Facebook that my wife has been complaining I don't share my feelings with her. Do I have to do this? I'm not even sure what my feelings are half of the time. Why is this so important to her?"

The way Allen found out that his wife was unhappy about their communication was sadly typical of the way social media influences our daily lives. Since he was "friends" on Facebook with his wife, he noticed when she responded to another friend who had complained about her own husband didn't he share his feelings by saying "mine doesn't either!" At first, he wanted to not take her comment personally, and tried to accept it as her stating a fact. Yet the more he thought about it, the more he realized that she was stating her unhappiness. While it made him sad that he was not providing his wife happiness in this area of communication, it frustrated him that she was bemoaning something so stereotypical and yet so difficult. When he approached her about her post, she looked a little sheepish but said, "I wish you told me more about how you feel. It seems that you've kept a lot of you from me."

Allen's wife, while asking for him to share his feelings with her, may instead have been asking for him to share more of himself with her. Women are adept at identifying and understanding their own feelings and then communicating them to other women. Because of this, they sometimes assume men are also good at this process if they choose to be. In fact, men are much more attuned to taking action than they are to feelings. Secondarily, they are attuned to paying attention to what they're thinking, which is often about some action they are taking. Identifying feelings is a difficult task for many men, in part because of the way their brains are put together (the bundle of fibers connecting the two hemispheres, the corpus callosum, is smaller in men than in women; this means it's more difficult for men to transfer information from the emotional side to the verbal side of their brains). Allen explained this difficulty to his wife and to react positively to her desire for more sharing. He offered to share more of his thoughts with her as he was aware of them. Although this was not the currency of sharing his wife initially had in mind, it made her feel more connected to him when he shared more of his internal process with her. Sharing thoughts may not be the same as sharing feelings, but if the desire is to increase sharing, this route may be easier and more practical for many men.

7 - What if I keep hurting her feelings?

Why don't men often show their true feelings?
Because they don't have any.

His feelings

If you guessed that a woman wrote this joke, you're probably right. At least it's likely that women will propagate a joke like this more than men will. Men rarely seem to understand women's feelings and can seem out of touch with their own. Do men even have feelings to understand? Well, of course we have feelings. It's like Homer Simpson says: "Sometimes I feel hungry. Or horny." See, we have feelings. At least that's what we call them.

Men are often more in tune with their bodily sensations than with their emotional states, a good thing for hunter-gatherers. You know how it feels to have a sore back after doing yard work. You know how something feels after you've sanded it smoothly enough for the final coat of paint. You know how it feels to look at the tempting piece of pumpkin pie, after eating way too much Thanksgiving dinner, which followed way too many appetizers. We can also cite Groucho Marx: When concerned about the well-being of a particular woman, someone asked him, "How did she feel?" To which he replied, "She felt fine to me!"

What if we're talking about emotions? Well, it turns out we've got those too. Who'd have thought? We're just not involved with our emotions the same way that women are. For example, you know how it feels when your team scores the game-winning field goal in overtime. You know how it feels when some jerk cuts you off in traffic. You know how it feels when your wife tells you, "Not tonight, honey. I'm just too tired." Believe it or not, most of us can even identify those emotions with certain names – excited, happy, irritated, and disappointed. Maybe also homicidal, depending on how work was that day, and whether the moron that cut you off on the freeway was driving a sports car or a sedan. We acknowledge an emotional world and we understand it's function. We just don't live there. At best, men are infrequent visitors to this land, and we often need directions to find our way around whenever we visit. As in the physical world, we rarely ask directions here, either.

Whether by inborn ability, social learning, or epigenetic trans-methylation (okay, I won't charge you extra for each of those big words – this means there can be changes to your DNA after your genes have already been set), men do not have the same relationship with emotions that women do. Men can have the same emotions as do their "more emotional" counterparts, even identifying them if necessary. However, to us feelings are more like a foreign language we can speak with some effort. It's clearly not our first language. Men are more aware of thoughts and sensations, and we experience these as rationally explainable phenomena. For example, even though we are capable of feeling happy, it's hard for most men to identify where in their bodies they feel it (more about happiness later in this chapter). It's those irrational, foreign, and mystifying things that women refer to when they say "feelings".

What if you don't understand why she's so hung up on feelings? One difficulty men have understanding women is that rational thought is on a different plane from emotions. Like two slices of bread in a loaf, these two planes do not intersect. You cannot use rational thought to understand emotions, nor can you use rational thought to refute an emotional state. Have you ever tried to talk a woman out of what she's feeling? Then you get my point. It's not only impossible, but you're likely to receive flak that sounds like, "Are you trying to tell me that I SHOULDN'T feel the way I do?? And who are you to tell me about my feelings? Mr. 'Doesn't-Even-Know-The-Difference-Between-Frustrated-And-Irritated!'" She has a point. Being logical and rational makes it more difficult for men to understand the world of emotions in which women live.

Her feelings

Women live in the world of feelings. Most things she does are influenced by how they make her feel. The clothes she wears on any day are designed to either echo how she already feels, or to make her feel a certain way she desires (or, perhaps, just because they're clean). She may do other things to avoid certain feelings (like feeling fat, scared or dirty). She might ask you to do things for her because she wants to feel nurtured. The decorations she chooses for the house, the car she drives, the friends she has and the things she talks about are all part of her life because of how they make her feel. To many men, this is similar to telling us that women live in the world of ghosts, and that everything they do is about paying attention to the ghost-du-jour. She might feel strong, or angry, or sad, or intimidating, or even puzzled. Notice that all of these words that describe different feelings are single words. This is a clue to whether things are feelings or thoughts: if it takes more than one word to describe something, it's probably a thought. If you say, "I feel like I want to go out," that's a thought; if you say, "I feel restless," that's a feeling. In general, "I feel that..." or "I feel like..." are thoughts, not feelings. While your thoughts may be important to you as a man, her feelings are just important to her as a woman. Start your education about feelings by learning the language.

We give each other what we want for ourselves

During close or especially intimate moments, does your wife ever turn her doe eyes to you, and with an ever-hopeful expression ask you, "What are you feeling?" And does she then seem disappointed in your bumbling response? This kind of question often frustrates men, in part because it requests we investigate something that is quite foreign to us. It's similar to asking men which flower or candle scent is their favorite. It might be similar to asking someone who is <u>not</u> a fan of Star Trek to name her favorite Klingon epithet. Most women know men are not facile with feelings, so why do they insist on asking about our feelings? Are they hopeful despite all evidence to the contrary? Possibly. It is also possible they are asking you what they would like to be asked themselves. Most women would be delighted if their guy asked, "What are you feeling?" so she might be thinking that if you were a woman, feelings would be important to you.

Men are not simply hairy women behaving badly, and we are much more likely (if we want to be vulnerable and sharing at that moment) to talk about our thoughts rather than our feelings. If she asks this of you, feel free to tell her, "I can tell you what I'm thinking right now, and this is it". Above all, this question often is a request on her part for reassurance, primarily reassurance that your relationship is still strong. Even if it's the truth, don't <u>just</u> tell her at that moment you are thinking about work, the big game, or your painful ingrown toenail. Tell her what you were thinking <u>about her</u> (and the game). If you choose to go into feelings, tell her what you were feeling <u>about her</u> (while you were thinking about the game). If you weren't thinking or feeling anything about her at that moment, then quick! Think about her (like how inquisitive she is, or how nice that she's interested in knowing about you) and tell her that. Whew!

You don't want to lie in a case like this, but it's a no-win situation for guys. When women ask what we are thinking or feeling, they want us to be honest, but they also have a desired answer in mind. At some other, out-of-the-blue time, ask your honey what answer she prefers to that question - the truth or something about her. You can always try out "I was thinking about the game, but now I'm thinking about you!"

<u>Stop asking her opinion about everything!</u>

As the feminine energy, women live in their emotions, and their feelings are things for which they want to be cherished. In contrast, as the masculine energy, men live with their thinking, and their thoughts are things for which they want to be respected. One form of your thoughts is your opinion, and most men can come up with an opinion with little difficulty. You may express your thoughts and opinions to your wife, and you want her to respect them by agreeing, asking for more information, or listening with rapt attention. This is your bailiwick, your wheelhouse; this is where you live.

Asking your wife for her opinion about a choice gets old for at least two reasons. First, she doesn't want to make all the choices, because for each choice she risks that you'll be disappointed. Additionally, choosing is a burden - save her from that. Man up, take the risk, and choose. Then ask her about her feelings about your choice. Second, asking her about her thoughts is the equivalent of asking you about your feelings. Not to say women don't have opinions – we know they do. However, if you ask her about her thoughts on something, you're asking her to leave her comfort zone and enter yours. This might include what she wants for dinner, what activity she wants to plan for the coming weekend, or which candidate is best suited in the upcoming election. She probably could answer this, but she might well be more comfortable hearing your opinion and then having you ask her feelings about that opinion.

This way, you get to express your thoughts, and she gets to express her feelings, each one coming from their own strengths. If she expresses her opinions and thoughts freely after you've asked, listen carefully to the feelings behind them. Respond to those feelings if you can. "It sounds like you'd be happy with anything at all for dinner, as long as it's simple," or "It sounds like you really want to focus on us just being together rather than on what we do." Don't wait for her to give you a solution if one isn't forthcoming – she might be trying to tell you what really is important to her. Focus on her feelings.

The last three sections have discussed her feelings as in her "feeling states". Let's now talk about her Feelings (note the proper noun).

Her Feelings (!)

Allison Armstrong uses the image that a woman has a special organ in the middle of her chest (stop staring!) that she refers to as her Feelings. When her Feelings get hurt, the result is as impactful as if a man has a migraine. She will be in pain, but it will be an emotional pain that recruits physical and sensory components; it will be as real as any pain that a man feels/senses. One common reason that women get their feelings hurt by men is that men and women make different assumptions in their communications. For example, men often to make practical assumptions about the reasons and outcomes of things they say and do. "If you ask me about my day, I will assume that you want the truth, and give you as much practical detail as I think makes sense." Women often assume that behind men's motivations, some desire for an emotional connection must exist; they get hurt when this assumption turns out to be wrong. Often the bottom line is this: a woman might get her feelings hurt by something a man says or does because she applies the same set of expectations and meanings to his response as she would to a woman's response.

Our old "asking like a boy/girl" issue is a good example: She asks, "do you want to go out for a pizza?" and he replies, "No, I'd rather have a burger." She gets her feelings hurt because if another woman used this reply, it would mean she didn't care about, didn't love, or didn't respect her friend. The man might mean something different ("I was just being honest"). Yes, it's based on a misinterpretation, because it might mean something very different just because a man said it (his motivations didn't match the stereotypical motivations of a woman in the same situation). Yet her feelings got hurt because she felt an injured or broken connection between the two of them.

It's this misinterpretation that often leads to hurt feelings. When that happens, the worst thing you can do is defend yourself. The second worst thing you can do is to explain. When a woman's feelings are hurt, neither is valuable at the moment. Imagine this example in reverse: in the kitchen your wife is gesturing with a knife in her hand, oblivious to the fact you are standing behind her, and she slices your carotid artery by accident. How useful would it be for her to defend herself ("but I didn't even know you were there!") or to explain herself ("I was trying to make a point!")? You're standing there spurting blood everywhere! A more useful response on her part that would to treat the wound by putting pressure on the cut, or ice, a bandage, or something similar. Perhaps she could call 911 or at least get you a bucket to bleed into. These would be more useful than explaining or defending herself.

The same is true when a woman's feelings get hurt. Defending or explaining yourself miss the mark and are often perceived as making matters worse. You need a response that addresses the wound. Since the wound is emotional and not physical, you need a response that addresses the emotions. "I'm sorry I hurt your feelings" is an excellent response. You'll be surprised at how much weight that carries and it saves you having to call 911, for either of you.

Why is defending or explaining so natural to men, and why does it miss the mark with women when their feelings are hurt? Let's start out with the sample argument and then analyze the situation:

She: You always forget to put the toilet seat down!

He: That's not true! I didn't forget yesterday morning.

She: But that's not the point! The point is you always forget every other time!

He: Well, since I didn't forget yesterday, that proves I don't ALWAYS forget.

She: You're so frustrating! You just don't get it! It feels like you just don't care.

Advice for men: when you're arguing with a woman, never _ever_ defend or explain yourself. It's not a good strategy. It might seem natural to defend yourself when you feel attacked or wrongly accused. Of course it does. However, you can quickly sound defensive when you defend yourself (duh!). At that point you are focused on your own needs, and she will notice this. Her sensitivity is tuned to whether you are attending to _her_ needs at the time.

It comes down to a matter of a cost-benefit analysis. What are the benefits of defending yourself? Well, if you are successful in defending yourself, you might set the record straight. You might establish the facts of the matter. These issues are important to men, who communicate to express facts and share information, and often argue to do the same thing. Women argue more often to express a feeling or to be understood more than to establish facts. This means that even if you are right, and even if you clarify the facts, she will still want her feelings expressed, and the argument will continue. For her, the "meta-communication," or the feeling of the argument, is more important than the facts. When Joe Friday of Dragnet used to say "Just the facts, ma'am, just the facts" he was being a typical man, frustrating the typical woman.

Another possible benefit is you might gain respect by proving you're right. Because respect is a currency valued by men more than women, this outcome is valued when men argue with other men. Her currency is more likely to revolve around feeling cherished, regardless of whether her thoughts are valued. Whether you are right will be of secondary importance to her. Until she can know that you heard, understood and valued her feelings, she will be dissatisfied with ending the argument. You might be finished when you've proven yourself right, but she will be finished when she feels understood.

What about the costs of arguing? One of the potential costs is that you create an imbalance in the relationship, from one that is equal to one that is hierarchical. And guess what? You end up being in a lower position! Whenever you are attacked, the attacker assumes a "one-up" position relative to you. By defending yourself, you are agreeing with the attacker that you are "one-down" relative to her. Defending yourself makes it less likely that you will gain the status you sought by arguing. A better strategy would be to keep the power balance being equal. To prevent this "one-up, one-down" result learn to reply from a peer position. This means acknowledge her distress, and ask what she is upset about, and above all do not get defensive. This verbal interaction maintains parity of power between the two partners.

Under conditions of heightened emotional intensity, women can think much faster than men. This is probably another outcome of their having a larger corpus callosum (the nerve fiber bundle in the brain connecting the two hemispheres) than do men. This means women can shift from logic to emotions and back much faster than men, so in an argument men are out-gunned. You're driving a semi while she's in a sports car; you're traveling through mud while she's on dry pavement. She's Olympic sprint champion Usain Bolt and you're - not even a bolt, just a lug nut. You won't be able to react as quickly as she can attack and defending yourself will cause you to sound even guiltier. Better to keep the high ground and invite her to express herself. Meanwhile, inside your head, you can remember that her comments are about her state of distress. They are not really about you. Ask yourself what her comments are telling you about her current feelings and state right then.

Sample argument, Take 2:

She: You always forget to put the toilet seat down!

He: You sound frustrated. What happened?

She: What do you think happened? I fell in!

He: Wow, I bet that was embarrassing and frustrating. I'm sorry that happened.

She: Yeah, it was! And I was all wet! And I was in a hurry. And it could have been avoided! Mostly I felt hurt and not cared-about.

He: You're right it could have been avoided. You have every right to feel upset about that. I'm sorry that I hurt your feelings.

She: Really? You're not going to tell me I should have put it down myself?

He: Nope. I just think I'd also be annoyed if it happened to me.

She: Well, I guess you get it at least. And thanks for hearing me.

And then, makeup sex! Or not. Either way, remember: defending yourself is a losing proposition. There is little to gain and much to lose. It's much better to learn a style that restores parity and equality, even in the midst of an argument. It's much more likely to diffuse the situation than defensiveness because you give her what she wants, which is feeling understood and valued. Remember, her feelings are as important to her as your honor and pride are to you.

Have you noticed how often a woman will want to resolve an argument right away, usually before you are ready (unless the roles are reversed here)? You might need time to "cool down," or at least to figure out what the fight was really about. You've done your best to "fix the problem" or figure out a solution to her displeasure, but you got frustrated too. You might need time for those feelings to go away, so you can regain your rational self and feel grounded once again. This might require some time in the "man cave," whatever that is in a physical sense. However, she wants to talk about it right away! The reason for this is similar to the reason women worry more about being liked by other people and maintaining friendships than do men. It involves two different modes of survival – historically, men survived by competing (and winning) and women survived by maintaining connections. These two modes conflict during an argument between a man and woman.

To survive, the man feels he must win (or at least not lose), while the woman feels the argument itself severs their connection. She will try to reconnect and resolve the argument as soon as possible because at some level it feels as though her survival depends on it. What can you do? You need to honor your needs, but let her know that you will try to meet her needs too. One example of this is to explain to her you need a little time to process your feelings, and then you promise to come back and resolve the situation with her. As a compromise, make the time spent in between less than you prefer (because what she wants is no time elapsed at all). Often, an hour apart is a nice round figure, a little too soon for him, but still tolerable for her. Then honor that agreement.

Happiness

Let's face it – as men, we pay a lot of attention too trying to make the women in our lives happy. When we think we can do it, it gives us motivation and encouragement. When she tells us what will make her happy, we are compelled (often with a great amount of pressure) to do that thing. Why is that? Allison Armstrong suggests that one reason for this motivation is that women's happiness recharges men. When the woman in your life is not happy, you don't get fed your life-sustaining "juice," and you might feel like you're starving. If this goes on too long, a man shifts his emphasis from "trying to make her happy" to simply "trying not to piss her off." And finally, if a man tries and fails to make her happy and to avoid upsetting her, and any other opportunity comes along (e.g., another woman who he thinks he can make happy), he will leave the unhappy relationship because his well-being depends on it. To avoid this outcome it's necessary to know how to make her happy with you.

With all that at stake, of course we try to make our women happy. Sometimes we don't get very far, partly because we don't know what she really wants. "Just tell me what you want!" I hear you bleat; we've all been there. There are several problems in getting an answer to this dilemma. The first comes from our sensitive side. Yes we have one, and it's located on the left. Despite the many stereotypes of men being insensitive, hairy beasts, we are often sensitive to a woman's happiness. This includes not only what she says about what makes her happy, but whether she says it with conviction, with that "zing" in her voice. For example, you ask her, "What if I take you out for dinner tonight?" and she replies with "Sure, that's great" in a flat tone. She may actually think she's telling you that this would make her happy. What you are likely to hear is that this is only okay with her, and won't actually make her "happy."

On the other hand if she replies with "Sure! That would be great!" you know she's actually telling you this would make her "happy." As odd as this is, this distinction is more apparent to men than to women because of the enormous emphasis we place on making women happy. Don't be fooled by the lingo that women use here. If you ask if she's OK with you going out with the boys instead of taking her to dinner on your anniversary, her response of "OK" might really mean you're in trouble; her response of "Fine!" rates as the woman's favorite four-letter F-word. Be wary of these subtleties.

The second problem with getting this information is women do not like telling anyone what would make them happy. Along with the rest of her feelings, a woman protectively guards her true happiness. For her to show true happiness, especially with emotion behind it, she has to reveal herself, to be vulnerable. Often "happy" is an absolute, the pinnacle of good feelings with nothing ever surpassing it, so it's very hard to state what would make her feel "the best possible." A woman has a hard time telling a man what would make her happy (this differs from telling him what she wants), so she creates something that would make her feel "satisfied" instead. Then starts the cascade of problems as you might predict. When she tells him in her language what would make her happy, he reads the emotion behind it and decides that she still wouldn't be "happy" so he doesn't carry through because he doesn't believe her. She then doesn't believe that he wants to make her happy because he didn't follow through, and round and round it goes. Instead of getting frustrated like this, try asking her what would make her feel "special." Women rarely find that question as difficult to answer, perhaps because it doesn't make them feel as vulnerable or perhaps it isn't such an absolute.

Finally, there are some women (thankfully in the minority) who are unhappy on purpose and in principle. These women are often so needy that they must be the constant focus of someone else's attention, and they believe that being chronically unhappy will achieve this goal. These women often self-identify as "victims" and wrap their identity around that theme. They are not people to whom bad things have happened, but rather people that see their lives as a series of bad things having happened <u>to them</u>. Unfortunately for women like these, men tire of not being able to make them happy, failing in every attempt. With any luck you have moved on past relationships with women like these by now.

A quick note about men's happiness as promised. We like being happy! It's easy for us to tell someone else what would make us happy. Winning, succeeding, being respected, being appreciated; all of these make men happy. When we are happy, we get a certain feeling of energy that starts in our chest and radiates down our arms. If we're really happy, that energy exudes from our fingertips, resulting in fist pumps, high fives, elaborate handshakes and effusive

90

gestures (just watch any athlete after a great play, and you'll see this fingertip energy at work). Just ask yourself: when you've succeeded at something you truly value, and find yourself saying under your breath, "yes!!" what goes along with that for you? A tightened fist? Spread hands above your head in the "successful field goal" sign? For most of us, it's something like that. Knowing you've made a woman happy feels a lot like this too. You feel like a hero. Or like you just won that chess game against your younger brother which, by men's standards, are approximately the same.

Lessons

1. Men and women have different relationships to feelings.

2. Men are more aware of thoughts and sensations, women are feeling-based. Men's being logical makes it hard to understand women, who are more emotionally focused.

3. Never defend yourself when she relates a complaint as that's staying in your rational world. Instead address her feelings-based world by telling her you're sorry that you hurt her feelings.

4. Women don't feel finished in an argument until they feel understood.

5. Don't ask your wife whether doing a certain behavior would make her happy (she might not want to be vulnerable enough to answer) and limit the number of times you ask her to decide what she wants to do. Instead, either ask her what would make her feel "special", or tell her what you want to do (decide) and then ask how she feels about it.

Example Problem:

"I come home from work and greet my wife in a friendly way, and instead of showing me she's happy to see me, she gets all huffy and tells me what I insufficient person I am. I'm just trying to get along with her! What gives?"

Mark and Mary have been married for over 22 years. Their two children are now of college-age, they have a fine home and are well settled in the community. When Mark comes home from his job as a high-level manager, he often greets Mary the same way he would greet anyone at work. He is aiming to be friendly, but does so in the male energy way of delivering mild barbs and putdowns and expects her to engage. It always surprises him when she gets angry. When she does, she reminds him of all the things he has not successfully done, and of all the ways he has hurt her in the past (and he thought he was starting a friendly conversation!). What Mark didn't realize was that he was trying to converse with Mary while he was still in his "male energy" state and was interacting with her as if she were "one of the guys." He was inviting her to compete. She took that as if he were severing the connection between them. Further, she perceived that he was a bit scary in his masculine state; to deflate him so he would be less scary to her, she emasculated him through criticism. How differently this conversation could have gone had Mark remembered to get into his "feminine energy" state before interacting with his wife. Instead of starting with a "good-natured" barb (like "We're not having that for dinner again, are we?" Or "I see we still have kids..."), he could have started with a connecting comment (like "Tell me something about your day" or "I'd like to do something for you. Tell me what might be helpful to you right now"). She would likely not perceive him as threatening or pressuring, would not be incited to diminish him for safety reasons, and might well respond with something like "Thanks for asking! I do have something to tell you about." Unfortunately Mark never learned that difference. While it's still important to be that "masculine energy" at home for most men, try to use the feminine, connecting approach to communicate with your wife. It's much more likely to produce contentment rather than conflict.

8 – Was Einstein right about men and women?

Women marry men hoping they will change, and they don't. Men marry women hoping they won't change, but they do. So each is ultimately disappointed.

Often attributed to Albert Einstein

What if you see change in your wife? What if you want to see change and you don't?

You've probably experienced this one, if not in your own marriage, then in stories you've heard from friends. She married him after admitting his faults to a girlfriend, saying something like "he can change." Perhaps he married the girl of his dreams and somewhere along the way she cut her hair, or became more assertive and less accepting, or changed something that initially attracted him to her. Was Einstein right that this is inevitable? This quote seems to suggest that both parties in the marriage are set up for eventual disappointment. Recent research suggests that none of us, neither men nor women, changes much regarding our goals and accomplishments; conversely, few of us are good at predicting how much our tastes and values will change. From where does this stereotype that women change and men don't come? How does it all relate to e = mc^2?

Over history, women have looked to men to provide stability and security. While that is less true now than in earlier generations, it may be partly responsible for the idea that men don't change. Many times men choose conservative values for themselves, choosing to conserve energy, momentum, action (doing things in the most efficient manner possible), etc. Men also seek a "most effective way" and then decide that that is the "best way" to do something. Once having found the "best way", why change it?

(Are you following along? So far this makes sense, right? Hang on, it's about to get weird.)

As a stereotype, women are attracted to the potential they see in men; this might especially apply to younger men. I recall a female nurse telling me that she always asks what his goals are when she goes out on a date with a new man. Some women may use this trait of looking at a man's potential as a way of minimizing their disappointment he isn't already what they are looking for; others may enjoy the process of "terra-forming" their guy. Sometimes women may try to make him match their ideal even though he hasn't changed for the other women before her. However, most men will find this attempt to change him to be undesired, unpleasant, and something to be met with active resistance. This, too, may facilitate the perception that men don't change. However, if you can put away the resistance and consider being influenced by her, you might find that some change can be a good thing.

<u>So what if she asks you to change?</u>

Of course men change. Really. Men grow taller and stronger, grow older, develop new interests and friendships, become more competent at their jobs, and take on new challenges and responsibilities. The majority of these changes result from one of two different things: either the man in question desires to learn something new, or circumstances have created a necessity for him to adapt. After all, Charles Darwin didn't say the smartest or the most powerful were the ones to survive. Survival was achieved by the "fittest", those most capable of adapting to circumstances. What frustrates many women is the observation that men don't change the way women want. A man is usually invested in acting a certain way by the time he meets a woman who is interested in him enough to try to change him.

Even men with the best of intentions, who might promise women they will change, face two immediate problems. First, we have repetitious practice in our history, habits built up after doing things a certain way repeatedly. Breaking these habits may seem a difficult and lengthy process, whether it's a habit of tossing dirty clothes on the floor until they pile up, or of assessing our needs first and the needs of others after. Second, we often have little understanding of the purpose of such a change. These together lower our motivation and ability to do things differently.

This presents a problem - resistance is not well received by the woman requesting the change. You want to be well received by your mate, but you also have an automatic response of standing your ground. While this might be defending your turf, it won't increase harmony in the marriage. You <u>can</u> ask her what the requested change might mean to her. She might just want you to look a bit more stylish or to be in better health. It might be hard to believe but she might want you around for a while. You won't know what her thoughts about this change are unless you ask her. Be sure to tell her what your old way of doing things means to you. If you can't come up with a good answer (other than "because that's the way I've always done it!"), then consider her request. If you've decided that you don't see a need for a change, ask for her indulgence while you assess whether this is a battle worth fighting. If so, then fight it fairly, with respect. Most likely her request comes from love and concern for you, and the change might be a good thing.

<u>What makes women change?</u>

Most women approach change differently from the way men do. While women appreciate stability in men, they often prefer novelty for themselves (this might be partly age-related, with younger women looking more for novelty than more "settled" women). Just look into the closets of a typical married couple.

He might have multiple versions of the same item (jeans, dark slacks, light dress shirts and light sport shirts), and someone will have urged him to buy a second or third pair of dress shoes. The woman's closet is more likely to have many types of apparel, each in several colors with a myriad of accessories to match. And shoes. Lots of shoes. A closet is a good example of how men gravitate toward routine, and women pursue novelty. When a woman is going out to an event, for instance, she may state "I have nothing to wear!" even if her closet is full. What she means is "I have nothing novel to wear" or "I have nothing to wear that makes me feel the way I want to feel today."

It is difficult for most men to understand that many women dress to reflect the mood they are in, even if their feelings change moment to moment. Once men understand this, it is easier to understand why women change. As people grow older, their values and perspectives change. Once a novelty seeker has gained, learned, or experienced something, it eventually ceases to be novel, and ultimately becomes routine. At that point, the novelty seeker will choose something else. This also means that novelty in your attire can make you more novel to her, and thus more appealing to her (hint-hint!).

A working woman may get many novel experiences from her job, especially if she is upwardly mobile, or if her job is otherwise somewhat different day-to-day. A woman at home may spend significant time decorating the house in (what seems to most men to be) "just the right way." This "rightness" will be sufficient for a little while until it, too, loses its novelty. She might then think about redecorating, not because the old way is no longer "right," but because it is no longer novel.

A mother (either a working mom or a stay-at-home mom) will experience novelty through the growth and changes of her children for many years. Eventually, though, there comes a day when either the children stop growing and are more routine from day-to-day, or they leave home and no longer provide novelty. Many women seek something new in their lives at that point. They may choose to go back to school or back to work, to get involved in community organizations, and/or to develop new hobbies or friendships. This is one way that women stay interested in things, how they feel fulfillment. Her husband might still think "just when I was getting the hang of things, ..."

Women see this kind of change as a good thing. Sometimes, they use the term "growth" in place of change. Often this is unfortunate because it is possible to have change without growth. Sometimes growth is refinement, meaning that one can be considered "growing" if one is getting better at something (e.g., in one's career, one's ability to perform artistically, or with one's intellectual acumen). These kinds of changes (or this kind of growth) may be more typical for men, and may represent an incremental approach to a cherished goal. This is especially true when that goal is one of success, but can also be true for goals such as retirement or happiness.

This suggests there might be two different ways of considering change, rather than that women change and men don't. The way men change may be slower and less dramatic, and may be goal directed. In contrast, abrupt changes (such as changing clothes or changing careers, lifestyles, friendships) may appear disruptive to goal-oriented progress. Men sometimes have difficulty understanding the motivation or rationale behind changes in life that women make. A man may feel that changes, such as a new career or going back to school, disrupt stability (a masculine energy value), and he might miss out on the novelty that this change presents (a feminine energy value).

In the best case, both of us change

Some of the changes men see in women and that women request in men are natural consequences of building a stable marriage. One change that helps create longer-lasting, more stable marriages is valuing your partner's positive traits while minimizing her negative ones. For example, choosing to view her bad mood as due to the day's stressors, instead of as a permanent character trait, might keep it from becoming a global impact on your marriage. Some argue this is unrealistic and biased, and it is. Yet this is what happy people do in their marriages: they stress the positives and minimize the negatives of their mates.

Another change that facilitates "good karma" in the marriage is a tendency to find the little things that the other person values and attending to

97

those. This might include picking up your socks or making your lunch before she leaves for work in the morning. It turns out it is important to sweat the small stuff. Perhaps it's even more important to create positives than to fix negatives in your marriage. This all means that certain changes may be required for us to grow together and to produce a healthy relationship. Be open to changes and let her convince you that some changes are for the best. Let yourself be influenced by your wife while you retain you own character.

Can I hope that my partner will (or will not) change?

An old joke defines second marriage as the triumph of hope over common sense. Given that 50% of first marriages fail, and that 65% of second marriages fizzle out, this might contain some wisdom. Isn't hope usually a good thing? Hope is often defined as the expectation that what is desired can be achieved. For example, a young woman might hope to get engaged, a young man might hope to get a job, each might hope to get married and raise a family. When a woman meets a man whom she believes to be of good potential, she may hope he will change *in the particular ways she desires*. When a man meets a woman to whom he is attracted, he may hope she stays as lovely, charming, and interested in him as she is. Each of these hopes is a wish for the new partner to become a perfect match for our expectations. As we saw in an earlier chapter, this match is unlikely, leading us to disappointment. Once again, it seems that Einstein was right. How we deal with these inevitable disappointments largely determines our marital happiness.

Life is not a smooth continuum, occasionally interrupted by spikes in randomness. At least most lives aren't. I suppose if you were a fly it might be true. There you are, happily buzzing around someone's living room looking for nice tasty meal of poop, when SWAT! Randomness. For most of us, life is a constant set of challenges and struggles, occasionally interrupted by a period of smooth sailing. Overcoming life's struggles requires resiliency; this is comprised of three traits: hope, a sense of purpose, and often, a desire to help others. Notice that this combination of attributes is like that required for happiness. Of these three, hope may be the most ethereal. It is hard to define, and much harder to gain if you don't already have it. The loss of hope (hopelessness or despair) is key in depression or in giving up. The presence of hope allows us to keep going, despite failures and setbacks, and sometimes in the face of all evidence to the contrary. Hope is essential for achieving long-term gains in the face of short-term frustrations. However, hope must be realistic or it can become a setup for disappointment. I can hope a new Ferrari appears in my driveway, but most likely I will be driving my Ford to work for a long time.

Marriage (and any other committed relationship) is all about long-term gains and is fraught with short-term frustrations and challenges. This makes hope an essential ingredient for the success of marriage. For what do we hope? We might hope that both of us live long, productive lives. We might hope that our parents like our chosen mates (and that our in-laws like us). We might hope that our children are happy, healthy, have lots of friends and do well in school. Many of these hopes are realistic and few are completely out of our control. We must manage the eventual outcome if we do not get what we hope for. Some people refer to this as "hoping for the best but preparing for the worst." That might be a little extreme; perhaps a gentler way to think is "hoping for what you want but being prepared not to get it."

As we saw in an earlier chapter, hoping that someone will meet all of your expectations is likely to result in disappointment. Hoping that a relationship you develop with someone will meet most of them might be more realistic. Accepting that someone might not meet one or more of your expectations is a sign of strength. This will probably mean changing one's expectations to fit the new information. This is what allows hopes to continue driving some people; these people have an ability to adjust their expectations and their hopes on-the-fly in response to the changing situation. Thus, their hopes may be changing as they adjust to incidental disappointments.

If you hope that your wife will not change during your marriage you will be disappointed, according to Einstein. Hoping she will continue to be happy in the long term might not be; this hope can be realistic even with incidental disappointments. Hoping that your wife will always be happy staying at home might not be realistic since she will require novelty in her environment to grow. However, hoping she will always want your validation, and that she will always be a partner in your relationship efforts might be very realistic. From these examples, let me suggest that hopes can be more realistic if they are flexible and can withstand incidental disappointments. Hopes might be unrealistic if they are inflexible (that is, black and white) and cannot be adjusted to fit new situations. Extreme examples of this lead to what I call toxic hope.

What is toxic hope?

One lovely young lady in her 30s began an online relationship with a Marine deployed in abroad. He was vigorous, interesting, brave and quite handsome in his uniform. She initially liked many things about him and grew to like more as the relationship progressed. Even though he would occasionally post pictures of his friends on Facebook, he almost never posted pictures of himself. He told her that his missions were far too secret for that kind of risk. He explained that his father had also been a Marine, killed in battle before he could achieve his final promotion. He explained that he wanted to achieve a similar promotion to honor his father's memory. He also explained that, on those occasions when he returned to the US, he was in training or taking care of his widowed mother. He explained that the way his voice sounded on the phone embarrassed him so they would never have telephone or video chat conversations. He also explained that he was socially awkward so they could never meet in person while he was serving. It was her hope that, with his hard work and her support, he could get over this awkwardness. Then they could not only meet someday, but end up together in a relationship at the end of his deployment. After several years she still had not heard his voice.

This woman might never know whether all the difficulties described by her Marine were true, or if he was a persona created by someone lonely for internet companionship. Either way, she was engaging in toxic hope. Her hope for them to be together was inflexible, and could not be adjusted as she received disappointment after disappointment. She went on hoping that things would change. This kind of hope is toxic because it drains away one's time or life force or both, all in the service of something unlikely to happen. Hoping for him to change (and become available to her as a potential partner) cost her years of her life, during which she might have been developing other relationships. In order for hope to be a positive force, it must be realistic and flexible, adjusting to new realities.

Your wife will change over time; hoping that she will not change won't alter this. Preventing huge disappointments might mean being realistic with your expectations, adjusting them when they don't match reality and being flexible with your hopes.

Lessons

1. Women change over time, in part because they seek more novelty than men do.

2. Be prepared to adjust your hopes for the future to match the ever-changing situation around you. This might mean adjusting your expectations of your wife.

3. Beware of toxic hope. Warning signs include inflexibility of your hopes and an inability to accept the eventuality that these hopes will not be met.

Example Problem – "Ever since we married my wife has stayed at home with the kids. The last one has moved out and now she's going back to college herself. It means that some nights I have to cook for myself and it's lonely at home. I don't like this - I want my old wife back!"

Patrick and Linda had gotten married right after high school; she was 19, he was 20. She had taken a year off after high school to earn money for college, but engagement and wedding planning pushed things back a bit more. When Linda got pregnant on their honeymoon, she realized that college would have to wait. Meanwhile, Patrick was working hard at his father's successful pest-control business. By the time their third child arrived, he had become the manager of day-to-day operations in the business and was doing well financially. Even though Linda stayed home to raise their children, she never lost sight of her dream to one day return to college and pursue her education.

The year that Patrick turned 42, their youngest son went off to college. He was very proud of all three children for continuing their education because he never attended college himself. He was a successful businessman in the family and had always done well financially. His expectation was that he and Linda would have more time together for travel, vacations, or to continue to build what was now his business. When she told him she wanted to attend college, he was confused and frustrated. This wasn't what he expected. For 20 years, Linda was home when he got off work, always cooked dinner, kept the household orderly and managed the children's day-to-day affairs. The three children led three very different lives and they always called upon Linda to help them out. This she did willingly but when they left she yearned for not only novelty but also finally to get her own needs met.

Luckily, Patrick's frustration was short-lived, as he realized that Linda's core values had not changed. The reason they could raise three children interested in education was largely because Linda promoted that interest in them. He realized she would want that for herself. Patrick decided to take a course in woodworking at the local college on one of the days that Linda had class. They made more of an effort to arrange date nights for the weekends. Linda's degree in journalism eventually allowed her to expand the advertising for Patrick's pest-control business. His ability to embrace her change, rather than resist it, eventually brought them closer together than ever.

9 – How do I know what my wife really wants in our intimate life?

Two buddies were sharing drinks while discussing their wives.
"Do you and your wife ever do it doggie style?" .
"Well ... not exactly." his friend replied, "She's more into the trick dog aspect of
it."

"Oh, I see; kinky, huh?"
"Well ... not exactly ... I sit up and beg and she rolls over and plays dead."

What if she complains about your sex life?

Guys, we need to talk about sex. Ah! There, done. "Wait", she says, "I want more than that - I want some understanding, not just the mention of the word". "Huh?" he says, "I'm ready to turn the page." Typical. So here's one of the many stereotyped differences between men and women regarding sex.

Did you turn to this chapter first? The chapter on sex and intimacy is where both a lot of our curiosity and our potential satisfaction lay. Why, oh why, isn't it that simple then? Maybe she (or you) is not satisfied with your intimate life, but how do you give her what she wants? These are subjects of countless books, poems, films, and jokes, and this means mystery. You're married now so you've, well, "done it". That mystery is gone, but the mystery of how to keep it special remains. There is no way to provide a complete treatment of this in one short chapter. The differences between men and women regarding sex and intimacy are like most other basic differences. That said, there are certain things that will come up during a relationship that you should know about. This will help reduce some significant misunderstandings and false expectations.

As an example, let's start with the common myth that men think about sex a lot more than women do. This probably isn't true over the course of a lifetime, and might be true at any particular time if we separate out sex from intimacy. During their younger years, men think about intimacy in terms of physical connection, what we refer to as "sex". We are attracted by how she looks, responding to those features that indicate child rearing potential (clear skin, healthy hair, ideal waist to hips ratio, round butt, etc.). We imagine what it would be like to touch her, but we also imagine what it would be like to be admired and respected by her (insert here the knight in shining armor motif). Meanwhile, young women are busy thinking about intimacy from the viewpoint of romance. They may also be attracted to the way a man looks, but are primarily evaluating his child protecting qualities (physical strength, status, power, wealth, etc.). They may think about what it would be like to be held by him, but also what it would be like to be cherished and desired by him (insert here the rescued Princess motif). In fact, young women often want much more to feel desired in the abstract sense than to be had in the physical sense.

While these basic themes can change over time, they form the basis of many misunderstandings between the genders. For example, when young women dress alluringly, their aim is to be desired because that makes them feel good about themselves. They rarely intend to have that desire acted upon. This may seem confusing and frustrating for the men around them, perhaps, but unless you're married to her, the rule is look but don't touch! Upon seeing an attractively dressed woman, young men may assume that this indicates that she wants what he wants, meaning completion of some physical act. When he is rebuffed his first conclusion is <u>not</u> that he had erroneous expectations. Instead he assumes she got more power out of being "a tease" and she exercised that power over him. She, when unexpectedly approached in a physical way by him, may also err. She might assume he wanted what she wanted but he chose not to control himself. In reality, she wants to feel desired but often wants it to stop there. For him, the pathway from desire to physicality is so short it might be difficult to interrupt. Because his emphasis is on the physical act, interruption of that path makes no sense to him.

This problem gets played out in schools, bars, front doorsteps, and sometimes courtrooms everywhere. The trouble stems in part from erroneous expectations, which are based on intrinsic differences. For most men, sex is an immediate act that leads to feelings of affection and love (if he can stay awake afterward). Younger men may not be aware of this, but all men intrinsically know it. It makes sense to them that the physical act should happen as soon as possible, as soon as there is "chemistry," because it starts something they wish to feel. For most women, sex is the endpoint; the feelings of love, appreciation and desire culminate in sex. This distinction has immediate applications to the expectations men and women have of each other while dating, but also for married couples.

Men want to have sex so they can feel connected to their wives; the feelings of love are generated as a result of having sex. They get turned on easily, with a glance or a touch, because the physical act starts the connection for men. The problem is that the physical act is the result of that connection for women. What does this mean about being a good husband? It means many things, but an obvious conclusion is that for many women, "foreplay" starts the day before (and you thought planning a vacation required thinking ahead). It includes all the things you as her husband might do to increase those feelings of connection. For a full 24 hours before the physical act, anything you do that makes her feel cherished by you and valued by you will count as foreplay. Take out the trash for her, sincerely compliment her outfit, or rub her feet at day's end. All of these things count as foreplay. If you wait until you're already in bed together, it's too late – you've missed most of the foreplay timeframe already.

Touch your wife. I know that might be a foreign concept to most men; after all, "eeeww!" Do more than just give her a kiss when you come home from work. Hold her hand, touch her arm when you're standing next to her, put your chin on her shoulder when you're looking over her at something in common. Give her a hug when she doesn't expect it. Sit within striking distance on the sofa (but snuggle, don't strike). These are some of the things that women count as generating feelings of love that may ultimately culminate in a physical sex act (hint-hint). Even if they don't, you gain points with her by doing these things, because they reinforce for her that you cherish her. More likely, you'll probably see your sex life improve.

By the time a woman is in a committed relationship like a marriage, chances are she thinks about sex as much as you do; she just thinks about it differently. While sex turns on loving feelings for men, and therefore lets men get in touch with their feelings instead of their bodies, it does the opposite for women. Sex allows a woman to get out of her head and into her body, something women yearn for but neglect over time. With all the demands put on a woman by real life, she will inhabit her body less and less. Sex allows her to re-inhabit her body and to rediscover the joys of being physical. However it takes romance to open the door to that possibility.

Alison Armstrong and others have suggested that women have a voice in their heads that tells them every day they are not good enough to be loved unless they're perfect. Quite an impossible standard! When they hear us tell them "you look pretty today" or "I really do love you", our words refute the daily voice inside her head. That's why she needs to be told every day. It's not that she doubts you or because she forgets. It's not even because she loves the sonorous tones of your masculine vibrato. For her, it's not a matter of knowing that fact, but rather hearing you say it as often as the voice in her head says the opposite. So tell her every day she is good enough to be loved because that contradicts her inner voice. This too counts as the beginnings of intimacy for her because it reminds her she is cherished.

Sometimes you, as a man, don't want sex. Well, ok, probably not often, but there will be times. You may prefer a stimulating discussion, a good laugh or a joint effort made on some mutual project (this is over and above the "alone time" that you might need). You may even prefer to go to sleep or just to read if you're feeling more like having alone time than intimacy. Women, too sometimes want alone time, even in bed. It might be she's had a full day of picking up Mae from preschool, getting back to work just in time to deal with angry customers before driving Random over to drama practice, and still getting a hearty kale-edamame salad on the table for dinner. She might also want a different form of intimacy than sex even if she still wants to be physical. For example, sometimes handholding or cuddling is sufficient. It reminds her you're connected to her, and it allows her to inhabit her body again.

Other times, she may want to connect by talking. In this case she may want to hear about your thoughts and feelings rather than about events of the day. Rarely will she want to engage with you in a spirited debate; you may think of that as an intellectual exercise, but she will think of it as competition that inhibits her feelings of connection to you. Leave the sport of debate for the office or for your time with the boys and seek instead to connect emotionally. Men often overlook this form of intimacy, because it's foreign and boring for most guys, right? At least it goes against our competitive spirit. Yet it's important for most women, and you want to keep your wife. So it's time to learn.

You might also find it difficult at times to initiate sex with your wife, even more than it was with previous girlfriends or more casual partners. For some men, the more emotionally involved a man is, the harder it is for him to initiate sex. It might seem that it should be the opposite, where more emotional involvement leads to an easier time initiating sex. But a man who is very involved emotionally with his wife may crave her approval, and the possibility of rejection may be too crushing. Sensitive men may have a harder time initiating sex with women they care about. Tell her about that if you can. That shared intimate moment will likely be initiation.

Then there's the myth about female orgasms.

One day Adam and Eve notice God standing before them, holding a bag.
"Hi, God. What's in the bag?" asked Eve.
"These are a couple of things left over from creation I thought you two would be interested in." God rummages around in the bag a moment. "Okay who wants to be able to

pee standing up?"

Adam immediately puts his hand up in the air, waving frantically. "Me! Me! Oh, PLEASE, God, let me have it! Just think of how much more work I could get done in the fields if I could pee standing up! And it would help so much when I'm out hunting! Oh, please, please let me have it!"

"Well, all right Adam," says God. "Now, let's see what we have for you, Eve." God rummages about a bit more in the bag.

"I'm sorry, Eve. All I have left is multiple orgasms."

For the longest time, many in the male dominated field of sexuality research didn't believe that female orgasm happened. But it does, and most women enjoy it. Some don't enjoy it, for a variety of reasons (they were traumatized sexually early in life, they learned to be ashamed of their sexuality, they were with men who didn't take the time required, etc.). Many women just learn to do without. Women value orgasms as much as men do; it's just that many women have become used to not having one because the men they are with do not take the time. Think baseball game instead of skeet shooting: lots of deliberate strategy instead of a launch and a blast.

Ever since Einstein, we've known that time is relative. But in the sexual realm, we see this notion taken to the extreme. For most men, "enough time" for an orgasm is often "as fast as you can go". Men generally don't take pleasure in prolonging things, and between 2 and 10 minutes between initiation and orgasm is standard fare for many men. And, much to women's consternation, that's the way we like it! It's a goal for men, an endpoint we cannot wait to reach. Having an orgasm is like finally arriving at a desired destination after a trip. For women, this not only just gets things started, but the whole concept is backwards. The enjoyment is in the trip itself, and while the orgasm is also desired, it's only as desired as the buildup to it was. Lionel Ritchie got it right when he sang about "All Night Long". "Slow" in the female sexual realm is measured in minutes to hours, not in seconds to minutes! Although all women differ, many women would be very pleased to be taken on an extended joyride of your sexual attention to her body. She might well see her orgasm as denoting the end of the trip. Men are often hanging out by the finish line cheering her on and waiting for her to arrive, having ended a similar trip quite a bit sooner.

The irony of the situation is that it makes men feel good to bring pleasure to their women. In fact, that is what we brag about when we are in a committed relationship (assuming we're finished with the immature phase of having conquests, something we might brag about in college). Think about it – one thing that makes us feel good about ourselves in the bedroom is how much pleasure we can bring to our women. Here's a quiz: which phrase from your wife makes you happier: "I'm glad you enjoyed yourself" or "That was the best I've ever felt!" OK, smart-aleck in the back, you can put your hand down. If she enjoys it, and you feel good about it, why wouldn't you want to learn how it works? It's not difficult, it's just different from the way it works for men.

It's possible for women to have an orgasm either by being stimulated internally (by intercourse or other penetration methods) or externally, usually by rubbing her clitoris. If you don't know where hers is, ask her - she knows exactly where it is, and will show you if you let her guide your hand. If not, then you'll both have things to discover. Remember, her orgasm is the end of her enjoyable trip. Take her on the "evening drive" first, after the romance, the attention to her, the efforts in her service to make her feel cared for. If you don't know what she likes as part of the trip, ask her. It might be kissing, it might be a neck massage or a foot rub, and it might be cuddling on the sofa. From there it might progress to caressing her skin, kissing her neck or ears (the vampires have it right - it's amazing how many women find that to be a turn-on). Finally you might get the better known erogenous zones of her breasts and vagina, but not until you've spent time on the rest of her! Remember, sex allows a woman to inhabit her body. You have to help her become aware of her body by touching her, and this might take 5 minutes to an hour depending on your wife and the circumstances.

Quickies are nice too, say up to 25% of the time. However you shouldn't wait until you both "want to" have sex, because it changes each other's lives, and it changes the way you relate to one another. Have sex even when you're too tired. Learn about what her experience is like by asking her things like "what is the experience of having sex like for you? How do you wish it were different?" This is not just about finding out how to "solve this problem" - she will hear these questions as indicators that you love her. The questions themselves will be part of foreplay (for tomorrow – foreplay for women starts with your attention to her the day before). Remember that there are biological benefits to having sex, besides that it feels great and that humans can't procreate without it. It's good for our hearts and it promotes better sleep. Men benefit by having reduced risk of prostate cancer with increased sexual activity, and women benefit by having increased release of the hormone oxytocin which provides a sense a well-being and connectedness.

Many men feel tired after their own orgasms, and they are less likely to have the energy to stay with a "road trip" for their wives in that state. The urge to fall asleep afterward can be very strong (even stronger than the cinematic cliché urge to have a cigarette). No problem - let your partner go first. Yes, this requires being patient with your own needs, but the benefits are well worth it. There's an added advantage to this strategy. Many women can experience multiple orgasms, either one right after another, or another one after only a few minutes break. The required refractory (or resting) period that men experience before having another orgasm doesn't exist for many women. You can either drive her to "50 shades of flushed" before you experience your own pleasure, or you can give her a repeat performance after you're done. Either way, she will appreciate it and you get to feel good about your connection with your wife.

One last note. In this age of universal connectedness and ever-present electronics, you might consider a partial ban on electronics in the bedroom, as they can be real relationship killers. Even if both of you are reading Facebook, an e-book, or playing a game, you'll be attending to the silicon in front of you rather than relating to each other. Kill the iDontThinkSo's (the iDevices) an hour before bed.

Lessons

1. Sex for most men is an immediate act and leads to feeling of love. Sex for most women is the culmination of feelings of love, and foreplay starts the day before (help her, listen to her and touch her!).

2. Sex allows women to be in their bodies and not in their heads.

3. Most women have a voice in their heads telling them all day every day they are not good enough to be loved. This is why they need us to tell them we love them so often – to counteract the inner voice.

4. Intimacy for women includes talking and cuddling – sometimes that's all she wants.

5. Women value orgasms as much as men do, it's just that many women have become used to not having one because their men are too fast. "Slow" in the female sexual realm is measured in minutes to hours, not seconds to minutes!

Example Problem – "Some nights I'm just too tired for sex, but most of the time it's my wife that says she's too tired. She must not look forward to it as much as I do or else she would find the energy for it. Because she says she's tired, I try to get it over with quickly, but that doesn't seem to make things any better. What am I doing wrong?"

Poor Derek! He was missing all the cues, wasn't he? In his attempts to connect physically with his wife, he initiated sex even when he might have been tired himself. When she said she was too tired, he "got it over with quickly," meaning he pleased himself and then went to sleep. He didn't understand that he wasn't doing his wife any favors. He was focusing only on the physical aspect of sex and neglecting the romance, which might build up her desire to be intimate. In their case, Derek worked long hours as a manager of a retail clothing outlet, and his wife was an at-home mother to their four teenagers. While Derek had some idea of what this entailed for her, his wife's actual day was hectic from 2pm on. She had to drive kids to sports and appointments, help with homework, and enforce family rules about friends, computer usage and more. By the time Derek got home, she needed someone to attend to her needs, not someone else whose needs outweighed hers.

He finally realized that his goal of having her be more interested in sex required him to spend time meeting her needs after work. He learned to listen to her talk about her day. He empathized with her frustrations about the kids and acknowledged what a good job she was doing in what seemed to be many no-win situations. She felt more loved and attended-to, felt connected to him in a spiritual sense once again, and was more interested in connecting physically again. She was still tired from her day, but she responded to his overtures in bed more when he responded to her feelings and connection needs before that. When he offered to give her a spontaneous foot rub at the end of her hard day, he got back many times his investment in her eagerness to be physical. He just needed to learn what currency mattered to his wife and then giving it to her was easy.

PART TWO - Oh, Those Special Circumstances

10 - What if we disagree about finances or

retirement?

A man complains to his wife saying, "We're so poor we can't even afford punch lines to our jokes!"
And she says

<u>What if she wants to save when you want to spend? Or worse, what about the reverse?</u>

How do you talk about finances with your wife? Do you pay all the bills yourself, keep her out of the loop (by trying to protect her from that painful world), or do you let her do the same to you? Do you acknowledge neither of you have money for anything and live off the land? Perhaps you have more than enough money for the expenses of daily living and for very large expenses (like college for the dog, solar panels for the outhouse and the yearly vacation to spend winter with the in-laws in Anchorage), so that most conversations about money are moot. Most couples fall in between these two, and this necessitates discussion of finances. There are many ways to do this well and several ways to do it badly. Some men leave their wives out of the loop regarding money, expenses and all matter of finances. Then they end up resenting their wives for spending "too much" or for not understanding the stress they feel. Other husbands badger their wives with their worries about finances, repeating how much better it would be if she got a better paying job or went back to work, how they need to cut back on their spending, etc. Either condition is extreme but they are examples of providing too little information or too much information to be useful to the partner.

Your wife loves to be a partner, even in running the corporation called your family. She can be your best ally with money but only if you're honest with her about it. Remember, her natural inclination is preserving and nurturing the family, and finances are part of that. Women often find that savers are more attractive than are spenders because savers show impulse control.

You might need to start by talking with your wife about why you work. Most men want desperately to provide for their families, and they get a lot of their self-worth that way. This is something women often misunderstand about men. Men will take on extra responsibilities at work, stay late, and engage in activities that will further their careers, all so they can be better providers. When women misunderstand this it's often because they see him staying at work late and they feel disconnected from him ("he doesn't care about his family"). Sometimes they feel frustrated when he complains about work ("if the boss doesn't appreciate you, why do you work so hard?"). You might have to explain to your wife why you work hard, and that you're working hard is <u>because</u> of your family, not <u>in place</u> of your family. However, your wish to provide for your family does not mean you have the same values about money that your wife does.

What do you do with the money you earn? Do you and your wife have similar values about how you spend? One example of differences in monetary values might be seen here:

Man to his buddy: We've become so broke that I've had to ask my wife to sell one of her kidneys to pay for Christmas this year. If it gets any worse, I'll have to cancel cable...

Financial priorities are a little easier to identify than emotional ones because money is more concrete. Understanding someone's financial priorities allows you to view the way they see things in general because they are good reflections of values. You can expect that some of these values will be different between a husband and wife. He might be nervous about money and expenses and be more inclined to save, or she might be concerned about missing out on life and be more inclined to spend her disposable income. He might value acquiring things while she might value having experiences. He might value consumables, like his onion-anchovy-garlic pizzas with Monday Night Football, while she might value collectibles, like the 55 First Edition American Girl dolls. There are many versions of these different financial values between partners.

Sometimes these differences in values can turn into an exercise in blaming one another. For example, she might be upset he spends money on cars, sports, or outings with his friends; he might be upset she spends extra money on clothes, private art lessons for herself or "knickknacks and frills" for the home. She might wonder why he doesn't work harder to be promoted to a higher level while he might feel he could have achieved more if she did not insist on his participation in all family affairs. Either one may accuse the other of wanting too much time with friends when they could have been working harder.

You might be in a marriage where you don't share finances. Maintaining separate bank accounts, investment strategies, and divvying up the joint expenses is more common than it used to be. Many of these earlier concerns will not apply to couples like that, but they come into play whenever you have a common income or common expense. This might be especially true for second marriages or relationships in later life, or when both people come into the marriage with ample financial resources. Maybe over time you've grown to understand each other's values and preferences enough to have built up an understanding and a trust in the other's spending process. You might still want to be informed of major financial decisions. Sometimes, it's enough to set a dollar limit below which you agree that you don't need informed consent from the other, but above which you make a joint decision.

For many couples day-to-day finances are a source of stress and they need to be navigated delicately. Even if your values are different, you are on the same team and should do what's best for the family and your relationship. Sometimes that will mean enhancing your individual happiness so you can bring more to the relationship. The question then becomes, what enhances your happiness, spending or saving (with budgeting being a thoughtful intermediate)? Working hard for the future or enjoying it now? When does enhancing one person's happiness lead to increased stress for the other one? Those are issues to navigate in the financial area.

One area of potential discord is the area of insurance. Most states require a certain amount of car insurance, most mortgage companies require a certain amount of property insurance, and the U.S. now requires most people to carry health insurance. The value of other insurances will depend on your degree of concern, either rational or otherwise. An umbrella policy to cover things like slip and fall accidents might be important if you live on a slope and have clumsy or litigious relatives. Most women feel somewhat comforted by having life insurance policies for their husbands because men are the traditional breadwinners. This has changed somewhat as women's earning potential has nearly matched that of men. Many women still find comfort in a life insurance policy, so that at least their financial needs will be met if you suddenly choke on that horrid Monday Night pizza. Extra life insurance might be important if one of you is much older, if you have children, or if you want to give your spouse a reason to consider whether you are more valuable alive or dead. However, each of these purchases, while bringing peace of mind to the worried, will create an "opportunity cost" whereby that same money cannot be used for something else. Be open with your wife and invite her to be open with you about which financial needs are "must-haves" and where the trade-offs might be.

Retirement or Not?

An elderly retired couple went to a doctor. The man said, "We want to know if we are making love properly. Will you look at us?"

"Go ahead," said the doctor. They made love in front of the doctor. "You are

making love perfectly," the doctor said. "That will be $30."

They returned six weeks in a row and did the same thing. On the seventh visit the doctor said, "What are you coming here like this for -- I told you you are making love properly! What more do you want?"

"Listen, doc, its retirement economics," said the man. "We both live in retirement communities. She can't come to my house and I can't go to her house. A motel costs $50. You charge us $30 and we get $24 back from Medicare."

Retirement used to mean stopping work and focusing on hobbies or travel. The main question then was not whether to retire, but when he would be home all day complaining about having nothing to do. These days, "whether to retire" is an important consideration, as the Great Recession negatively impacted many households. They may now be struggling with lower home values, lower retirement portfolios, and even lower pre-retirement incomes. Many couples will delay retirement; for others, it will be nonexistent. With a few exceptions, the current time has seen an end to many corporate sponsored retirement pensions, and an increased emphasis on self-provision of retirement funds. Retirement looks different now than it did in the recent past, and it will probably look different in the future than it does now. Retirement will also look different for different couples, depending on where each of them worked and whether they will retire at the same time.

The traditional retirement scenario might see the husband retiring from a long work career somewhere between ages 55-65. His wife might have been working, often in a part-time capacity or in a lower-paid or at least less-structured position. She might have taken significant time off to raise children, and she might either retire at the same time or to continue working at a reduced commitment. This means many things will change, both for him and for the couple. They will ask themselves some unusual questions, and they will define some new ways of being during changes.

First, as Armstrong says, men operate on the 3-P principle. These 3P's stand for procreate, protect, and provide. This means that men seek first to produce progeny, then protect them from the dangerous world, and then provide for them. This can be extended to the relationship with a wife by

119

recognizing that protecting her becomes a priority before providing for her. Presumably, you've provided for her all your working life (remember, this is in the traditional scenario). After retirement, this history of providing becomes the new protection (you've protected her against the future difficulties inherent in retirement). This leaves open a big question: how do you now provide? What you do feel productive and useful? It might mean you take up a hobby, volunteer work or get involved in some social clubs. Realistically it might also mean you go back to work, perhaps in a job somewhat related to your previous one, or perhaps in something completely different. It might also mean you spend untold hours in the garage "organizing" the decades of tools and hardware you've accumulated. As a result you produce a grand artwork devoid of function except that it keeps all of the hardware and tools off the garage floor. Either way, being productive is often how we men define ourselves; we have, as Schwalbe puts it, an "instrumental orientation towards life"[13].

This brings up another question: if you retire and she doesn't, will you feel inferior? You might feel this way if you're not pulling your weight or being an equal partner; it could also lead to feeling that your relationship is now a hierarchy instead of a partnership with you being the base level upon which everything trickles down. This also brings up the less traditional version of a retirement scenario in which each partner has worked and provided. Maybe your wife will either return to work (or continue to work) after you retire. This might be her biology telling her it's time to be productive, or maybe that you're just too annoying to have around the house all day. You too might continue working, albeit in another job or even another career. These types of considerations should be made together, with honest and open discussions about each other's needs and dreams. Your expectations about how things will be might not match with hers, and your happiness in retirement will depend on your being honest about them. Talk about what you expect before the Big Day happens. As Tom Magliozzi ("Click" of the Car Talk radio show on NPR) famously said, "Happiness equals Reality minus Expectations".

Eric Erickson outlined a series of life stages in his developmental psychology. Around the time of retirement comes the stage of "generativity vs. stagnation." This mean it's important to generate something or give back to society, or else one risks feeling stagnant (I know, it sounds like he's talking about energy production and pond water). Presumably, this is one force that drives retirees toward altruistic endeavors, like philanthropy or volunteer work. Often retired couples will engage together in these kinds of activities, but it can be for very different reasons. For example, men are more likely to engage in an activity to feel productive, while women may engage in the same activity to connect with others, or because it makes her feel good. One peculiarity of this is that men might sometimes engage in something they don't enjoy (but makes them feel productive), much to the bewilderment of their wives. This is especially true of playing golf.

One stereotypical fear women have is that their newly retired husbands will not know how to occupy themselves at home, and will end up being needy or underfoot all day. It used to be her domain during the day; now the two share this space. However, he might not know all the rules of daily household activities she has developed. A similar concern can come up if both people retire at the same time. You might not be used to spending so much time together, and it's possible that too much of a good thing will still be, well, too much. It will be necessary and important to establish new sets of expectations and agreements about things, like how you each spend your time and individual and mutual priorities. Of course, it's very likely that the household chores will need to be redistributed, since the balance of effort in the partnership will have changed. Remember to ask her about how she feels about all of these changes and don't just plan new roles for each of you.

Similar issues need to be addressed under other circumstances. For example, if one of you decides not to retire, it's time to reevaluate expectations in the partnership. Less traditional versions of this might include you continuing to work part time, her deciding to go back to school and start a career after raising a family, or both of you starting new careers. Obviously, there are many variations on the retirement theme, each one representing a change for at least one of you and therefore a change in the partnership. Discuss it before you collide on the way to the coffee maker or the bathroom.

Lessons

1. Get on the same page financially. Even if you have one person routinely in charge of money, make sure that you both understand the basics of your household finances.

2. When your values are different about money, make sure you each discuss the dreams that are tied up with it, and what money decisions mean to you.

3. Retirement means that a man has to change the way he provides.

4. If retirement is coming soon, make sure you discuss what that will mean for each of you in advance, and as it's happening. This is a lousy time to be trapped by assumptions!

Example problem (Spending) – "I'm worried about upcoming college costs for our kids, and I have to work some overtime to make sure we have enough. The other night I came home late on our anniversary, and my wife exploded! It turned out that she had spent a lot of money on a surprise anniversary outing that included a dinner cruise and tickets to a show, none of which we could get to on time. Doesn't she know we can't spend and save at the same time?"

Anton and Shanique had been married for 22 years. Both were hard-working individuals on the job and as parents. Anton's job on the police force was the primary income in the household, and they managed to make ends meet without very many luxuries. They each had a car, and as the kids learned to drive, they helped each child buy a good used car by matching the funds that the children had saved. Shanique worked at the office in the High School her oldest kids attended, and she often heard the other people in the office talking about the trips they took or the events they attended. She tried not to get envious and reminded herself that she and Anton were in a different financial situation from the others in the office. Of course, she didn't pay as much attention to those office workers who said that they too stayed home most summers and kept their belts tightened. For many years they told themselves things would be different

122

when the kids left home.

Their oldest was a senior in High School with a Junior and a Freshman right behind her. All three kids showed significant potential in academics, and they all wanted to attend college. Even with scholarships, Community College, and living at home, the financial burden was going to be significant. So much for the children leaving home at 18! The kids all had after-school jobs, but produced only enough income to pay for their pocket money, half of their cars and a bit toward insurance. Anton realized that the only way he could cover the upcoming college costs was to work more overtime, so he started taking every shift that he could. He was often exhausted but still managed to be present for family events. He was so focused on earning extra money that he was completely caught off-guard when Shanique wanted to do something more than simply go out for dinner.

Shanique wanted both of them to have some of what her colleagues at work were getting. She wanted to live the good life and to surprise Anton as well since he really had been working hard. She never thought that his exhaustion would cause him to misread all of her cues about doing something special for this year's anniversary. In reality, it was less his exhaustion than it was his belief that he and Shanique were on the same page about financial priorities. Of course, some of Shanique's disappointment was about Anton seeming to prioritize work over his family (and especially his marriage), and some was about the spoiled surprise. Anton was initially angry that Shanique seemed to foil his hard work by spending money that was "supposed to" go for college. After he had a chance to calm down, he explained how much effort he was putting into the future of their children. Shanique then took the time to explain her intention was to celebrate their joint effort in raising their family. She also wanted to reward Anton for all of his hard work and it became clearer that they were on the same page. For each one, the family was of utmost importance; they were simply using different methods to show it. As a compromise, they agreed to spend a little on themselves while saving the majority for college costs, and they gave themselves a budget for these personal expenses. It might mean saving for college would take a little longer, or that the kids needed to work the first year, but this way everyone's needs would be recognized.

Example Problem (Retirement) – "We both retired last year and thought we would have lots of time to be together now. Boy, do we ever, and we're getting on each other's nerves!"

Byron had worked for the Post Office for 30 years and looked forward to the day that he could retire. He had become tired of the routine of his delivery route and of the long days with little recognition for all of his reliability and effort. He expected that he would spend more time reading, growing his orchids in his indoor nursery, and spending time with Anjie on activities they both enjoyed. Anjie had worked in sales and had managed a clothing store in the local shopping mall. She too looked forward to retirement; although she enjoyed her interactions with the customers and fellow employees, she felt the drain of working later in the day to accommodate prime shopping times. She generally got home in time to make a quick dinner and then enjoy one show on TV with Byron before he had to go to bed as his day started very early. She was anticipating that they would spend a lot more time together after retirement, making up for years of lost time together.

They had planned everything well financially. Each of them had medical coverage and a retirement package that included matching funds in their IRA accounts. When retirement day came they recognized that neither of them needed to get up early or stay up late any more. For the first month they ate together, gardened together, went to the movies and spent time reading during the afternoons. By the second month, Anjie was craving more social time as she had when she was still working. She kept requesting that they get together with friends, or even that they join a group or activity that would bring more social opportunities. Byron was already getting more social time than he was used to just from being around Anjie all day since his mail delivery job was so isolated. He didn't understand why his company wasn't enough for Anjie. Her constant requests for social time began to seem like nagging to him, and he spent more and more time in the garden. She began to feel lonelier around him than she had at any other time in her life.

Byron and Anjie took the time to understand that their own different experiences in the work world had set them up with very different dreams and expectations of what retirement would be like. They realized that a compromise was needed to preserve their relationship. Byron agreed to participate in more social activities as long as they didn't exceed a certain number per week, and as long as Anjie took responsibility for planning them. Anjie agreed to join a woman's book club that met in the afternoons to get more social interactions. The couple learned to savor their interactions with each other as they used to before they developed "too much" time together. They could see that their starting assumptions had been biased toward their own needs.

11 – What if we disagree about children, returning children and grandchildren?

One day, the phone rang, and a little boy answered in hushed tones.
"May I speak to your parents?" the caller asked.
"They're busy," the little boy whispered.
"Oh. Is anybody else there?"
"The police."
"Can I speak to them?"
"They're busy."
"Oh. Is anybody else there?"
"The firemen."
"Can I speak to them?"
"They're busy."
"So let me get this straight -- your parents, the police, and the firemen are there, but they're all busy? What are they doing?"
"Lookin' for me."

What's all this about having children? Don't manly men just eat their offspring?

If you are intending on keeping a wife, then you will need to love her children. Even if they are yours. If she doesn't have kids already, then you can expect to discuss at some point in your relationship whether eventually to have kids. Kids and family are still part of a self-definition of womanhood for many. There is still truth to the "biological clock" that ticks loudly in a woman's brain sometime between her late 20s and late 30s. As a man, it's possible you've never even considered whether you want to have kids. Having a relationship with a woman will change all of that. Many wild type males (this is how scientists refer to unaltered males - these would be males of other species, of course) would rather eat their offspring than raise them. Keeping peace in your relationship will mean learning how to value nurturing kids in the feminine style and therefore feasting instead on kale, wheatgrass and other manly fares.

Make no mistake: raising kids is the hardest job there is (even harder than maintaining a good marriage, which comes in at #2 on my list). Someone once said that deciding to have kids is like getting a tattoo on your face – you have to be committed. Because of this, it's important that you and your partner are on the same page about many things, some of which you cannot predict until they come up. At first, it will be enough to be on the same page about the basics. This might include whether to have kids; how to split parenting chores during the first six months and then also until they enter school; which religion (if any) to introduce them to during their formative years; and what values you want to teach them (like whether to watch professional hockey).

Most people fall into one of two different categories regarding parenting styles. People either want to raise their children as their own parents raised them or differently from the way they were raised. Discussing your own childhood experiences with your partner is something you've already done when you were getting to know each other. It might now be important to revisit that conversation with emphasis on what you would do differently.

Maybe your different childhood experiences would lead the two of you to have different expectations for raising your kids. For example, perhaps you were raised in the city with permissive parents who always let the kids sleep in late on the weekend. She may have been raised on the farm, having to get up early to take care of the animals. Blending these together might make you ask whether you should expect to let the animal sleep in on the weekends. Perhaps your parents raised you with an allowance to teach you how to budget and save money. Her parents may have raised her without an allowance, but being paid for grades. You may try to decide whether to send your own kids off to work before, or after, they start school. It's so important to be on the same page!

Kids don't come with an owner's manual, and you may just have anecdotal stories about what to do for these human seedlings. You're supposed to nurture and care for them and protect them from harm (including the self-induced kind). You must teach them things that matter to you like values, sports, independence, and compassion, and prepare them to become functional and capable adults. You'll be doing this in partnership with someone who may not share your exact values or ideas of how to accomplish this. Be prepared to give in a lot as she will do the same. That's an awful lot of responsibility, with less and less control, as they get older.

Raising kids is a much harder job than being CEO of a corporation. You have many trusted advisors, but they won't be there at your moment of need and the need changes quickly. It's the one job you cannot resign from (well, some guys do that, but we don't call them real men); once you're a parent, you are a parent for life. And because much of child rearing is a job, most men approach it like they would any other job, with their masculine energy traits at the forefront. For example, you may be competitive either with your kids or about your kids (in the first case, we use the euphemism "teaching;" in the second case we call it "pride"). Men also look for problems and then apply potential solutions, and this is often exemplified by the doling out of rewards and punishments. Problem: "What? You got into a fight at school today?" Solution: "You're grounded this weekend!" This is the masculine approach to things, applied here to child raising.

Your wife may not see things quite the same way. She is likely more interested in building a trusting and supportive relationship with her kids than she is in solving problems. And sometimes, your solutions will be in direct conflict with her trusting relationship. This highlights the basic difference between many men and women regarding interacting with kids. You, as a man, may want your children to respect you above all else. Heck, even the Romans took the approach of "we don't care if you like us as long as you respect us." Okay, the more accurate quote is "we don't care if you like us as long as you fear us," but you get the idea). Your wife may want her children to love her and to love each other above all else. Notice how similar these two desires are to what you desire to get from each other? It's one of the many things that lead us to take different approaches to parenting.

According to some, we have seen a feminization of our culture over the last few decades. Because of this change in attitudes, the holders of this opinion suggest that we are more focused now on teaching children feminine energy attitudes. This includes attitudes like "make sure everyone feels good" and "your feelings about certain things are as important as those things are themselves." If this is true, it means that our children are learning more about how to feel and how to connect than they are about how to think and to compete. We will leave whether this is a good or bad change for others to debate. However, it produces certain outcomes of which fathers should be aware, including that your wife may be quite convinced that teaching them about feelings and connection is crucial.

If you play any games or sports with your children, in most cases you will teach them to deal with winning and losing. Although current culture may give every participant an award for just showing up, the competitive worlds of business and general life will reserve the greater rewards for the people and teams that win. Teaching your children how to win is important. It might be even more important, however, to teach them how to lose, so it becomes an expected outcome and an invitation to continue trying. Otherwise, when they apply for their first job, your kids may start out feeling good about their resume and the fact they sat for an interview. They might then go home feeling good about their efforts even though they failed to get that particular job and end up expecting their rewards while having no food to put on the table. It gets harder to feel good about things when you're hungry.

This distinction may be more important for raising boys than it is for raising girls, in part because the ability to tolerate losing is a necessary skill for developing a traditional masculine energy. If one is to be an initiator and a leader, one must know persistence and dogged determination. Boys get in touch with their honor through the experience of things like losing and shame, and from learning how to recover from those. It's part of learning how to put aside their testosterone-driven competitive traits and settle in to a more civilized life. Anyone can win a game of chance or game of sport, and perhaps not experience losing for a long time. I know fathers who are very proud to say that their son's baseball team has never lost. However, to be a winner in life will mean to be resilient, and resilience is all about the ability to recover from loss and proceed. If your wife comes from a different point of view, you might need to explain to her both the world you occupy as a man and the lessons you are trying to teach. You will also need to listen to her points about how social connections allow people to live longer, healthier lives.

There are other ways in which raising boys differs from raising girls. At the risk of using generalizations that border on stereotypes, little boys are more active than little girls and sometimes their activity borders on fearlessness. Early on, they may already compete for status and for favor with their friends or siblings. Little girls may seek approval through their connections with others (this changes for girls in middle school when their competitive back-stabbing can put a ninja to shame). Social research has shown this to be the case for most children in Western society, even when given equal access to various toys and play opportunities.

Boys learn to connect with other boys using this competitive motif, including bonding through sharing insults and derogatory comments they later find communicate affection for one another. This can be problematic later on if they use this same style with girls or women in their lives. These ladies will see these comments as offensive and might not respond well to defensive comments like "I was just joking!" There will be certain things about raising boys for which both of you might assume you have more expertise just because you were raised as a boy. Equally, there are certain things about raising girls about which she might be assumed to have more expertise just because she was raised as a girl. These assumptions may not be accurate, though, because the influence of your respective parents, siblings, and friends when you were growing up also comes into play.

Raising kids will impact your relationship with your spouse even if the two of you have very similar values and views. The primary relationship in the lives of most men is with their spouse. For many women, the primary relationship is with their children. I once heard a young mother tell me, "My husband is my husband, but my baby is my baby", and I knew exactly what she meant. This alone can startle most men, who are prone to assume they are as important to their wives as their wives are to them. It's surprising and painful to get displaced. Men often feel left out unless they can communicate this to their wives and have them make extra efforts to connect with their husbands. It's important that you understand your wife's bond with the kids, and that you keep attempting to connect with her anyway.

Sometimes, astute kids will notice this difference, and some even try to leverage it to their advantage. For example, if your child uses a line like, "well, mom lets me do it," he or she is leveraging that difference. Their positioning of themselves between you and your wife is called "triangulating," where the child is the apex of the triangle and the parents are the two legs. The result is that the parents are pitted one against the other, with the child being the only one who might benefit. All too often, no one benefits at all.

This is a time to draw upon your strong relationship with your wife. Defer any action or response to your child until you've had chance to relate to her behind closed doors. If your child brings up an apparent discrepancy between you and your wife, check it out with your wife directly. If you disagree with your wife about how to handle something about the children, always bring it up behind closed doors. Try not to air out your differences in front of the children. This does not mean, "never let them see you fight," because it's important that kids learn that all couples disagree. Rather, this means try to take your disagreements about the kids behind closed doors. This is boundary setting that will prevent, or at least minimize, their attempts at triangulating. While this might astonish them at first, these attempts are likely to continue until they learn that their parents act as a unit.

Sometimes triangulation occurs because of the actions of the parents, and the child is the unwitting pawn. For example, a couple that doesn't get along might develop an anxious or sickly child. Both parents might focus on the problems of their child (medical problems, behavioral problems, social or school problems) instead of addressing each other and the difficulties in their marital relationship. Here, the same advice applies: take it behind closed doors. Once you're there, however, don't neglect paying attention to your relationship and how it is being affected by whatever difficulties your child might have.

Parenting is the one responsibility you cannot discharge. You don't stop being a parent when your child turns 18, you can't quit, you can't get fired and you can't get a refund. At least I haven't found a store that will take them back. It's a decision not to take lightly because parenting is for life. Barbara, the mother of a young adult, once told me, "Whenever I look at somebody else's baby, I think to myself 'Boy, that's false advertising!'" She meant that kids don't remain adorable cherubs forever, but no one thinks about the difficulties of raising older children and young adults when they're dealing with a baby. Another mom, Pat, once told me, "The hardest time to be a parent is after the kids leave home – you have the same sense of concern, but none of the control." Women worry about their kids for a lifetime, not just until they launch. This concept is illustrated in the following anecdote:

Betty is a 95-year-old widow in a nursing home. One day she receives a telegram, and upon reading it, lets out a deep sigh.

"What's wrong?" asks Bill, the attendant. "I can finally relax," said Betty. "The last of my children just died."

What if your kids don't leave home when they become adults? On the other hand, what if they leave home (for college or to start a job) and then they come back when they find they cannot make it on their own? This latter situation people refer to as having "boomerang kids," because they come back, not because of their shape. For some families, that's natural and well tolerated. These families seem to value togetherness and cooperation. Here, thriving as an adult does not include independence. In other families, returning home as an adult is seen as something between a temporary inconvenience and a complete failure. Those families value independence as an adult above other styles of interaction, and this behavior of not seeking independence is known as a "failure to launch." Just like, well guys, you know. Whether this represents a failure or not depends on your point of view. This can impact your relationship if the two of you have different viewpoints on having adult kids at home. This is another thing about which to keep on the same page as your wife.

Parenting adult children comes with its own set of difficulties. The most common set of difficulties seems to arise when the adult children want all the permissions of being an adult ("Dad, I'm an adult now; I don't need a curfew"), but also insist on having only those responsibilities they had as children ("what do you mean I have to pay rent and utilities now? I moved back here to save money!"). Even though they are adults, it is still your house. You and your wife are still the executive function of the family, and you still get to create and enforce the "rules of the house." Your adult children don't have to like it, but they have to abide. This transition should be something you, your wife and your adult child have talked about and prepared for well in advance. This would be a good time to involve a written contract, so that there are no quarrels later on about mistaken assumptions. Your wife will want to make sure that the children are okay mentally and physically. She may err on the side of extra permissions even if she wishes she could enforce rules of the house. In that case she would be happy if you can be the "heavy" if a need arises, enforcing the responsibilities that come along with adulthood.

Grandchildren

A doctor that had been seeing an 80-year-old woman for most of her life finally retired.
At her next checkup, the new doctor told her to bring a list of all the medicines that had been prescribed for her.
As the young doctor was looking through these, his eyes grew wide as he realized she had a prescription for birth control pills.
"Mrs. Smith, do you realize these are BIRTH CONTROL pills?"
"Yes, they help me sleep at night."
"Mrs. Smith, I assure you there is absolutely NOTHING in these that could possibly help you sleep!"
She reached out and patted the young Doctor's knee.

134

"Yes, dear, I know that. But every morning, I grind one up and mix it in the glass of orange juice that my 16 year-old granddaughter drinks. And believe me, it helps me sleep at night."

A short note about grandchildren and their affect on your relationship: most of the things I've mentioned about the impact of children on your relationship still apply. Here the issues become a bit more complicated, in part because you're now dealing with two generations of kids. Each of them will impact you and your wife. Remember, being a grandparent means also being a parent at the same time.

First, if you're old enough to have grandchildren, you may also be old enough to notice that decline in testosterone. That will make you a little mellower and a little more interested in feelings and communication than you used to be. Your son (or son-in-law) may still be in his competitive male energy, and he may still very much need your respect. This will be true even while your youngest grandchildren still need you to cherish them if they are girls or younger boys. This can be a tough balance. You will be called upon to respect your offspring and their parenting methods even if you don't agree with them, all while you are doting on your own grandchildren. Your wife may have her opinions about how her daughter-in-law is raising your grandchildren, but she too will occasionally have to bite her tongue. Remember, your daughter-in-law is living with a child you raised, so she knows how your methods of parenting work out.

In the best of all situations, grandchildren can be a lot of fun. Being a grandparent is nurturing something that hasn't had a chance to disappoint you yet. As the grandparent, you often get to take part in the activities and fun times of the child's life without having to provide the discipline. It might also mean taking over the parental roles when the actual parents either need a break or can't parent any longer. Unfortunately, grandparents are raising the kids more and more these days. This can be because either Mom or Dad is ill, in jail, deceased or divorced, causing the primary caregiver to work more than he or she planned. Here it will be time to go back to the cooperative posture on raising kids with your wife as discussed above.

While being a grandparent can be lots of fun, it can also be stressful if you and your spouse have different views on how the kids should be treated. You have mellowed and become more interested in communication than you used to be. It's still likely that you still want respect from your grandchildren, while your wife may still want to feel loved by them. This sets up a slightly different dynamic, and your different desires may cause different interactions with the grandchildren. For example, you may tell them stories about your history, try to teach them skills and facts, or engage them in challenges and adventures. Your wife may read to them, listen to them, bake with them and do crafts with them. While all of these are common grand-parenting activities, they achieve two separate groups of goals. Practice remembering these different desired outcomes when you think about the kinds of activities you each will do with your grandkids.

Lessons:

1. Raising kids is the hardest job there is – be sure you're on the same page!

2. It's possible that your primary relationship will be with your wife, while her primary relationship will be with the kids, either yours or hers. That doesn't mean there's anything wrong with your marriage, it just means you must let your wife know if you're feeling left out.

3. You want your children to respect you, and she wants the children to love her and each other.

4. Kids can get in the middle of the couple, causing triangulation. Be sure to take your discussions about kids behind closed doors.

5. You're a parent for a lifetime, not just until launch. This might affect how you look at "launching" itself.

6. Even as a grandparent, you might still want respect from your

grandkids, while your spouse may prefer to feel loved by them. Keep this in mind when you think about to which kinds of activities with the grandchildren you are each drawn.

Example problem (children) – "Our son is in team sports, and it seems like nobody loses any more! Every team gets a trophy regardless of their record. My wife thinks this is fine because she wants no one to feel bad, but how are we supposed to produce winners if there aren't any losers?"

Roy was being as good a father as he knew how, attending all of his son's soccer matches even if it meant working later on a weeknight to take Saturday mornings off. He played both football and basketball in high school himself and recalled his time doing team sports with a lot of pride. His basketball team won a local championship when he was a high school junior, and 20 years later, he and his previous teammates still reminisce regularly. The team's fourth place trophy his son brought home confused and irritated Roy. Fourth place isn't winning! His wife Nancy tried to explain that everybody gets a trophy now and then, and sometimes feeling good about yourself is more important than winning or losing. His concerns have merit, however, and there is a current debate about whether this approach does more harm than good. On the one hand, kids who are taught to lose as a matter of course are less likely to get frustrated and give up if they don't win. However, they are less likely to try to win if the reason is not very motivating. This might be more important for boys than it is for girls, especially when boys measure their sense of self-worth by their productivity and competition. Roy put his son in an additional sport through the local club soccer system besides his school sports because the club system would teach the more traditional competitive values. That way, Roy believed his son could choose for himself which system of values left him feeling better in the long run. Nancy agreed and saw the value in exposing their kids to both sets of values.

Example Problem (grandchildren) – "When our kids bring the grandkids over to visit, we always get along. I just don't like the way my daughter handles my granddaughter when the little one is tired and cranky. Not the way MY dad taught me! I think I should say something before my daughter spoils my granddaughter. My wife says to back off and let my daughter be the parent. Who's right?"

Alan and Barbara worked very hard to raise their son and daughter. They wanted to instill a set of values that would last their own kids a lifetime, so their parenting style was strict but forgiving. Both had been good students, had many friends, and were hard workers. Alan was thrilled when their daughter Julie announced her engagement to Tyler, her boyfriend of three years and the president of a small labor management firm. Two years into their marriage, the young couple had a daughter, Kelsey. Alan and Barbara visited the young family often, enjoyed taking part in family outings, and watched as the little girl passed one milestone after another. By the time Kelsey was four, however, Alan noticed that Julie was accommodating to her daughter Kelsey when the little girl was irritable, and even when she was outright disrespectful. Alan confided in Barbara that he feared Julie's tolerance of that disrespect would eventually create a child disrespectful to her parents. He knew that Tyler was working hard to build his own business for the sake of the family, but it meant that there was no firm hand at home to discipline Kelsey. Alan felt sure that Julie just needed to be reminded of the parenting style he and Barbara had used, especially because it worked so well for Julie and her brother.

It surprised Alan that Barbara objected to any intervention that he might make. "Why wouldn't Julie want to learn the right way to do this?" He asked. "You won't be as permissive toward Kelsey as she is, will you?" Barbara had to remind him that, parenting was a privilege of the biological parents (and not of the grandparents). Mothers are often less concerned about feeling respected by their children then are fathers. "Remember that most of the time, Kelsey is a cooperative and pleasant little girl," Barbara said. "It's just when she gets upset that this behavior comes out. Julie's belief is that treating this irritability with compassion will let Kelsey work things out for herself. It's just a different style of parenting." In time, Alan came to see that his response to Julie's behavior was mostly due to his own desire to feel respected by children, and not that it was "the right way."

12 - What if there's "trouble in Paradise"?

Alimony – A Latin term for removing a man's genitals through his wallet.
Robin Williams

What if your marriage is in trouble?

Perhaps you're reading this chapter because a "friend" of yours has a troubled marriage. You found this book early in your relationship and have used it in a preventive way; you've learned how to do and say the things that let your wife know that you value and cherish her. Perhaps you've also learned not to take her occasional upsets too personally. You've kept the ship of your marriage righted and on track. Very sad for your "friend" who blundered along in these treacherous waters! Now how bad is it for him? Are frequent fights enough to make him worry about the long-term stability of the marriage? Is he noticing his wife pull away from him, or perhaps he feels nagged by her. Worse, perhaps he never saw it coming, and now his wife has informed him that either they go to marriage counseling or she finds an attorney. What on earth happened and how did it get so bad?

In his book "The Seven Principles for Making Marriage Work", John

Gottman suggests that he can tell the outcome of the conversation between two spouses within the first three minutes of an interaction with 96% accuracy based on their styles. He also states he can determine whether a couple is likely to divorce in the next five years with 91% accuracy.[14] There are certain features Gottman looks for in these predictions. First, he looks for what he calls the "harsh start up," or a negative and accusatory beginning to an argument. Second, Gottman cites four different kinds of negativity that couples use in an argument he calls the Four Horsemen of the Apocalypse (criticism, contempt, defensiveness and stonewalling). If these run amok during an argument, the end is near. Third, he looks for what he calls flooding, or being overwhelmed by your spouse's negativity. Fourth, body language reflects the physical outcome of being flooded. This is a sign that a person's adrenaline level is high enough to invoke a "fight or flight" response. Fifth, the "repair attempts" that couples make to de-escalate the disagreement are hijacked by one of the Four Horsemen (here, stonewalling is more commonly a masculine move and criticism is more commonly feminine one). And sixth, the memories about the relationship are weighted toward the negative ones and any positive memories are diminished in value or significance. At that point, survival is all that matters, and any chance for resolving the issue is over.

These features show that the way a couple argues is much more important than whether they argue, as all couples will argue. Your "friend" may have been prone to acting defensively when arguing with his wife. Perhaps he was guilty of stonewalling her by refusing to engage after he felt flooded by her criticism of him. Even if their arguments were few, the marriage could have been in trouble because the couple neglected to do important positive things that keep couples together. What can he do now?

When do you need help and what kind of help do you need?

What if your "friend" has come to you seeking advice? What kind of help does he need? Let's suppose for a moment he's not ready to consult an attorney and you've already helped him out by hosting him on your sofa. Since he ate all of your snacks and drank all of your beer, you may now want to refer him out to some other kind of help. Unless there's some serious pathology on either side (like one of them uses drugs or alcohol, or one has a serious personality disorder), just learning to communicate will not solve their problems. Herein lies the rub - men and women rarely communicate the same way, and many marriage therapists are trained to facilitate communication by teaching "active listening". However, while learning to communicate is necessary, it alone is not sufficient in most cases.

Can't you just hear your "friend?" "I <u>know</u> what she's saying - she's very loud and very clear!" If your "friend" sees a marriage therapist, he could increase his chances for success by asking the therapist if she knows about the tools for making marriages work and not just about how to communicate better. Gottman focuses on learning to change yourself and not on trying to change the other person. Sometimes, though, changing the other person might seem like a good idea, as in the following joke:

Dan married a woman with an identical twin. Less than a year later, he was in court filing for a divorce.

"Tell the court why you want a divorce" said the judge.

"Well, your honor, every once in a while my sister-in-law would come over for a visit, and because she and my wife looked exactly alike, every once in a while I'd end up making love to her by mistake," said Dan.

"Surely there must be some difference between the two women!" the judge said.

"You'd better believe there is a difference, your Honor. That's why I want the divorce."

Usually we think about changing the other person's character or behavior, not changing the other person into someone else. A common version of this is that we want our partner to become someone who will meet our expectations even if we don't tell her what these are. This effort requires us to believe that this change is possible and desirable (more than just to ourselves). Further, we have to believe we have enough control over the situation to effect this change. Changing ourselves is much more likely since we <u>do</u> have control over that. Help your friend find a book, a coach or a therapist who will help him change <u>himself</u> to know and value his wife's life and character more. He will need to find things about her to appreciate and learn to show that appreciation for her in ways she values. This means he has to learn what her currency of appreciation is (does she value compliments, gifts, help, hugs or...?).

He might need to re-evaluate his expectations of her and assess whether they are realistic. He must learn to make his own decisions, but to include her input on them and feelings about them. They both will have to learn the difference between solvable problems (and then how to solve them to benefit the marriage, not just to benefit one person or the other) and irreconcilable ones. They must also learn how to navigate the irreconcilable differences so they are accepted and not fought over. The final thing your "friend" can do to put effort into his marriage is to create a shared value in life. This might be either a lifestyle or a purpose they can both work toward and from which both can benefit (for example, engaging in a joint hobby or volunteer position).

What if she mentions divorce - is she serious?

Maybe. At least she probably is at the moment. But she might mean something different in the longer term. Remember that she's likely telling him what she is feeling at the moment. At least it means she's either really angry, very frustrated, or feeling hopeless that things will change for the better. It's well past time to take action! And by that I do not mean time to protect his assets and to defend himself. Remember this is a book about keeping a wife, not about strategically how to leave one. It's time to start paying attention to her distress, asking her what her feelings are and what they mean. Then he needs to listen, closely and without rebuttal. She at least needs to feel heard by him and the clues to keeping her will be embedded in the things she tells him about her feelings. Even if she's at the end of her rope, she will tell him what she needs, often encoded in the emotion of her complaints.

According to Armstrong, women get to this point when they have lost two things: 1) affinity or connection with her man, and 2) respect for him. The first loss makes her feel alone and the second loss results from her not feeling safe with him. Unfortunately this is often part of a cycle that involves her feeling hurt or scared and then her emasculating him. For example, she might put him down to try to make him seem "smaller" if she's scared by him, or to punish him if she's feeling hurt by him. This leads to his inevitable angry reaction, followed by her losing respect for him (and not realizing that she was, in part, the cause). This means he needs to find a way to not take things personally when she's telling him she wants a divorce, not to defend himself, and to not react angrily when she tries to emasculate him. I've heard women say that after a "talk" where she could express her discontent without his rebuttal, the very next day her assessment was that she now felt more connected and more hopeful about the relationship.

Whoa. Hear all of that and not take it personally or get defensive? Is this even possible? If so, is it a good thing? Isn't it both natural and essential that we defend ourselves if we feel attacked? I hear you; this not only sounds counter-intuitive but also very hard to do. It will take preparation to start and practice to get better at it. You'll want to focus on the idea that all communications are about the speaker. This means that when your wife is talking about anything (yes, even about you), she is telling you something about herself. Most of the time, she's telling you about her feelings; sometimes she's telling you about her thoughts. This means she's not really talking about you.

For instance, if she says, "I think what you did is pretty stupid!" she is telling you about her thoughts on the matter. If she says, "I'm so disappointed! I just don't think you understand," she is telling you about her feelings. In cases like these, defending yourself would not just be a bad idea, it would be out of place. Up till now, the conversation was about her thoughts and feelings, not about you. If you suddenly make the conversation about you (by defending yourself), she will know that you didn't pay attention or her. Listen to her thoughts and feelings and do not take things personally. You might need some of the tools in chapter 19 on Dealing with an Angry Wife.

When your marriage is in trouble, it's important to try everything you know to save it (unless you discover there are things with which you simply cannot live). This proposition is more limited than most people realize, because there's a big difference between doing everything you know and everything there is. It might be time to learn about the other things you can do to save your marriage. This might or might not include marital therapy (a scary option for many men). For instance, marriage education can be a very workable substitute for therapy when treating common marriage woes. Reading a book on relationships together, going to hear a speaker or attend a workshop on the realities of marriage together, or working with an educator or coach can help reset each party's expectations of both the marriage and of each other. This often makes a big difference in marital satisfaction.

For example, it's interesting to note that a common source of dissatisfaction for wives comes from not what the husband does, but her belief about why he does it. Acting on the belief that "if he were a woman and he said that, she would mean it to be critical and hurtful," a wife could get her feelings hurt by a comment made by her husband. However, she might recognize that "since he's a man, that comment probably came from a different place and therefore had a different meaning behind it." In this case she is less likely to get her feelings hurt and to see him as a jerk. And for guys, learning how to hear your wife is much more important to the relationship than learning how to communicate better yourself. Marital educators can point out some of the common differences between men and women, leaving it up to the couple to assess that information and decide which parts of it fits their marriage.

Don't forget that most of the reasons for which she married you are still there. It's important to find out what things she perceives to be missing now (perhaps because these missing things might just have been part of her dream in the first place). You wouldn't be reading this book now if you'd didn't want to try everything to save your marriage. You can still resolve this issue, figure out this problem, and even win this battle as long as you're willing to put your best masculine skills to work. This might include being open to learning things you didn't know before (about her, about yourself, and about marriage), but it shouldn't require you to "redefine yourself".

When to run

Although by far the majority of women are decent well-meaning beings, even when they are angry, there are a few women that need to be avoided at all costs. It's better if you can learn to spot them while you are dating (that's when it's time to run). If having your marriage in deep trouble results in you learning you are married to one of these women, then it's time for some alternative considerations. These women are referred to as "Nightmares" (the technical term), and are typified by having most of these traits: 1) A long-term pattern of unstable relationships, extreme rages and bouncing between extremes of seeing a particular other person as ideal on the one hand and hateful on the other; 2) a pattern of impulsive behaviors that might include excesses of sex, money, food or substances; 3) an internal sense of emptiness that creates a fear of, and anger at, being left alone; and 4) dramatic crises typified by threats or acts of self-harm, including self-cutting or substance overdose. Scary, huh? Add to that these women are often very sexual and flirtatious, manipulative and deceitful; they make false allegations and seek revenge for even the smallest of perceived slights; they demand that others love them and sympathize with them, even as they justify their difficult behavior by claiming that they are the "victim." Women like these aren't crazy, just crazy-making. I once knew a woman who decided that her boyfriend didn't love her "enough," despite her spending almost three years haranguing him to get what she wanted from him. After she left him, she described her plan to ruin his home, his work and his closest relationships on her way out the door. "If I can't have him," she told me, "I want to destroy him."

If any of this sounds familiar, then there's more trouble in your paradise than for most men. You've probably wondered if you're the horrible person she claims you to be. If you're still in the dating stage, then run the other way. Fast. Don't even think about collecting your things, but rather consider these items to be the cost of experience, while you contemplate how much more you still could lose. If you're already married, start out by looking for a copy of "Stop Walking on Eggshells" by Paul Mason and Randi Kreger or one of several other books written for people dealing with loved ones with this personality type. There IS hope and treatment, but only if she accepts that she's part of the problem. But you will have to learn how to preserve yourself while the long slow change involved is ongoing. That will involve understanding that while she might be doing the best she can, you still need to set boundaries that will preserve you.

<u>Lessons</u>

1. If the specter of separation has reared its' head, or you hear signs she might have one foot out the door, it may be time to get outside help.

2. This help does not have to be a marriage therapist (although sometimes that's a good start). If it's easier to listen to a relationship coach, to take a couples workshop together, or even commit to reading a relationship book and talking together about how each part relates, that might be enough.

3. Most of the time saving your marriage will involve you changing your behavior, but not changing your character (possibly besides other changes, like your responses and attitudes).

4. There are certain types of women from whom you should run if possible.

Example Problem - "My friend Larry has been staying on my couch for the last two weeks, ever since his wife Kim asked him to leave. Larry thinks Kim is serious about ending the marriage this time, and he seems kind of desperate to figure out what to do. It sounds like the problem comes from Kim being jealous when Larry talks about his old girlfriend. He does this a lot in the company of his guy friends because Larry's ex-girlfriend was a model. Larry doesn't want to lose his marriage, but he's afraid that a therapist will just side with Kim and make him the bad guy. How can I advise my friend?"

Poor Jorge has an extended houseguest; his friend Larry has been couch surfing for far too long, and it sounds like there's trouble in paradise. Jorge's best friend since high school, Larry was the high school quarterback and prom king, and always enjoyed having an audience, especially his "guys." After college, Larry dated a model for about two years, and although the breakup was hard, it was always a boost to Larry's ego. He seemed to gain status among his guys by bragging about his past relationship. He was indiscriminate about bringing her up, especially when they were out drinking. This continued even after Larry got married to Kim, a woman who was sweet, intelligent, and capable, but who felt inferior in the looks department by comparison whenever Larry brought up his ex-girlfriend. Kim had explained to Larry often how she felt, and they had even gone to therapy together to resolve the issue. By Larry's account, the therapist implied that he was insensitive to his wife's feelings, and that he either needed to rein in his braggadocio or risk losing her. Larry's most recent offense came at a party thrown at Larry and Kim's home, ostensibly to celebrate their third anniversary. As the party wound down, and the alcohol flowed, Larry found himself surrounded by his "guys" in the living room, while Kim and the "girls" were primarily in the kitchen. Once again, Larry brought up how impressive it was to have dated a model, but this time his voice was loud enough that it carried all the way to the kitchen. Kim was ashamed in front of all her friends, and the next morning she asked Larry to leave.

Larry loved Kim and did not want to lose his marriage. He simply had astonishingly poor self-esteem, never quite being able to live up to the "King of the Hill" position he occupied in high school. He occupied Jorge's couch and bent his ear for 14 evenings in a row, and Jorge finally sought help for his friend. Luckily, Jorge knew a relationship coach, and this coach knew of a workshop being held in a nearby city the following weekend. The workshop was on "male-female communication - the many ways we stick our feet in our mouths while trying to get our needs met." Jorge recommended this workshop to Larry and took the extra step of recommending that Larry attended by himself without Kim. This proved to be insightful and especially impactful to Larry. He was a single man at a couples workshop where he was surrounded by couples dealing with different communication issues. He explained his own situation to a small group of men during the workshop. These men were learning their own lessons about communications with women and saw right through Larry's facade into his insecurities. Unlike Larry's "guys" (most of whom were the "yes-men" that he had surrounded himself with since high school), the men at the workshop called Larry out on his insensitivity to Kim's feelings. They pointed out to Larry that he was cheating on his wife with the memory of his ex-girlfriend. When the men explained it to Larry that way, Larry saw why Kim had asked him to leave and how he had jeopardized his marriage by continuing to references his ex. At the end of the workshop, Larry went home and asked Kim to join him the following weekend at the same workshop, even though the workshop had moved on to a different city. He explained to her some of the things he had learned, and he asked her to join him in his attempt to learn more.

Larry and Kim attended two more workshops that year on similar topics and eventually enlisted the aid of a relationship coach. While Larry's behavior may have seemed to meet his primitive needs for status among his peers, it was poisoning his relationship with his wife. It took several months of deliberate practice to change that behavior, but it did end up saving his marriage (at least that time).

13 – What if we have "irreconcilable differences"?

A life long supporter of the Republican party was lying on his deathbed when he suddenly decided to join the Democratic party.

"But why?" asked his puzzled wife, "You're conservative through and through ... Why change now?"

The man leaned forward and explained: "Well, I'd rather it was one of them that died and not one of us."

What if we have pretty significant differences?

Even if you were happy with the way things were, your relationship needs to grow. Just ask your wife, or go back and re-read Chapter 10. Conflict in a marriage is not just normal it is essential. It is through resolving conflict that growth happens. Conflict can occur in many areas in a relationship where two people have at least some different values, opinions or interests. Common areas of marital discord include in-laws, sex, money, children and chores. When any of these areas are contested, the resulting discussion all too often ends up with each party trying to express his or her feelings and be understood. This sometimes comes at the expense of the otherwise natural ability of the partners to see each other's point of view.

For example, he says, "I don't think you're understanding it's really important that I play pinball with the guys for an hour or so on my way home from work!" She might respond with, "But you don't understand it's important that you come straight home when you have melting ice cream and our 4-year old in the car with you!" Neither of the two is listening to the other, but rather each is trying to be heard. The ensuing angry dialogue (or silent hostility) can easily produce hurt feelings that can injure the relationship. Often these result from differences in values and sometimes these differences can be significant. Learning to navigate these differences not only reduces the hurt and tension between the partners, but can also enhance the feeling of "joint effort" in a marriage. It might also prevent the 4-year old from having to eat all the ice cream before it melts, much to his dismay.

What is a "solvable problem?"

According to marriage expert John Gottman [15] only 31% of marital conflicts fall into the category of solvable problems, ones that can be rather easily resolved without compromising one's values. The rest, by far the majority, fall into the category he calls "perpetual problems", ones that divorce attorneys might call "irreconcilable differences". These might be hard to differentiate, but solvable problems are primarily acute and can be addressed with some behavioral compromise where each partner gives a little. Suppose she wants more input on the finances of the family while you've traditionally been the one paying the bills. OK, let her pay the bills, and you celebrate one more chore off your back. Suppose she wants to have a regular night out with the girls, perhaps playing Mah Jongg or else going to the Chippendale's club. Ah, this is a different issue, one that requires your tolerance, forbearance and negotiating skills. You realize that she needs her time with female company, and that the cost to you of giving her this is babysitting duty. Remember the little guy eating the ice cream? He's old enough to be educated about sports during babysitting time, and there is baseball in the summer, football in the fall and basketball in the winter.

Suppose she wants to visit her family for the same holiday you wanted to spend with yours. There are several ways to resolve this one. If there is an obvious reason to go visit one family over the other, perhaps a special event occurring on that holiday, then go visit your family. Just kidding; visit whichever family is the more important one. This will be an issue to negotiate, as each family will likely be more important during certain times. Figuring out which one that is will require finesse. If you saw your family last, it might be time to see her family next. This need not be a tit-for-tat scenario, but rather there needs to be away to make your visits even out. This can be by alternating visits, making a coin toss, or letting age, health, and distance factor in.

Most differences are solvable differences

Solvable problems are the minority of couples' issues, are usually acute, and are easily resolved by minimal compromise. No wonder these are what most marriage therapists focus on! Examples of solvable problems include her taking "too long" to get ready in the morning because they stay up too late at night watching their favorite programs; him forgetting to pick up her dry cleaning the night before her important meeting; her wanting to engage in the community Bunco game on the night that has been when he goes to the gym with his buddies; she feeling left alone and taken for granted after they both get home from work because she's cooking dinner while he watches the news on TV. These are situational and have less to do with the other person's character than her actions. Therapists often address solvable problems by teaching clients to practice "active listening" and to validate one another. While useful skills, these are difficult for most people to master, especially when they are in the middle of a conflict. While most conflict resolution skills require patience and practice to master, Gottman offers steps that might be easier for most couples to manage[6]. They include:

1. Soften your startup (approach your partner with positive regard and compassion even if she is starting out with a harsh approach).

2. Learn to make and receive repair attempts (make efforts to put the brakes on or stop the cycle of the argument and notice your partner's attempts to do the same).

3. Soothe yourselves (let each other know when you need a time-out

and take time to do self-soothing activities to avoid feeling flooded by negative thoughts and feelings).

4. Compromise (be ready to accept influence from your wife, to consider her opinion and to give in, so she can give in too and achieve a common goal).

5. Be tolerant of each other's faults (by not expecting perfection from the other you will be able to compromise successfully).

Applying each of these can lead to resolving most of a couple's solvable problems. Learn to do that by looking for compromises instead of assuming there is no area of compromise or assuming she has to find one.

What is a "perpetual problem?"

Unlike solvable problems, perpetual problems are chronic, the source of the same argument over years, and usually involve some aspect of the couple's character. She likes a clean house, you want the flexibility to "live in the moment." She wants you to go back to school at night to get a better job with more status; you enjoy your job because it's with guys you appreciate and you don't want to be pushed. She wants a baby and you're "not ready for that kind of responsibility" (and maybe never will be). She wants sex four nights a week, and you...say OK. The key to moving past any conflict is recognizing that you don't have to resolve all your differences, but rather you learn to keep your differences from becoming generalized.

Each relationship will come with it's own set of problems you'll deal with over time, and no relationship is without them. As some might say, different spouse, different problems. To do this, you both need to communicate to your partner that you accept the basics of their personality. Think about it - you're much less likely to respond to advice or requests for change from someone if you don't feel valued and understood by them. If you feel judged or rejected by your partner, you'll be more likely to dig your heels in, and less likely to empathize with HER point of view. The psychologist Carl Rogers believed that the basis of preparing people for change was "unconditional positive regard" from the therapist. It turns out to have been right on the money and it applies to partners, friends, family members, and therapists. It presents a truth that seems paradoxical - people will only change if they feel liked and accepted as they already are.

Marriages that fail often do so because the perpetual problems are ones that one partner or the other cannot deal with or that color the entire relationship. If she wants a clean house and you're, well, not so clean, this perpetual difference could kill the relationship, if you insist on maintaining your "randomness" and she insists that you change. That dynamic could become an ongoing source of tension between you. "You know that pile of papers on the living room table you keep promising to clean up? Well, those tickets to the baseball game you thought you lost 4 years ago are in there". This could be successfully navigated if each person recognizes the other's point of view (for you to try to be more organized and for her to try to relax a bit). Keeping a sense of humor about these differences is important as is trying to focus on the positive aspects of your partner's character and minimizing the negatives. "Boy, I guess I should have listened to you and picked it up long ago. It would have saved me from having to buy the team!"

There are truly irreconcilable differences

The majority of problems between married partners are what Gottman calls "perpetual problems", ones that are ongoing and representative of differences in core values or personality styles. These are a couple's "irreconcilable differences", so-named because they cannot be reconciled or "solved" in the traditional manner. You want to travel, she's a homebody. She wants kids, you don't. She considers her faith to be important to her and wants you to go to church with her; you're science born and bred and consider most faith to be "foolishness". You drive fast and value getting to places "on time" or even early; she always takes extra time to get ready and therefore runs late. These are differences that speak to the core of the person and will always be present. What can be done about them? Are you doomed to either fight about these each time they come up, or at least to become resentful and passive-aggressive toward each other, as did the following couple?

His wife came home late at night and quietly opened the door to the bedroom. From under the blanket she noticed four legs instead of two! She reached for a baseball bat and started hitting the blanket as hard as she could.

Once she finished, she went to the kitchen to have a drink. As she entered the kitchen, she saw her husband there, reading a magazine.

"Hi darling," he said. "Your parents have once again come unannounced to visit us, so I let them stay in our bedroom. I hope you have said hello to them!"

As a man married to a woman, you chose a life partner who is different from you. You did this on purpose. You realized that her personality traits complement yours rather than match them. Even if she has a lot in common with you, that she's a woman and you're a man means there are differences. Learning to celebrate these differences is important, rather than to insist that she be like you in all ways. This means that the goal of dealing with these kinds of differences is <u>not</u> to eliminate the difference, but to learn to dialogue about it without requiring change. This solution often represents a difference of personal dreams and expectations, or possibly learned values and experiences.

For example, let's say she's liberal and you're conservative. It might mean you disagree on who should run the country and that you rarely vote the same way. It also means you should be wary of "spirited debates" about politics. She might even try to avoid the debate by dismissing politics as "show business for ugly people." In the broadest sense, liberal thinking (about the common good, about connectedness and emphasizing equality) is inherently feminine. On the other hand, conservative thinking (conserving energy, resources and keeping things the way they have always been) is inherently masculine. This doesn't mean all men are conservative or all women are liberal. It does mean there is a basic "political" difference between masculine thinking and feminine thinking. So there is a good likelihood you and your wife might have different political views just based on gender differences. Listen to what each of these views means to the person holding them, and don't try to convince each other of a different point of view. Remember that being "different" is not the same as being "wrong." Remember also that masculine thinking is not only for men – women do it all the time in the workplace, and many of them are masculine thinkers at home. Honor those differences without trying to convert the other person.

What if you have differences involving life style, habits or beliefs? What if she wants to raise the kids Catholic, and you want to keep them "free from religion"? What if you want to have sex three to four times a week, and she wants to have sex only on her schedule? What if she wants to save money for future needs and security, and you want to "live in the moment?" These types of differences are truly irreconcilable, and can cause what Gottman calls "gridlock"[17]. The fact is that all couples have differences of this nature and having "irreconcilable differences" need not be a reason for divorce. However, they require a different strategy for resolution than the ones used to resolve your "solvable problems."

According to Gottman, having different plans, religions or politics are all just examples of "gridlock" or places where couples can get stuck. Much of the time, getting unstuck means learning to live with differences. This is much easier to accomplish if each of you can tell the other person what your position and the conflict means to you. Telling her why your position is important to you, what it means to you personally and to your family historically, might be difficult if you've never thought about it yourself. Then get her to do the same. Gottman calls this discussing each partner's "dreams," exploring what the concern means to each partner in the context of how they grew up and what values they hold. Here each partner would take turns being the Speaker and the Listener. The Speaker tells what the issue means to them and why it's important, as if one were explaining this to a friend. The Listener must suspend judgment and listen impartially as if a friend were telling about their life dream. Once this is accomplished, it's important for both parties to feel relaxed and soothed, not flooded or defensive, prior to looking for a temporary solution and common ground from which to move forward.

So-called "irreconcilable differences" are those differences that cannot be "solved" and must be lived with, just as one of you is male and the other is female. They need not be grounds for divorce. Try to understand her reasons for having these differences and try not to be "right" in an argument. When one person is right the relationship suffers. These fights are about feelings, like feeling respected and validated, feeling taken for granted, feeling disregarded, or not feeling understood. Take responsibility for your own feelings in a conflict despite the tendency you might have to feel the fight was the fault of your partner. Seek to understand your wife's position before you explain yours.

Lessons

1. Solvable differences our acute and usually can be dealt with by compromise.

2. "Irreconcilable differences" are chronic and must be lived with. This means they will always exist, but need not derail the marriage.

3. To help each person tolerate unsolvable problems, explain the meaning of your positions, including their history and relation to your respective values.

Example Problem – "I'm conservative and my wife is liberal. I love debating politics, but my wife won't engage with me. It cuts me off from one of my real passions. How can I get her to enter the ring with me on this topic?"

Marcus grew up in a liberal California family, but his views swung toward the conservative side of the political spectrum soon after leaving home. He supported himself by doing contracting work through college and continued this trade after graduation. His gift for gab made him a good conversationalist and a smooth salesman with his customers. However the exchange of ideas he encountered in college left him hungering for more. He enjoyed debate with his contracting crew members and with his best friends. When he met Jin, a single mom working as a secretary to support herself and her son while she went to nursing school at night, he was smitten. They seemed to have much in common, as she was raised in a liberal Californian family, and while still politically liberal, shared many of Marcus' views of life.

After just 4 years of marriage, Marcus was disappointed when he tried to engage Jin in debates about political topics. She had tried to discuss both her views and his views with him at first, but then stopped taking part and told Marcus that she felt that this was an area where they would always disagree. It seemed to her pointless to argue about it. Jin took the time to explain that her liberal upbringing and her desire to pay attention to the needs of society had guided her into the nursing profession. Marcus responded by telling Jin how he had learned that the difficulty of earning a living in the trades and the importance of preserving it led to his fiscal conservatism. Each explained their dreams and related how these dreams influenced their ability to preserve and protect their new family. It became apparent that they both focused on the same outcome but were using different methods to approach it. Marcus could remind himself of why he chose Jin in the first place as a compassionate and understanding woman. He resolved to try not to change her but to recognize that these differences were part of what he cherished about her.

14 - What if one of us has unrealistic expectations in our marriage?

How many women with PMS does it take to screw in a light bulb?

ONE!! And do you know WHY it only takes ONE? Because no one else in this house knows HOW to change a light bulb.

They don't even know the bulb is BURNED OUT. They would sit in this house in the dark for THREE DAYS before they figured it OUT. And once they figured it out they wouldn't be able to find the light bulbs despite the fact that they've been in the SAME CUPBOARD for the past SEVENTEEN YEARS!

But if they did, by some miracle, find the light bulbs, TWO DAYS LATER the chair they dragged from two rooms over to stand on to change the STUPID light bulb would STILL BE IN THE SAME SPOT!!!!!

AND UNDERNEATH IT WOULD BE THE CRUMPLED WRAPPER THE STUPID #)&~!@.!! LIGHT BULBS CAME IN.*

WHY???

BECAUSE NO ONE IN THIS HOUSE EVER CARRIES OUT THE GARBAGE!!!! IT'S A WONDER WE HAVEN'T ALL SUFFOCATED FROM GARBAGE THROUGHOUT THE ENTIRE HOUSE. THE HOUSE!! THE HOUSE!!! IT WOULD TAKE AN ARMY TO CLEAN THIS HOUSE!!!

Not all women suffer PMS to the same degree. For example, I am one of those lucky men whose wife has few monthly mood or irritability symptoms associated with her period. A little gloom or a little whininess perhaps, but rarely noticeable. Your wife may be different. Anyone can be irritable or cranky from time to time. It's one of those unpleasant but natural human conditions, and it can get worse if one's expectations aren't being met.

What if you have different expectations in life and marriage?

Why include PMS (or any irritability) in a chapter on expectations of marriage? Much of the time our expectations of marriage are set up by the relationship of our own parents, the stories we hear growing up, fantasy relationships in books and movies, and our own ideas. The interaction style we develop when we are dating is another contributor to our expectations. Even if we know otherwise, we project this forward into our married life. Of course this is unrealistic. When we are dating, we not only put our own best foot forward, but our partner does too. Dating is exciting, so we bring our excitement and happiness into the relationship. We also leave the darker, more frustrating and more ordinary aspects of our lives behind in a different realm, away from the new relationship. Assuming married life will imitate dating relationships is like assuming that real life will imitate being on vacation. Assuming that your spouse will never be irritable or cranky in a marriage just because she shoved that part of her aside when you were dating is equally irrational.

In his book "Getting The Love You Want," Harville Hendrix presents the compelling thesis that we carry around in our heads an image of the ideal mate he calls the Imago[7]. This image is built from the positive and negative traits of both of our primary caregivers (typically, mom and dad). He suggests that we are consciously drawn toward people who have both our caregivers' positive traits, but we are magnetically attracted to those people who combine our caregivers' negative traits. In this way, the negative traits influence our romantic desires[8]. The upshot is the following dating advice: if you're at a party and your eyes meet across the room, when you feel the thrill of love-at-first-sight, turn and run the other way! That initial rush of good feelings about your mate, yourself, and the rest of the world is partially biochemical. Hormones and other chemicals flood the body and create a profound sense of wellbeing. This is what we refer to as romantic love.

In Hendrix' view this occurs because our brain tells us we have found a relationship through which we can master the old difficulties of childhood and potentially be nurtured and whole again. Since the very traits we had not mastered in childhood drew our interest, we created an opportunity for ourselves. Other less refined observers might say we feel this rush because we've found boobs, beer and pizza. Either way, it's a set of expectations. This hope for fulfillment in the face of a set of familiar negatives occurs during what Hendrix calls the unconscious marriage. During this period in the relationship we engage in fantasy and denial. We over-emphasizing the positives of the relationship and minimizing the potential negatives as we relax into the comfort of the new relationship. It is also a time during which our expectations of future years get hardened.

What kinds of expectations are we talking about? Primarily, expectations that our needs will be fulfilled; this is the reason we got into this relationship. These expectations are based on the needs that are unfulfilled from childhood. These can include the need to be independent, or the need to impress your younger sister's friends with your juggling skills at their sleepover. These needs are coupled with the traits in our partner that remind us of those un-mastered challenges. Just a thought, but you probably still won't score any points by juggling two dirty diapers and a hamster in front of your future wife. At a certain time, you're done "shopping" or trying on this relationship to see if it's a good fit, and you're ready to make a "purchase." When the commitment stage begins people naturally desire those expectations for the future to come to fruition. This means we act on our expectations. Husbands might have the expectations that their wives will cook and clean for them. They will run the household, take care of the children, and still have both time and energy to pamper and provide sex for them. Wives may have the expectations that their husbands will take out the trash. They will work hard toward financial stability, repair the house and car, and still have the energy and desire to provide the travel and romance of her dreams.

Each of them is likely to have unconscious expectations, based on those unmet challenges from their own childhoods. For instance, a woman's father might have worked so hard that he was rarely a part of her life. She may now expect she will have a husband who not only works hard, but still comes home on time and give her a foot massage each night. Perhaps she will help change him into a more relaxed person by teaching him the benefits of delivering said foot massage. A man's mother might have been depressed or anxious during his childhood. He may now expect his wife to be playful, funny, demure and alluring, but also as emotionally stable as a rock. Perhaps he expects that he will rescue her from some distress, probably by offering her a foot massage.

Most couples do not share their conscious expectations with one another during the dating phase of their relationship. It's the rare couple who asks questions as explicit as, "Will you be willing to cook, clean, run the household and take care of the children while I am away at work?" More often, people aren't even aware that they need it, or they try to get at this information passively. They might ask about the dynamics within the other person's family of origin (for example, "What did your Dad do for a profession?" or "Your Mom got married how many times?"), talk about their priorities and interests, or listen for clues to the answers they hope to hear, even if they're not aware of the real questions.

All of these unspoken expectations, the conscious ones and the unconscious ones, set us up for disappointment. In fact, the only source of human disappointment is expectations. Without expectations, you would never be disappointed. Just look at the Cubs. 'Nuff said. Your friend invites you and six other friends over to watch the game of the week. He sits you all down in front of a 19-inch computer screen (he's the one telling you all about how proud he is to "cut the cord") and it's a big disappointment. This can be mitigated if at least he has good beer and killer nachos. This means that other people, events, and situations do not disappoint us. The failure of our own expectations to get met is what disappoints us.

If you are disappointed in an event or an outcome, it means you didn't have your expectations met. You might not have known what these expectations were at the outset. You might not have known that you had any expectations; these might be unconscious. When you are disappointed about an event or thing, do a little internal investigation. Examine what your expectations might have been. It is irrational to insist that there must be something wrong with reality if nature did not meet your expectations. More rationally, it means that your expectations were too high given the conditions that prevail. Does that mean that to avoid disappointment you might need to lower your expectations? Yes, but first you need to investigate what they are and how they fit (or don't fit) with reality.

The same is true if you feel disappointed in another person, and especially in an ongoing relationship. Let's say that your child does not perform up to your expectations - he only gets Bs and Cs on his report card, or he isn't finished with potty training by his 4th birthday. You could trade him in as a defective model, but chances are that your wife has already gotten attached to the Little Disappointment. Perhaps the neighbor does something other than what you wanted him to do, or if your wife takes a different course of action than the one you believe to be "obvious." You might be disappointed "in them." Your disappointment is authentic, but that does not mean they did anything wrong (well, the neighbor probably did). It simply means that your expectations were not in line with their abilities, needs or the prevailing situation.

Many men have a difficult time with this idea since men's competitive nature drives them to strive to meet expectations. These men can well believe that reducing one's expectations is equivalent to accepting mediocrity. However, when the price of not accepting reality is disappointment, one possible avenue is to investigate whether your expectations are in line. This is especially true of your expectations about your wife. If you've never verbalized these to her, she has little chance of meeting them. If she doesn't (or can't) meet them, it's time to re-evaluate those expectations. Strive to find realistic expectations that she can achieve. Set her up to succeed instead of to fail and then brag about her ability to meet your expectations to anyone who will listen. This will please her, satisfy you and astonish your friends.

<u>Boredom</u>

When I get real bored, I like to drive downtown and get a great parking spot, then I sit in my car and count how many people ask me if I'm leaving.
Stephen Wright

One condition that often occurs in marriages (and in most lives) is that of boredom. Boredom in a marriage does not have to be boredom (or "bored him") <u>about</u> the marriage. One can be bored with the daily routine, with one's job, with having the same food to eat each day, or with having the same commute. Boredom can come about from failure to grow or a failure to progress toward a certain end. For instance, if you never set goals for yourself, it's easy to get into a routine where nothing changes and you never advance. As they say in dog sledding, if you're not the lead dog, the view never changes. Even if you do set goals for yourself, without some kind of accountability it's easy to get into a routine and get off track from your progress. The same thing can occur later in life if you've met your stated goals and have failed to set new ones (for example, this happens often during retirement). Being bored primarily comes from insufficient goals, or insufficient progress toward your goals.

Boredom in a relationship is a perception. There are no objective qualities that denote boredom, but it's always a matter of what the participants experience. When boredom is about the relationship, it usually indicates the interaction between two people have become routine. They might have felt new love fade away and have not yet fallen in love with the real person they are married to. They might recognize that their expectations are not going to be met and they fail to adjust those expectations to reality. They might recognize that these expectations are a defense to keep the other person distant or they might have accepted the status quo without enjoying it. They might be tired of consistent power struggles yet are unwilling to be influenced by each other. Perhaps one or the other is depressed, where boredom is just a symptom of a larger mood problem.

Like gardens, relationships need constant tending and attention, and they need a way to include novelty regularly to stave off familiarity and boredom. Like you are right now, reading these same old predictable words written here until, suddenly, Burma! Something unexpected happens (a hat tip to Monty Python for invoking that former country and the aftershave - the rest of you can go look it up). Novelty keeps our attention better than sameness. This does not mean you need to find someone new, but you might need to find something new about the one you're with. After you have been together for a while, you might feel you know each other pretty well, and you fall into a routine. Under these conditions, it's easy to get bored. Each partner needs to bring something novel to the table, and that's easier if each of you have somewhat different experiences during your lives.

If you've fallen into a routine, you might need to create different experiences for either or each of you individually, or for the two of you together. Some people take up new hobbies or have new social encounters, and many couples try to infuse novelty using vacations or travel as new experiences to be shared. Often, when men get bored, they need something new to <u>do</u>. When women get bored, they often need someone new to do things with, or at least to share things with. Often this takes time away from the couple and that can lead to its own difficulties. In the best cases, each partner engages in new experiences, either together or separately, and then comes back together to share those experiences.

New experiences can be had in the bedroom, with role-playing, nights out away from home, sex dates, etc. All of these are sexual ways of adding novelty, but novelty can exist in many forms. Again, finding yourself in this state does not mean you need to find someone else. Your woman really wants to be your "everything" and sexually that's a good thing. Try out new positions, new places and new identities. Also try out new activities, new foods and new hobbies with each other. Sometimes you might need to have other activities like poker nights with the guys or hiking with a buddy. In these cases you should expect her to find something social to do with another friend. As you both experience new or different things, you will become slightly different people than you were before and this change will help contribute to keeping the relationship new.

Blaming in a marriage

I never blame myself when I'm not hitting. I just blame the bat and if it keeps up, I change bats. After all, if I know it isn't my fault I'm not hitting, how can I get mad at myself?

Yogi Berra

Blaming someone else is basically a way of stating that they are responsible for your distress. For some people, blaming is a primitive coping mechanism. These people cannot take responsibility or regulate their emotions, or both. Even those of us who are healthier can blame others when we are in acute distress or despair. When we are feeling desperate for love it's possible for us to use negative approaches to get our partners to be more loving or to meet our expectations. We might become distant (giving someone the silent treatment), critical (invalidating our partners successes and emphasizing their struggles) or blaming.

One version of blaming and attacking is asking questions that are not really questions, but rather are scoldings. For example, when one asks, "What were you thinking?" or "Why do you always do this to me?" we are not searching for an answer, but are scolding someone in disguise. More direct blaming can sound like "You made that same mistake again, and now I'll have to fix it!" Either way, it gets us to give away our power over things and to hand it directly to the other person. If she's standing there with the cord in her hand and the smoking plug is still in the wall socket, the astonished look on her face might say, "I didn't pull it out by the cord!" In that case a little blame might be hard to resist. Try to find the humor in it even if the appliance in question is your brand new $1500 Miele vacuum. "Uh, OK, we'll just get the plug out now" is all you need to say.

Notice that in these cases blaming is about the past. This helps us to differentiate it from taking responsibility. Taking responsibility is about the present and the future: now that something's happened, what can you do about it? Blaming is about assigning fault for the past and does nothing to resolve the issue. If you blame someone for something, you admit that they have control over that thing. For example, if you blame someone for how you feel (telling your partner "You really made me mad!" or "You hurt my feelings!"), you admit that they have control over your feelings. In this way, blaming someone else is always dis-empowering to you. It says they have control and you don't.

Blaming someone else for your feelings comes back to a matter of expectations. If you expect someone to be complimentary and they say, "I don't like your outfit", you might get your feelings hurt. What if the person who said that was a three-year-old child? You probably would not be hurt. In part that's due to your lower expectations of the child. Even getting your feelings hurt is largely a matter of your expectations, and therefore your feelings are always controlled from inside. There's a novel idea - no one hurts our feelings, it's always an inside job. Like blaming the guy on the bar stool next to you for spilling his drink in your lap when you're actually so drunk you've peed your own pants. It was an inside job. If only your friend would have peed for you when he got up to use the facilities, like he promised. All he reported after he got back was, "I guess you didn't have to go!"

If you blame someone else for something, you give them control over that thing, or at least over how you feel about that thing. If you blame yourself for something without also taking responsibility for it, you are choosing to feel guilty instead of choosing to take action. Blaming anyone (yourself or someone else) dis-empowers you. Blame, like worry, is a waste of time and mental energy. If you can't take action or make a plan, then worrying is a waste of time. It's a way of trying to reduce your anxiety about something when there isn't anything else that you can do. Blaming is a way of trying to address an unfortunate incident or feeling after the fact, when it's too late to do anything else. Don't fix the blame, fix the problem.

Instead of dis-empowering yourself when something unfortunate happens, try expressing your feelings about the matter. Saying "I'm hurt by that," or "I'm feeling frustrated right now" are ways of addressing something in the present tense. This can occur after the event has happened but without trying to assign blame, especially to your partner. It also reinforces that you have the power to change your feeling regardless of whether she changes. You might be frustrated, for instance, that your partner is not meeting your expectations. That isn't her fault and blaming her only increases ill will and decreases your satisfaction. Your distress and frustration are real; more than likely, though, they are due to expectations you had based on your experiences from childhood and your hopes and desires for the relationship.

When blaming someone for not living up to your expectations, why would you think being critical, blaming or distant would get her to be more loving? That's likely to produce the opposite of what you want, and it's likely to make you fail to meet her expectations. Therefore blaming your spouse for not meeting your expectations, or blaming yourself for having those expectations in the first place, are both nonstarters. Becoming more intentional will likely lead you to the satisfaction you desire from your relationship. This will mean developing a more realistic appraisal (and therefore, more realistic set of expectations) of both yourself and your partner, and becoming more purposeful and communicative in your relationship. Accept that every good marriage will have difficult times, and that the benefit of having a good relationship is worth the cost of putting effort into it.

Lessons

1. Expectations are the sole cause of disappointment. If we are disappointed in our relationship, it's primarily because our expectations did not match reality.

2. Our expectations of relationships are based on our leftover challenges from childhood, combined with hopes and desires created during our dating experiences. Because of this, no partner can match our expectations at least until we make them more conscious.

3. Relationships are like gardens - they need tending and nurturing, but they also need novelty to keep from growing stale. Do new things individually or together and let the experiences add to your relationship.

4. Blaming our partner for not meeting our expectations, or blaming ourselves for having those expectations in the first place, prevents us from getting what we want in our marriage.

5. Resolve to learn about yourself and about your spouse, to become more realistic in your appraisal of each other, and becoming more intentional and communicative in your relationship.

Example Problem 1 (Expectations) – "I'm routinely disappointed in my son because he's not as good at school sports as he could be. I work hard to coach his team. He isn't working hard enough himself but my wife defends him. How come we're not all on the same page?"

Clay grew up in a family of four boys, all of whom enjoyed sports. His mother and father went to all their sons' games and supported their efforts to try new sports. Although all four boys were decent students and the parents stressed academic performance, achievement in sports received most of the parental enthusiasm. Understandably, Clay expected that he could share that enthusiasm with his own son, and was eager to be even more involved than his parents were. Clay's son Mark enjoyed playing games with his dad and even enjoyed sports activities but did not show the competitive spirit that Clay expected. Instead, Mark appeared to value the companionship more than the competition, and often amused himself by doing things Clay referred to as "goofing around". Mark did not work out or rehearse his skills and often reported being bored or tired when Clay tried to drill him one on one.

Clay's wife Ling grew up in a very different home, with her parents also stressing academics but where they urged each child to find his or her own area of interest. Lynn's brother and sister tried out music, acting, chess and writing en route to finding their own areas of interest. Ling's dream for her son was to watch him grow and help him determine what things he might be interested in. Ling was often frustrated with Clay for having such an emphasis on sports, seemingly at the expense of other possible interests. Even as late as middle school, Mark had shown little interest in any of these pursuits except video games and hanging out with his friends. She became frustrated that Mark was not finding an area of interest in which he could excel.

Clay and Ling each had expectations that their new family would follow the pattern they saw in their own families of origin. These expectations, while understandable, were the source of their own disappointment. Clay came to realize that his new family would differ from his family of origin, and that Mark may not have the same interest in sports that Clay did. Likewise, Ling eventually realized that Mark might need a little more guidance than members of her original family did, and that some direction was helpful to Mark. Letting go of these sets of expectations and embracing the opportunities of a new environment allowed all three of them to experience less disappointment and more optimism.

Example Problem 2 (Boredom) – "My wife has been reading this book about '50 ways of being sexually crazy' or something like that. Now she wants to change our sex life. What gives? I thought it was OK before."

Hank and Linda had been married for 15 years and had 2 sons, ages 10 and 12. They got along well, both worked at jobs they enjoyed and spent most weekends together. They either watched their sons play baseball, watched their favorite reality shows on TV, or went out for dinner. Hank found that the routine they had settled into was comfortable and predictable. He knew that Linda read books in her spare time and was amused when she found a series of books she devoured in just a short time. Hank was surprised when Linda approached him with requests to try out some of the, well, less exotic things she had read about. When he asked her about her desire to try out new things, she at first responded that she was just curious. When he resisted, she acknowledged that she had gotten bored with the routine their lives had gotten into, including their intimate lives.

While Hank saw the routine as comfortable, Linda found it boring. He was at a comfortable level of stimulation while she needed more novelty. When Linda explained that she still wanted only Hank in the bedroom with just a bit of "newness", he realized that Linda was not expressing dissatisfaction with him but rather asking for more of him. That made him feel more desirable, and he was willing to put more effort into keeping the relationship new. Even if it didn't include whips and chains.

Example problem 3 (Blame) – "We never got as financially secure as we needed to be before we retired. I blame my wife for this since she retired after I did. My wife thinks I'm being silly and takes no responsibility for our situation. She wants me to get a part-time job to help pay the bills, but I just want her to accept the blame!"

Nathan's idea of retirement was to retire first since he was older than Emily and had been working longer. He expected her to continue working for another 5 years after he retired. This would not only bring in extended income but also give him a little extra time alone at home to "putter around" with no one to hold him accountable. Nathan was a High School principal and Emily was a public works official, both working for many years at the same jobs. When he retired in 2005 he expected that their savings would last them a long time. Surprising Nathan, Emily decided that she would also retire because she "wanted to spend more time with Nathan" than they had during their working years. Two years later, when the Great Recession hit, they lost about 40% of their investments, putting their retirement plans in jeopardy.

Nathan's disappointment at having his previous plans foiled was easy to understand. Placing the blame on his wife was less so. Rationally he knew that she didn't cause the recession which produced their retirement distress; Emily knew that she had no control over how the economy affected their plans. Nathan couldn't get past the thought that "if only she hadn't retired, we wouldn't be in this much of a mess even with the Great Recession!" Blaming Emily was a primitive way that Nathan externalized his distress, since as bad as it was to have Emily responsible for things, it was far more difficult for Nathan to have the cause be "random occurrence" or "fate." These were tough to take because they indicated there was nothing Nathan could do about it. Instead he blamed Emily as a substitute for doing anything else. Once he came to terms with the idea that blaming was a substitute for other action, Nathan dropped his requirement that Emily accept the blame. He decided it would benefit him to have something more to do during his days than just putter. He did some consulting for private local schools on a part-time basis. This, combined with letting Emily off the hook for something over which she had no control, greatly improved their relationship.

15 - How do I deal with role reversal at home?

Little Red Riding Hood goes out into the forest, but this time she's hiding a .44 in her package of goodies, ready for action. The wolf follows her into the woods and grabs her from behind. "Now that I've got you I'm going to f*** you until dawn," he growls. But Little Red Riding Hood pulls out the .44, holds it to his head and announces calmly, "No you're not. You're going to eat me like the story said."

(included in Blanche Knott's Truly Tasteless Jokes)

<u>What are the different roles in a stereotypical relationship like?</u>

Albeit in pretty tasteless humor (like the rest of her book, thankfully), this joke is important. It is one of few jokes that puts the female in such an assertive position, making a demand backed up by threats of violence. This represents a type of role reversal from the typical male and female roles, which can happen in relationships. Luckily, most role reversal between men and women need not involve violence.

We are interested in a different role reversal here, the reversal of the masculine and feminine energies. In her books, "Getting to 'I Do'" and "Staying

173

Married and Loving It," Patricia Allen illustrates how having both a masculine energy and a feminine energy in a marriage to complement each other works out the best. Most frequently, the man embodies the masculine energy and the woman embodies the feminine energy, although this historical stereotype is giving way to new models and awareness. Either person can carry either energy, and people can switch from one to the other during the day. While it can become complicated to determine who wears the pants and who wears the skirt, it can be downright embarrassing if you have to switch clothes in the middle of the supermarket.

Let's start out by defining what it means to be feminine or masculine in terms of energy. This has little to do with anatomy or sexual orientation and more to do with ways of thinking and behaving. According to Allen,[10] men have traditionally been portrayed in Western culture as the protectors, leaders, and doers. Men have traditionally brought status to women and have been the providers of security. On the other hand, women have been the domesticators, followers, and responders. They often make themselves available to men, change their life plans to follow those of men, and respond to the needs of men, often at the expense of their own needs.

By these terms, the masculine energy is functional and pragmatic. It initiates action, does things, and is productive. It represents starting, leading, taking control and pursuing. A continuing example of this in our culture is the marriage proposal itself. Despite many varieties of marriages and roles within marriages, certain symbolic gestures are very resistant to change. In the marriage proposal, the man traditionally gets down on one knee (perhaps a sign of respect or proof he is not a threat, or perhaps he simply needs a rest). He enjoys a culturally sanctioned few minutes to express his feelings and asks his intended for her hand (he gets the rest of her too, which is sometimes more than he bargained for). This is one example of the masculine energy taking the lead. The feminine energy is passive and receptive. Its strength lies in waiting and responding. It uses emotion and morality as a check on behavior and focuses on relating. In the example of the marriage proposal, the feminine energy is restricted traditionally by waiting for the man to be ready, perhaps hinting but traditionally not demanding. "Marry me, dammit!" is not as often heard as you might think. During the proposal itself, it's her position to listen and then respond with her feelings about his request. This is a receptive and passive position.

It's important to recognize that men and women each have masculine and feminine elements. To make a marriage work, these two parts must complement one another. This means that there can only be one masculine and one feminine energy at any given time. If both partners want to lead, there are two masculine energies, and they will compete. If both partners defer to the other, then both are choosing the feminine energy and they will take no action ("what do you want to do?" "I don't know, what do you want to do?"). It will be important to recognize which of these energies is a better fit for you and which is a better fit for your partner, so you can choose which role you will inhabit most often.

There are other traits that go along with these energies. For example, thinking is primarily a masculine energy trait, while feeling and emoting are feminine energy traits. Seeking to be respected is a masculine trait, and seeking to be cherished is a feminine trait. If you prefer to have your thinking respected, you are choosing the masculine energy; if you prefer to have your feelings cherished, you are choosing the feminine energy.

Verbal communication comes from the masculine energy. When the two of you meet, whoever speaks first (being verbal and taking action) is choosing the masculine energy. Nonverbal communication comes from the feminine energy. Flirting by smiling, glancing, and moving your body (being nonverbal and receptive) is choosing the feminine energy.

At this point you might think, "Wait a minute. I do a lot of those things, like waiting for my wife to take the lead and listening when she's talking. Are you calling me a girl?" No, Bubba, I'm not saying that; you can put down that ax. I'm just suggesting that those are the times you are coming from the feminine energy position. Most of us trade off from time to time.

Giving, widely admired in our society, is a masculine energy trait. After all, giving is an action and shows initiation. Giving back (that is, reciprocating) is responding, and therefore a feminine energy trait. A masculine energy man will be the first to give to his feminine energy partner, whether the giving involves gifts, information, opinion or pleasure. A man who insists that his partner give to him first is choosing the feminine energy. True masculine men are generous with their time, money and effort. If you're the guy, give first.

Feminine energy women are receptive to their men's needs and ideas, and in return for giving their respect, they desire to have their feelings cherished. They will put their relationships and home life ahead of their career goals (these will be ""women with a career" as opposed to "career women"). They will be supportive of men's ideas and decisions as long as they are not morally or ethically tainted. They will want to be listened to as this is their primary way of expressing their emotions to you. Feminine energy women will expect masculine energy men to speak first so they can reply, to take the initiatives on planning vacations, family activities, and romantic interludes (like date night and initiating sex). They will expect their men to express their thoughts so they can tell you their feelings about them.

There are certain environments that call for certain types of energies. For example, being at work in business is an environment that is best handled using one's masculine energy. Work environments place an emphasis on productivity and practicality, and often on one's competitive nature. Taking initiative on things is rewarded as is taking action. All of these are masculine energy traits. Your wife might be busy coming from her masculine energy all day at work and then come home to a different environment. If so, you might expect her to have some carry over of continued masculine energy at first; she may want to slip into a more familiar feminine energy role as she relaxes.

Certain jobs, like those in the helping professions (doctor, nurse, therapist, teacher, etc.), place a little higher emphasis than most on feminine energy traits (like listening and being receptive). These people are still somewhat consumed with the business end of things. Taking care of younger children is almost exclusively about feminine energies. This involves nurturing and assisting rather than competing and jockeying for position (taking care of older children might demand a little more leading and negotiating). Sometimes dads let their masculine energies come into play with child rearing. We see this when we compete with our son in the guise of "teaching him to be a man" (that is, at least until he wins these battles regularly; we then retreat to "I'm too mature for this kind of horseplay!").

What if you're the feminine-energy man and you have a masculine-energy wife?

What if you are the husband, but you're the feminine energy at home? Gender alone does not determine your primary energy state. As Patricia Allen wrote, "masculine energy likes to make money and wield power and prestige. Feminine energy likes to make love, build families and play."[11] That means that if you have a masculine energy wife to complement you, she is likely to both make and control most of the money. You may choose to protect your manhood by making enough to cover expenses like gifts and dinners out, or by requesting that she put some of her income aside for your purposes. This not only allows each of you to function independently as adults, but also allows you to be the masculine energy when society demands it. It also means you are the one who values feelings and yearns for feeling cherished by her while she may value her thinking abilities and feeling respected by you.

You may be predominantly a feminine energy man if others have considered you "too nice." Perhaps you always had a tendency to "give in" rather than confront or had some feminine energy women consider you "not a real man." Of course you are, in your loving and playful way, a real man. This just means that your energies are most naturally directed toward connecting and nurturing rather than competing. You would probably feel most comfortable with a masculine energy woman to be your complement. Other women might question why she "lets you stay home" while she goes to work, and your own buds might well question whether you're being dominated. Sometimes couples that hear this feedback from others question their relationship roles and even try to change them. The important thing is whether the way you complement one another works for you both.

There is nothing wrong with being a feminine energy man at home (or at work). You may need to be confident and secure enough in yourself to allow your wife to be the leader, to decide, and to take the initiative. If your masculine side tries to compete with her or to demand respect, learn to recognize this tendency and set it aside at home. It means you will support her needs to go out of town for business, extra lunches or dinners with ""the girls," and longer hours at the office. It means that you will be the one responsible for playtime at home between the two of you, keeping a social calendar and nurturing her growth as a leader.

Just because you are the feminine energy most of the time does not mean you are always the feminine energy. It's okay for you to be assertive when you are out with the boys, enjoying recreation with your sons, or interfacing with the rest of the world (like taking care of the cars, dealing with service personnel, etc.). You may occasionally be competitive and direct even if this is not always comfortable for you. Nor does being the feminine energy at home mean you are weak. If you don't like something that is going on, you must tell your wife about it even if it means speaking first. It will be her job to listen and attend to your feelings on the matter. If she is spending too much time away, or placing an uncomfortably high priority on her career, you must let her know that too. Women can also get too wrapped up in their careers and neglect their duties to their primary relationships.

As I mentioned earlier, certain biochemical and hormonal changes occur to both men and women as they get older. Many men, somewhere around midlife, tend to "mellow out," become less competitive and confrontational, and become more interested in connecting, socializing and being receptive to the ideas of others. I suppose this might have produced the idea of the "kindly old grandfather."At least in part this is because testosterone starts to diminish and it plays a smaller role as men get older, leading to a larger influence from the bit of estrogen men have. Many men notice that their feminine energies are more predominant as they get older. Luckily, the reverse happens to most women, although it might not happen at the same time. Their estrogen levels diminish, leading to a larger influence of their naturally occurring testosterone. When this happens, women enter (or re-enter) the workforce, go back to school, or become a stronger force at home in determining things like finances, investments and healthcare. In some ways, the "role-reversed" feminine energy younger man is just ahead of his time.

Being the feminine energy, many of the things you must do to keep your wife happy will differ from the advice given to masculine energy men. Some of the advice will still apply since she will likely still be the feminine energy at home. It means you must treat her with respect for her ideas and be receptive to her requests. She will tell you what she thinks and what she wants, and you will be the one telling her how you feel about those things. She will expect you to do more than the average share of housework, especially if she is the primary breadwinner. However, that may be one thing you truly enjoy. She may have a lot more sexual energy than you do but you will still need to be receptive to her sexuality. That is the vehicle through which she will connect to you.

She may spend long hours on her work, but is more likely to be giving in terms of small gifts and experiences. It will be up to you to give back, especially nurturing things like having dinner ready or offering to give her a foot massage. If you have kids, you are more likely to be engaged in the bulk of childrearing than many men. The chores could be split, with her helping with homework and you administering meals and bath time. If one of you is respected and giving and the other is cherished and fun, it doesn't matter which is which; it can work out beautifully! Remember that these roles can shift back and forth during the day.

Lessons

1. Gender alone does not determine whether you represent the masculine or the feminine energy in your relationship.

2. Masculine energy is the leader, is competitive, likes to make money, takes initiative, is giving and requires respect for ideas.

3. Feminine energy is receptive, values connection and communication, is fun, submits to the needs and wants of others, but requires having feelings cherished.

4. Marriages work best when these energies are both present as they complement one another.

5. If you're a feminine energy man, embrace your role when you're at home. Appreciate your wife's leadership and energy and respect her thinking and decision-making. Don't forget to value your own feelings, give her feedback about her ideas and ask to be cherished in return.

Example problem - "My wife is now a full partner in her law firm and she brings in the big bucks. It allowed me to go back to school to pursue my PhD, and to do lots of writing I always wanted to do. However, when I try to tell her I'm not satisfied sexually and I want her to be more feminine, she gets annoyed."

By the time Chuck and Linda met, they were both professionals and had spent significant amount of time pursuing their careers. Chuck had several prior, long-term relationships with feminine women, which he found sexually, but not intellectually, fulfilling. Linda kept him on his toes, being a very competent attorney herself, and ended up being the one pushing him to get married. Chuck had not been happy in his accounting career for some time, and with Linda's income, he could quit his accounting job and pursue his PhD in literature. More than anything, he enjoyed writing book reviews. As Linda's career blossomed, Chuck did his writing, took care of the household, fetched coffee and dry-cleaning for Linda, and took care of the dogs. He respected Linda a lot but always felt unsatisfied with their sex life. He was frustrated that she resisted when he asked her to wear high heels more often and to wear sexier outfits in the bedroom. His frustration was significant enough that he thought about leaving his marriage and pursuing someone new that might be a better match for his sexual fantasies.

He didn't consider this option for long once he realized that the role he chose in the relationship was the feminine energy. Being the primary breadwinner positioned Linda as the masculine energy in their relationship. Chuck took the role of the feminine energy, which meant that he needed to be receptive to her ideas, including those about sexuality. The more he insisted that she be feminine in the bedroom, the more his attempt at masculine energy conflicted with her masculine energy, leading to a stalemate. Ironically, once he allowed himself to remain as the feminine energy and allowed her to make her choices about sexuality, she ended up choosing to be more overtly sexual with Chuck. It was then up to him to be sensual. With the stalemate broken, their love life could get back on track.

16 – What if we have a hierarchy at home instead

of a partnership?

Smith goes to see his supervisor in the front office. "Boss," he says, "we're doing some heavy house cleaning at home tomorrow, and my wife needs me to help with the attic and the garage, moving and hauling stuff."

"We're short-handed, Smith," the boss replies. "I can't give you the day off."

"Thanks, boss," says Smith. "I knew I could count on you!"

<u>What if you disagree about the distribution of power in your marriage?</u>

Workplace relationships are almost always based on hierarchies. Here we will define a hierarchy as a relationship where one person has more power than another. Sometimes, as in the situation above, this can work to your advantage. Typically you have a boss (about whom you love to complain), and you have peers (many of whom are slackers, and never do as much work as you do). You might even have people underneath you (who always seem to make you look bad). The rest of a man's world is full of other examples of relationship hierarchies. In school, you have the teacher (the boss) and the class. In sports, you have the coach (the boss) and the team. In the military, you have the commander (the boss) and the servicemen. The stereotypical competitive man will even strive for hierarchies in social environments. Here one man may try to prove that he is stronger, more influential, wealthier or more adventurous than other men around him. Put another way, men often strive to present differences between themselves and other men. This orientation is part of the way men prove themselves to be fit for leadership or fit for a mate (or just superior to the dick-wad down the street).

Each of the examples of hierarchical relationships above also includes examples of peer relationships, the relationships between equals. Coworkers, classmates, teammates and service mates are all examples of peers. For example, in the military people wear "uniforms" to enhance a sense of sameness; that is what the word "uniform" means. Men have experiences with both hierarchical and partnership types of relationships even if they may identify more with one than the other. We support our team even at the expense of ourselves, and sometimes we bond by griping about the boss.

When men get into relationships with women, the confusion about expectations begins. In a man's world it is clear to other men whether their relationship is hierarchical or a partnership (where both parties have equal power). In a woman's world the expectations are different. Women focus on similarities between themselves and other women, so there is a preference (and an expectation) of peer relationships. Women have experiences with hierarchies in all the same situations that men do (work, school, sports and the military). However, a woman's social world is more structured in terms of partnerships, at least after high school ("Mean Girls" was a good example of hierarchies in a girl's world). A relationship between a man and a woman, like a marriage, can either be a hierarchy or a partnership, and either one could work well. Problems here often arise when one person expects a hierarchy (where one has more power than the other) and the other expects a partnership (between equals).

These different relationships may actually be present without being overt. For example, a gentleman named John once told me, "Of course our marriage is a partnership! We each have our role, and we each have our jobs to do. Lots of times, though, she won't know the right way to do something until I tell her, and then I'll have to correct her somewhere in the middle. Between the two of us, we get the job done!" It was a shock to John when his wife told him she didn't think that was a partnership, and she was right. At least, it wasn't a partnership the way she understood the word. For her this seemed like a hierarchy because John often told her what to do or how to do things. Plus, in her way of thinking, it couldn't be a partnership if it didn't feel like one. At least after high school, the feminine world is organized largely by partnerships.

Men's interactions are mostly designed to foster and enhance individuality, and this comes into play even in the concept of "doing something together". John's comment of "we each have our role" meant that whenever he and his wife had a project to work on, he would do his part and she would do her part, at the same time but separately. When I asked his wife one day if that was what she meant by "doing something together", she replied, "Oh no! When I think of us doing something together, I mean together! We do the same thing at the same time until it's done. He wants us to work separately. That's not together!" Clearly they had different ideas of what working together meant.

In contrast, Antoine and Belinda had a marriage that seemed very much like a partnership between equals. Antoine was an accountant and worked long hours until he got married, at which time he made it a point to come home every day by 6:00pm. Belinda was a schoolteacher at the local high school. They did most things together, including making dinner, house cleaning, doing yard work, going to church and related activities, and traveling. They were fond of taking travel pictures. They collaborated on creating not only the best versions of each picture but also composing a narrative to go with each and uploading them to their own travelogue website. There were certain things that Antoine was more familiar with than Belinda, but she had no problem asking him for help when she needed it. He had no problem asking her for help when he required her expertise either, and neither one offered help without it first being requested. Each one seemed aware of the needs of the other.

One place that Antoine and Belinda had difficulties in their marriage was when they needed to decide something that neither one had a vested interest in. This included decisions like where to eat (or what to eat), what movie to watch or where to go on a weekend vacation. Each tried to pay attention to the wants and needs of the other, and each tried to avoid having unequal power. This brings about problems when neither one wants to take the lead. It's a good thing that there actually is a restaurant called the "I Don't Care" Grill; that's where they usually end up going for food. The lesson here is that, even in an equal partnership, sometimes someone has to lead.

Accept influence from your wife

When the media heard about John Gottman's study[18] on partners accepting influence from one another, the sound bite that made the headlines was "Anything you say, dear". The jokes and parodies were non-stop. My own uncle, on the occasion of his 50th wedding anniversary, said to his audience that this phrase was part of his secret to remaining married so long (my aunt said that her secret was that after 30 years, she stopped trying to change him). However, this was not what Gottman meant. He did not mean to suggest that men should give up all of their power (what kind of partnership would that be?). Instead, in "the happiest, most stable marriages" the "husbands actively searched for common ground rather than insisting on getting their way" when the couple disagreed about something.[19]

Accepting influence is the key to a good partnership - decisions are made by a committee of two, not by an autocrat of either gender. The majority of women in Gottman's study responded to their husbands' negativity during a conflict by either matching their tone or by reducing it. Men escalated their wives' negativity, something that might be a strength in a competition. These men often imported one of Gottman's Four Horsemen of the Apocalypse (criticism, contempt, defensiveness or stonewalling) to try to win the argument. Using one of these was a sign that the husband was resisting accepting influence from his wife. Gottman's data suggest that men must be more careful than women when using one of the Four Horsemen to escalate conflict (he does not explain why the gender difference exists). Perhaps, he speculates[20], it has to do with the tendency of most wives to accept influence from their husbands. Men must be more carful than women to practice accepting influence if only to keep the partners on equal footing.

Agreeing to accept influence in a partnership like a marriage is equal to agreeing to share power. If you're in a partnership and not a hierarchy you will share power, decision making, authority, etc. This is all that accepting influence means. You might get your way only half of the time! When a man accepts influence from his wife, she is less likely to be harsh with him when difficult topics arise (See? There's a benefit to letting yourself be influenced!). When she is less likely to be angered or frustrated, she is more likely to discuss things without excess criticism, and there is a foundation set for establishing compromise. These things bode well for survival of the marriage.

Men can learn a lot from women, including being skilled in listening and emotional intelligence (primarily because women have been practicing these skills much longer than men, on the average). Being influenced this way means becoming an emotionally intelligent husband, one who has learned to override at least some of his caveman traits. For example, giving up competing at all times as if it's life or death, getting annoyed when she wants to discuss something in the middle of a football game, etc. It means choosing the "team" good over the individual good.

Accepting influence from your wife may help you become a better father too; the same tools that allow you to be better connected with your wife will allow you to connect well with your kids. You might want them to remember you as fun to be with and not just someone who was unavailable because he worked all the time or was over-involved in football. Instead, having these interactions with family means they will be more supportive when you do have to work especially hard because everyone will be on the same team. Since more and more married women are in the workforce, the gender roles are changing to more egalitarian partnerships. Adapting to these changing roles means agreeing to share power. That means you have to learn to yield as an individual for the team to have a win. Even if you're "right", yielding power can score points because if you insist and thus "win", the team loses.

Avoid defensiveness

A common way men avoid accepting influence from their wives is by getting defensive. Defensiveness is one of the Four Horsemen that Gottman says portends doom in a marriage, and it is one that men use to significant effect. Many of us were raised to believe that defending ourselves was a noble endeavor, and hearing it is something we should learn to avoid might seem counterintuitive (What? Be like Obi-wan Kenobi and let yourself be struck down?). Few things are as damaging to good communication and team building as defensiveness. Yet this is a natural and engrained, even automatic, mechanism of self-protection. We use it when we perceive that we are being attacked, or when we perceive that we might lose something like our own self-respect (if there's truth in the criticism) or the respect of others (if we feel the criticism is unjust). So what can you do to help yourself avoid being defensive? There are several things that can help:

1. If you notice you're becoming defensive, mention it. You might need time in the man-cave to cool down enough to have a productive discussion. This differs from having your wife call you out on it - this can be perceived as another attack and will probably not help. Don't ask her to notice your defensiveness and point it out to you (but she could use help in knowing how to respond when you are defensive).

2. Don't take it personally. Remember, all communications are about the speaker, so hear her complaint or criticism as a statement about her perceptions. Accept that her view might be true for her, and yet false for you.

3. If you know criticism is coming, give yourself a dose of self-worth in advance (remind yourself of things you respect about yourself).

4. Seek to understand her, listen carefully, and try not to respond. Use self-calming tools like mindfulness or deep breathing if you need to.

5. If there is truth in the criticism, accept it. You aren't perfect and aren't supposed to be. File it away for future assessment and change.

6. When you respond, use "I" statements (e.g., "I feel hurt by that" or "I think I was misunderstood, so let me try again"). Your response will be about you, not about her. Own your own feelings.

Above all, remember that this is a partnership, a team. One part of the team criticizing another part is meant to improve the team. Even if you "lose", the team can still win. Your partner should have a very similar perception and you wouldn't be married to her if she didn't. It's unlikely that her long-term goal is to hurt you. You might need time to plan your response so that it isn't simply a reaction to her criticism but a thought-out response. Let her know that you need time and that you'll come out of your man-cave once you're ready. Then follow through. It turns out to be quite un-burdening to learn that you need not defend yourself, and you'll score points by listening to her feelings.

Household responsibilities

Housework is something you do that nobody notices until you don't do it.
(Somebody somewhere must have said this)

Whose job is it to cook in your household, to do the laundry, the dusting, or to mow the lawn? How about doing homework with the kids or looking after the cars? Whose job is it to watch every episode of The Simpsons carefully and in order? In most households, there is a division of labor concerning the chores of common interests or common areas. In some two-worker households, he mows the lawn, maintains the cars and takes out the trash; she cooks, does the cleaning and does the laundry. In some single earner households, she works at the office and does homework with the kids while he takes care of the house and yard duties including meals and bath time for the kids.

This division of labor gets its start from expectations that the partners developed during their growing years. Because these expectations will be different, there will be some negotiating of duties at first. It will be easy to decide that he will cook if he likes to cook and she doesn't, for example. However, if neither one is accustomed to doing laundry, then one or both of them will have to take on an unfamiliar chore. If both are familiar with the laundry and both are picky about it, then one will need to relinquish control about how the laundry gets done. Perhaps each will do their own laundry. Many different negotiations are possible, at least at first.

In evaluating different approaches to household chores between men and women, it might be important to recognize that men and women have different relationships to their environments. Men live in their environment but independently of it. They focus on the single task at hand, like repairing the car, or playing a video game. Meanwhile, tools can be strewn about, grease can be deposited on towels or on sandwiches, trash cans might become over-filled (and so can sinks). It might look as though men have a higher tolerance for disorder than do women. In reality, men have less interaction with the disorder and are less impacted by it. Women interact with their environment routinely, and the environment has an enormous impact on how a woman feels and what she thinks. Some experts have referred to this characteristic as women "being called to" by the environment, as if the trashcan is calling "Empty me!" and the furniture is crying out "Dust me!" To men, this seems as strange as insisting there are ghosts in the room upon which we must not sit. This difference between men and women is part of the problem involved in distributing household chores, responsibilities and tolerances.

Over time, household responsibilities become more and more fixed and routine. You might each do the things that are natural for you, but then you continue doing them out of habit. Before this habit sets in, or perhaps during a transition phase (like moving houses), establishing the division of labor is rather important. This division rarely changes much after that. If he starts out cooking simply because he's a better cook, it will probably remain that way, even if she learns. If she starts out doing the laundry, even if he is capable, it will probably remain that way. So it's best to divide the chores as soon as you decide to live together. Here are tips for making that possible:

1. List all the chores. Have a brainstorming session where you write all the chores involved in running the household on a single piece of paper. Include all those chores having to do with cleaning, organizing, shopping, maintenance, automobiles, yard work, pet care, childcare, cooking, etc.

2. Set household priorities. You might have different priorities for these

tasks. For instance, cooking might not be very important for you if you are used to and comfortable grabbing anything out of the freezer for dinner; changing the oil every 3000 to 5000 miles in the car may not be very important to her. Make sure you come to a consensus on the household priorities you will share as a couple.

3. Set tolerance levels for each chore. You might have different tolerances for things around the house. For instance, you might have a much higher tolerance for dirt and germs than she does. You might also have a higher tolerance for a full trashcan than she does. She might have a much higher tolerance for that rattle sound under the dash than you do. As best you can, come to a consensus on what the household tolerance levels will be for each task.

4. Choose who will be responsible for each task. Include two caveats to this assessment. First, if the person responsible cannot do the chore (if he is sick or if she is out of town), then the responsibility falls to the person secondarily responsible. Second, the person responsible for the task also has control over it. This means it will be important not to micromanage the other person on the progress of their task.

5. Be flexible and expect to compromise. You may have to tolerate more or expect less than your standards if it's her task. As long as the task is done acceptably, who cares if it's perfect? Remember, this is a joint effort between two vice presidents and there is no CEO.

6. Don't nag or compare; use praise and appreciation instead. Try to resist the urge to compete by explaining that you did your task even though she forgot hers. Although this might make you feel more competent, it will diminish the partnership. No one got to be great by pointing out the smallness of others. Try catching her "being good", say "thank you", and express how you benefit from her doing her tasks. A little appreciation goes a long way.

7. When situations change (moving, birth of a child, etc.), revisit the chores list. Household chores may remain constant for a long time, but there are certain things likely to create changes. Lifestyle changes are some of those.

If you move to a new place, if one of you starts a new job with different hours or requirements, or if you add a child (or a dependent parent) to your family, it's time to revisit the chores list. You might have to add new chores like helping with homework, going to school events, taking mom to her doctor's appointments, etc. You might also have to reassign some of the chores that one or the other of you can no longer do.

8. Teach children to have their own chores as soon as they are able. Teaching children the value of chores early will not only prevent them from growing up entitled, but will also help them learn the value of responsibility and helpfulness. It's not too early to expect a three-year-old to help you with small things like setting the table, throwing away trash, or putting away her toys. As kids get older, make sure their chores are within their ability, and praise should be the only reward they receive for doing these chores. Keep allowances separate from household chores, as the purpose of allowance is to teach fiscal responsibility, while the purpose of chores is to teach mutual effort in a partnership.

Remember, doing your share around the house is not about "fairness," it's about teamwork. Behaving as a team will assure that she won't end up feeling taken for granted. Good things will flow to you like manna from heaven.

Lessons

1. Men and women often have different ideas of what constitutes a partnership. Be sure you are on the same page with this distinction.

2. Men (and workplace environments) are more comfortable and familiar with hierarchies and define partnerships in terms of independent efforts. Women are more familiar with peer relationships between equals and define partnerships in terms of joint efforts.

3. Men who learn to accept influence from their wives (e.g., to share power) have happier, more stable marriages in the long run.

4. Learn to avoid defensiveness, in part by learning not to take her criticism personally (communications, even criticism, are always about the speaker's perceptions).

5. Learn to share household responsibilities. Having a husband increases a woman's household burden by 3 hours a week on the average, while having a wife decreases a man's household burden by an hour per week.

Example problem 1 – "My wife often complains that I don't do her tasks with her, but they're her tasks, and I have mine to do. How can I get her to be more independent?"

Jacob was a busy house painter by trade and enjoyed doing tasks around the house that made use of his manual skills. His wife Robin, 10 years younger than Jacob, was a social worker in the early stages of her career. She, too, enjoyed doing things around the house, primarily crafts, decorating, and providing "finishing touches" on projects that Jacob had produced. For example, when Jacob created a faux finish on their dining room ceiling, Robin hand-printed a scrollwork design around the edges. Because she wanted to feel part of the team and to feel valued by Jacob, she would ask him to participate in the craft chores she had selected. While Jacob didn't mind helping his wife, he sometimes got annoyed that working with her kept him from working on projects he desired.

Jacob didn't understand that Robin's concept of working together was working on the same thing at the same time. Jacob's concept of working together was working on two independent parts of the project in parallel. While this made him feel more productive, it made her feel less connected and less part of the team. Once they learned about their two different understandings of the concept of partnership, they could come to a compromise. Jacob and Robin still work in parallel on the same project, but he takes time to appreciate her work and praise her effort so she feels the partnership of teamwork.

Example Problem 2 – "My wife tells her girlfriends I'm just one of her children because I don't notice the little jobs around the house. I tell her I don't mind the little messes but I do mind her comment."

Justin and Cindy married young and had a relationship based on fun for the first two years. They were each playful, spontaneous and clever, enjoyed surprising one another, playing games and teasing. The next two years saw the arrival of two kids. They decided Cindy would be a stay-at-home mom while Justin continued to work to support the new family. As the kids grew older, it became less and less possible for Cindy to keep up with the mess that the two youngsters created. When Justin came home after a long day at work, Cindy would expect him to help with dinner, help with bath time and help pick up the house. While Cindy had always wanted children, taking care of them took much more of her time and effort than she had expected. It exhausted her by the end of the day. While Justin loved his new family, he missed the fun he and Cindy used to have, and would frequently try to engage her in some sort of play. He wanted their old style of interaction back, and she wanted help with the housework.

Justin's continued clamoring for Cindy's attention (and competing with the children for her time) sometimes led her to see Justin as just one more person who needed her attention. In conversations with her friends, she would refer to Justin as ""one of my three kids." When she observed Justin stepping over toys rather than picking them up, her perception worsened. From Justin's perspective, Cindy was still his primary relationship, and he was simply trying to interact with her; the mess of the house was of secondary importance to him.

Justin and Cindy needed to see there were now two more people who needed time and attention. Even though the needs of their primary relationship with each other had not changed, this resulted in a frame-shift of understanding for both of them. Because Cindy was the stay-at-home mom, primary responsibility for attending to those two new people fell on her, and she needed to divide her time between them. Justin spent more time attending to either the new household chores (cleaning up the mess created by the kids) or the kids themselves (helping out with dinner or with baths). This let him take some of the burden off Cindy and freed her to spend a little more time with him. This was an important example of two people each having valid needs and working at cross purposes to get them met. It was also a good example of how important it is to revisit the list of household chores once there's a change in living status (like the birth of children).

17 – What's an appropriate amount of time to spend with friends vs. with my wife?

One evening Mike went over to his friend Terry's house to play cards with some friends.

Mike sat directly across from Terry's wife. Mike dropped a card on the floor and bent down to pick it up. When he looked across the table he saw that Terry's wife had her legs open and no panties on. He sat up and was flushed.

He went into the kitchen to get a drink of water. To his surprise Terry's wife had followed him into the kitchen and said, "Did you like what you saw?" Mike said "Yes I did." She said, "Well you can get more of that but it will cost you $500." So Mike thought about his financial situation and nodded. She said, "Come here tomorrow at 2:30 because Terry will be at work then." Mike agreed.

The next day, Mike came over, they had sex, he paid her and then he left. Later, Terry came home and asked, "Has Mike been over here today?" Thinking she had been caught she said, "As a matter of fact, he did." Terry said, "Good because that fool came by my job at lunchtime and asked to borrow $500 till this evening, and he said he would leave it with you."

What if you have different social needs?

You might want to share lots of things with your friends, but you probably wouldn't share your wife with them. If so, there are other books for that kind of issue. We want to focus on how to have the best relationship with your wife that you can. What if you want to spend more time alone and she wants to be with you every minute? Can the "overly attached girlfriend" become the "overly attached wife?" What if she wants most of your leisure activities to be ones you do with other couples, and you want to do things by yourself or with the guys? What if she wants to go on trips to Las Vegas with "the girls" and you don't think a married women should go out alone, or at least without you? Virtual reality (VR) promises virtual vacations tailored to your own personal desires. You'll be able to have just the kind of trip you want while she has just the trip she wants, but that's not here yet. How do you navigate your social time until then?

While you're dating, especially when you first meet each other, it's easy to want to spend a lot of time together. The relationship is new and exciting, and you enjoy both getting to know her and teaching her about yourself. Once you've dated long enough to determine that this relationship has legs (umm, yep), spending time together is necessary for building this third entity you call a Relationship. It takes both of you being together, usually at the same place and time, to build a relationship because you both contribute to it. If only one of you is contributing, you're building a fantasy and not a relationship. Commonly people in new relationships neglect their friends, family, and even themselves to instead spend that time with each other. "We want you to come bowling with us," say the friends. "Or won't she let you have your (bowling) balls?" Friends might even let us know that they miss our company but our attention is elsewhere. This happens on the female side of the friendship equation too, with girlfriends reporting, "Once you started dating him it's like you dropped off the earth!" Our social energies seem to be all consumed by building this one new relationship. So what can you o to find balance?

Building a relationship never stops because people never stop growing (well, some stop, but they don't have to). This means that you'll have to be putting energy into this relationship forever, but not at the same pace as when you're dating. One person cannot meet another person's total social needs, and the desire for "guy time" (and for her, "girl time") returns eventually. Sometimes that desire is accompanied by feelings of guilt for wishing to spend time with other friends. This can result in attempts to include both the relationship and friendships in the same activities. Tolerate that guilt and go out with just the guys anyway- you need your guy time! Other times, that desire begins with spending time alone with friends and evolves into spending time together as couples. This can include double dating (something that, in ancient times, used to occur before marriage) or meeting in small groups. Either way, the character of social time has to change to include other people, and this usually means spending leisure time with members of the same gender.

When guys get together with other guys they relate in a specific way. They punch each other, tell fart jokes and generally act as if they were still in Jr. High school. They compete, verbally joust with each other, tease each other and tell stories designed to impress and "one up" each other. All of this is understood to be bonding rather than distancing behavior. Men's stories are typically about work, adventure or conquest. Guys need this kind of interaction to remind them what it's like to be a guy. If guys try to do that with women, however, women interpret this as being distancing, awkward and even rude. Guys need a different style of relating for interacting with women.

When women interact with other women, they usually focus on similarity, empathy and feelings, and their stories are designed to show connection and familiarity. Women's stories are about emotions, nurturing or connection (and sometimes, emotions about the lack of connection). If women try to talk this way with a guy, he will tend to wonder when she will get to the point and what she wants from him. He might try to listen for the problem in her story so he can offer a solution. Women need this kind of connection with each other to remind them of what it means to be feminine.

Guys need "guy time" and girls need "girl time." When you're in a relationship, it's important that both parties know and respect this essential fact. How much time are we talking about? This varies from person to person. As a general rule, guys might need less social time than women need because of the functions that social time serves. When your lady wants to go out to meet her girlfriend for lunch, meet "the girls" for happy hour, or even if she wants to go dancing, give her your blessings. There's no point in being jealous as she most likely isn't looking for someone else to date. She's looking to renew her femininity and that can only be good for you. If she isn't doing anything with girlfriends, you might encourage her to do so. Her friendships with other women will end up benefitting both of you.

Similarly, you need to go out with the guys for a Monday Night Football beer (unless you're rooting for any of my Least Favorite Teams, in which case just go home). You might prefer a Saturday morning hike or Thursday night bowling league. You need your time to be reminded of what it means to be a guy, even if you must remind yourself that you've given up your "birthright to polygamy" to be in this more civilized relationship. This means you're not going out looking for women, but rather that you're seeking adventure or comparing stories of old adventures. Try explaining that this will help you by providing guys with whom to compete so you don't have to compete with her; hopefully she will understand the benefit of male bonding the way you understand the benefit to her of female bonding. As your relationship matures, keep the notion of time for "you two together"" current and relevant; date nights are important ways to keep nurturing your relationship. Remember that feeding a relationship is just as important as feeding the dog. It has to be done every day, and after a few days of "I'm sorry I didn't feed you today," it will wither and die. Keep dating your wife as long as you're married.

The actual amount of time you spend with your wife vs. with your friends will depend on your respective needs. Some people need less time together and more time with other friends; some couples prefer to spend most of their time together. You'll need to understand each other's needs for friends and find a compromise. This will partly depend on your understanding of what spending time together means and what the goal of that activity is.

A guy went to his travel agent and tried to book a two-week cruise for him and his lady friend.

The travel agent said that all the ships were booked up and reservations were tight at that moment, but he would see what he could do.

A couple of days later, the travel agent phoned and said he could get them onto a three-day cruise.

The guy was disappointed that it was such a short cruise, but booked it... and went to the drugstore to buy three Dramamines and three condoms.

The next day, the agent called back and reported that he now could book a five-day cruise. The guy said, "Great, I'll take it!" and returned to the same pharmacy to buy two more Dramamines and two more condoms.

The following day, the travel agent called yet again, and said he was delighted that he could offer bookings on an eight-day cruise.

The guy was elated and went back to the drugstore. He asked for three more Dramamines and three more condoms.

The pharmacist looked sympathetically at him and said, "Look, I'm not trying to pry... but if it makes you sick ... why do you keep doing it?"

What if you don't agree on how to spend leisure time?

Leisure time could include any activities (or in-activities) that an individual can imagine and finds pleasurable. Some leisure activities can occur in the home by oneself (reading, watching TV, internet activities, video games, writing, crafts, gardening and home decorating, etc.). Other activities require the interaction with another person (talking, sharing food or drink, playing dirty word or board games, sex, etc.). Many activities either require, or are easier to do, being away from home (most sports, working out, walking the dog, shopping, taking a drive, etc.). Travel is a special category, in part because it both requires being away from home and can include many other categories of activities, so we will deal with travel separately.

In the initial stages of your relationship, the emphasis might be on spending time together and not dependent on what the activity is. Sharing meals; hanging out; watching TV, "watching movies" (and all that euphemism implies); spending time on, uh, your texting device; working out together or going for walks are all examples of how people spend time together. You'll have spent a lot of time participating in each other's favorite activities (she watching football and he going shopping) just to be together. This served to strengthen your relationship. Later on in your relationship or marriage, social time is still important but it might not be as interesting to do activities that one of you doesn't care for. Doing these things together will help maintain your connection to one another. In part, your social activity strengthens your relationship if you understand this as a goal of the activity.

Social time means adding novelty to your relationship. It means not only enjoying each other, but also each other's company during an activity or in a special location. Novelty keeps the relationship fresh. Deciding "what to do" with each other is the second question to be asked; whether to do anything or "just be together" is the first question. As a general rule (everyone is different and your mileage may vary), when people "do something together," men focus on the thing that is being done, while women focus on the idea of "being together." If a man and woman go for a jog, it's common that the man will focus on the importance of the jog itself and may even desire to run on ahead, or at least run at his own pace. The woman may see this opportunity as a way to be together and the jog is just the activity providing the vehicle for togetherness.

If you do something together, remember that for her the important part may be the "together" part, while the activity itself may be important to you. Make sure you agree on the main point of the adventure, whether it's to do the activity or to be together. Also make sure you show her appreciation if the main point is to do the activity. Show her that she's not just there to observe you doing it. Compatibility is a measure of how much you like each other and less whether you like doing the same things. If you're going rock climbing, make sure you relate to her on the ground, during the climb and at the top. If you're going to run a race and the point is for you to have a personal best time, then relate to her at the start. Then run your own great race and relate to her again at the finish (for example, shout her name in ecstasy as you set the record for the 10-mile mosey).

Related to this is a concept that comes up often in dating whether it's pre-marriage or post-marriage. This involves observing whether you are enjoying each other or if you are each enjoying a third thing, like watching TV or a movie. Having dinner while conversing is a good example of the first: while dinner exists in the background, the main interaction is between the two of you through your conversation. Watching a movie is a good example of the second: since talking is rare in the theater, you may hold her hand but you will enjoy the movie in parallel with her. Both types of leisure activities are fine but it might be important to discuss each of your needs and expectations prior to activity. Interacting with each other creates a kind of intimacy that having the two of you interact with an activity cannot. If you're both running with the bulls at Pamplona, it's probably not the right time to try holding her hand and gazing into her eyes. Misunderstandings about this can lead to the classic football game disaster: he wants to watch the game and have her do the same while she wants to talk while the game is in the background. ""I want to WATCH the game together while you want to BE TOGETHER while we watch the game." The problem is that these two desires can conflict with one another (although the bulls might like it that way).

Is Travel a "be" or a "do"?

Now what about travel? In this discussion, we assume that travel is for vacation (travel for work or family obligations - or to get out of those obligations - may include some of the same issues, but they are more goal-directed situations). If you don't know whether you are compatible as a couple, traveling together will often tell you; however, traveling creates such unique stresses and expectations that doing so with an incompatible person can be a horrible experience. Part of all travel is time spent en route to a destination. Some travel (like a road trip, some cruises and some tours) is all about being en route, while others are about enjoying a destination. The actual time spent traveling will be more enjoyable if you appreciate each other's company. Much more of the interaction will be between the two of you as opposed to between you and the destination. It's possible to see both the best and the worst in another person while traveling.

Different people look at travel and vacations differently. Some go on vacation to "do" or to "see," preferring to pack as many experiences into their available time as possible. These are the people who come home saying that they "now need a vacation from my vacation," but they enjoy the novelty and the stimulation. Other people prefer to go on vacation to "be" or to "rest." These are people who come home feeling rejuvenated but are sometimes bored while away. Either approach to vacation is fine, but you might need to discuss the purpose of the trip ahead of time. If one of you expects to "do" and the other one expects to "be," disaster may ensue ("Come on dear, it's time to get up to go zip lining. I know you wanted to sleep in, but it's already 4:30 am, and we're on vacation!"). Make sure you discuss how you will divide your time between these two vacation desires before you go.

These days travel requires a great deal of patience, understanding, and tolerance for the unexpected. Delayed flights, long lines at the airport, unplanned travel changes and unavailable options can bring out stress and irritability in even the most patient of us. Just navigating the airport can tell how each of you operates under stress. Whenever you see this in your travel partner, it's prudent to remember that this response to stress is in her general repertoire. If she manages this with an easy-going attitude and a sense of humor, she will probably be good under most stressful conditions. If you are the one doing the grousing and the chewing out of the inattentive waiter, it's good to appreciate her level of tolerance for you.

Perhaps you like fishing and she likes sitting on the beach. Perhaps you like meeting people in new cities and she prefers observing the architecture from the hotel window. Perhaps your idea of a vacation to Australia is bungee jumping and diving the Great Barrier Reef; her idea of the same vacation is photographing wallabies and learning to play a didgeridoo. Why shouldn't both of you enjoy it? Just make sure you discuss this before you leave and that you both voice your expectations about which things you will to do together versus separately. If you agree with her to do something together that isn't your normal fare (perhaps in exchange for something she agrees to), don't back out. Keep your commitment and do it for the sake of being together. Your relationship will be stronger for it. Expect her to honor her commitment as well.

Lessons

1. Social time means time together as a couple and individual time for each partner, "guy time" and "girl time" with same-gendered friends. All components of this are important to the health of the relationship.

2. Define whether a joint activity focuses on the activity itself or on "being together". Different people will assume different priorities and being open about this will help avoid hurt feelings and false expectations.

3. People travel for all kinds of different reasons. Learn to appreciate and tolerate the reasons she travels even if they're different from yours. Make compromises about priorities where appropriate.

Example Problem (social time) – "We retired about 10 years ago and my wife has gone back to work part-time in a new career. I've focused on my friends and our club activities. Now my wife is complaining I can't say 'no' to people and that I'm over-committed. She wants more of my time and she thinks I should take better care of my physical health. I don't know if she's right, but I don't really want to change back now - I'm enjoying myself!"

After serving in the Navy for four years, John took an Honorable Discharge and continued to work for the Navy as a civilian until he retired. He enjoyed his work and felt intellectually stimulated by it. Rosie stayed home to raise their four children until they were ready to leave home and then went back to school to get a degree in social work. All the time John was working, Rosie ran a household, raised the kids, and organized their social life. This primarily comprised meeting other Navy couples for dinner, attending functions at the Admirals Club, and going to school functions with their children. When John retired, his first concern was that he would be both bored and lonely without regular contact with his workmates and without some planned function to structure his life. This became more concerning when Rosie went back to school as she was not around to keep him organized. John decided that he needed to take matters into his own hands and he volunteered for committees that provided both club and civic service. This included parades, pancake breakfasts, youth outreach programs, etc. After a while, he was busier with his new social life than he was when he was working. Although John enjoyed cooking and took over most of those chores, he did not take over the house cleaning chores, which still fell to Rosie after class time.

John enjoyed his new social functions, but Rosie felt they were drifting apart since they spent less time together now than they did when John was working. Rosie found that John was spending a lot more time with cooking and eating, and not very much time exercising or being active. She was concerned when he gained a little weight as he had been trim his entire life. Although John reported that he was happier now than he had been in a long time, Rosie prevailed in getting him to go for an annual physical (it had been 8 years since his last "annual" physical). When the doctor told him that not only was his cholesterol too high, but he was now technically overweight, John was stunned. He hated the idea of going on cholesterol-lowering medications. He realized that the pancake breakfasts he hosted for the club, along with the rich desserts to which he was treating Rosie, came at a significant cost to him. He vowed to his doctor he would have both situations in line within 6 months, and the doctor agree to hold off on the medications. John didn't want to give up his social life, but didn't want to have health problems make him give up his whole life either.

Coming to terms with their new life roles meant revisiting their activities and preferences. John took on a few more of the cleaning and gardening chores around the house and became the default social chairman for the couple. His cooking became much healthier and focused on creative use of fresh produce, even for dessert. He still hosted the pancake breakfasts, but stuck to the fresh fruit and egg whites instead of the pancakes and syrup. They made a new plan about how to spend their time together that included John meeting Rosie for lunch once a week at work. They would spend one hour every Saturday morning organizing the house together and take a walk around the neighborhood every weekday morning before John's first social activity. After 6 months John revisited the doctor and reported that he was actually enjoying his new task of looking out for his health and fitness. In fact, he had gotten a few of his buddies from the social clubs to march in the parades with him instead of riding on the floats. His cholesterol was back in the normal range though he still had a few pounds to lose. New life roles required new agreements for the relationship and a new focus on preserving health, and both of them ended up being happier for the negotiation.

Example Problem (travel) – "We have enough money for some travel now and again, and we both enjoy it. I like to go to the cities and explore everywhere; my wife wants to go to the beach or the hotel pool and read a good book. That doesn't even seem like a vacation!"

Salvatore was the owner of a large and very successful dance studio. His team of instructors taught many styles of dance, put on many competitions and exhibitions, and had acquired several generations of clientele. Stephanie was a mid-level manager at the port of entry in their Pacific coast hometown. They had each worked very hard to get to where they were and had reached a point where they felt financially stable. Both had opportunities through their careers to meet people from other places and were enthused by the possibility of seeing other lands firsthand. They agreed on their priorities for life at home and had an fair distribution of effort in the household and with the family. On their first significant vacation together, they took a 10-day cruise in the Mediterranean, with all expenses included. They could engage in many activities and they found it simple to do some things together and do other things individually. They always met for dinner to discuss the different opportunities they had explored.

The next vacation proved somewhat more problematic. They planned a trip to Rome, where Salvatore's expectation was that they would spend all day and evening being as active as he was when they were on the cruise. He was disappointed when he realized that Stephanie only joined him for tours and explorations on some days, She preferred to spend time on other days and evenings at the café or by the poolside relaxing. "Why did we come all this way?" Salvatore said in frustration. "Too much walking tires me out!" replied Stephanie. "I like exploring with you, but I came here to relax."

Salvatore and Stephanie had different ideas about this trip. He wanted to "make the most of it" while she wanted to relax in addition to explore. This difference occurred on the cruise but wasn't as noticeable because they could each partake in the activities they desired without interfering with the priorities of the other. Neither one was correct; different preferences and different priorities may equally well suit different people. To make this divergent style work for them, Salvatore had to learn to do things on his own while Stephanie was relaxing. In exchange, Stephanie needed to be explicit beforehand about which activities she would participate in and which ones she would skip. That way Salvatore would have a fair chance to arrange his independent schedule, and they both would end up with pleasant memories of the trip.

18 – What if one of us has a health issue?

Two elderly gentlemen had been friends for many decades. Over the years they had shared all kinds of activities and adventures. Lately, their activities had been limited to meeting a few times a week to play cards.

One day they were playing cards when one looked at the other and said, "Now don't get mad at me....I know we've been friends for a long time.....but I just can't think of your name! I've thought and thought, but I can't remember it. Please tell me what your name is." His buddy glared at him. For at least three minutes he just stared and glared at him. Finally he said, "How soon do you need to know?"

In the middle of a busy waiting room at the doctor's office, a man rushes in and shouts, "Doctor! I think I'm shrinking." The doctor looks up and says calmly, "Now just settle down. You'll have to be a little patient."

What if one of you has a health issue? Or if one of you thinks the other has a health issue?

If you're like most men, you probably don't think much about changing your lifestyle for the sake of being healthy. This might change if you get injured, notice those pounds creeping into your midsection over time, or determine that some bodily function is not working the way it used to (or that some bodily part has spontaneously fallen off). Health issues can happen at any time in life, but they seem to become more frequent as we get older. Staying healthy is something we should practice all of our lives but we don't. Men care little for going to the doctor, in part because it's about asking for help (we don't even like asking for directions much less for medical help). This is because we don't like feeling vulnerable and because we really don't want to hear any bad news. We would rather hear no news at all and assume there is no bad news.

We do, however, like to know that we will be taken care of if necessary. The other time we <u>consider</u> (although not guarantee) changing our routines to stay healthy is when the woman in our lives makes it a request or a requirement. In that case, it's common for us to increase our exercise routine or even trying the latest craze in organic diets and supplements. So why do women nag us about going to the doctor? Can't they just take our word for it we don't want to go?

While men take comfort in <u>not</u> knowing if there is anything wrong with them, women find that to be more anxiety producing. Remember, a sense of security is important to many women. If she perceives that you are about to croak, or worse, that you will mostly croak (and she will have to take even more care of you), that will erode her sense of security. In her mind, it's better to send you to the doctor to find out how everything is. If you have a health issue after all, she will be there to help you out. This, too, will increase her sense of security. Whatever the health issue is, be prepared to share it with your wife. Let her know what she can do to help and what can be expected. Also let her know how you plan to take care of yourself. That might include getting more exercise, sitting less, improving your eating or sleeping, getting on or staying on the medication routine, or having occasional time with your own thoughts. Here is where the figurative meaning of the term "man cave" comes into play. This refers to the mental space you might need to inhabit to figure things out, to come to terms with things or to decide what to do about them. This does not require a literal "man cave", usually a dark room filled with audio equipment, computer screens and Batman memorabilia, but occasionally one facilitates the other.

What things about your health might arouse your wife's attention?

There are many things that your wife might ask you to pay attention to for the sake of your health and her mental well being. Here are a few of them, along with ways to respond that she will appreciate when she does notice:

1. Your diet – This might refer to your need to lose weight or to her desire to have you eat more healthfully, perhaps forgoing a few of those cheeseburgers, beers or ice cream sundaes. Please. If you're like many guys, you may be thinking, "This salad tastes like I'd rather be fat!" Not all salads need to taste like of a bowl of grass. There are many tasty ways to eat more vegetables. Work with her on this. It probably really is a good idea to eat more vegetables than you do already, and perhaps a little less red meat. Chips and salsa, French fries, hops and chocolate should not count as vegetables. You can find veggies you like, and if she enjoys smoothies made of kale, banana and ginseng, you might choose to enjoy something different. Let her know that you appreciate her attention to which things you are putting into your body. If you're packing a few extra pounds these days, mind your portion control. It's never too early to limit your overall intake of sodium and cholesterol. The good thing about changing your diet (and by this I mean whatever you eat, not that you need a specific "diet") slowly is that you will come to prefer these foods. Besides, your wife will notice your efforts. If they aren't noticed, make sure you point out to her when you eat less or when you choose something healthy from the menu. She will be happy you are taking good care of her investment. If your diet is better than hers and she is still making the request that you eat more healthfully, make sure she's on the same page. This is not so much that there's a need to be "fair" about your diets. It's just easier for you to avoid temptations if she is not having that bowl of Gooey Fudge Mint Chip Swirl in front of you.

2. Your fitness and exercise routine – You may have heard people call exercise "the poor person's plastic surgery;" my father used to say, "pushing 50 should be exercise enough!" You might already have an exercise routine that includes sports, going to the gym, running or walking, or using home exercise

equipment. If so, bravo! Keep it up. This is a good habit you will want to maintain throughout your life, and one that your wife will appreciate. However, we live in a culture that is far too sedentary, and sitting as much as most of us do leads to all kinds of health problems down the road.

There are more advantages of exercising every day than simply that when you die others will look into the coffin and say, "Well, he looks good, doesn't he?" Exercise benefits every system in your body. Your improved muscle tone will be able to support your frame and keep you limber enough to avoid many accidents. Improved cardiovascular tone will decrease the likelihood of heart attacks and stroke. Your digestive system will work more efficiently, your sleep will improve, and your stress level will decrease. Improved blood flow in the brain will preserve your memory as you age and make it less likely that you will develop dementia. You will decrease your likelihood of developing depression or anxiety problems and your likelihood of stress-related diseases will decrease. You will, of course, also become a more charming and likable fellow.

Your wife might request you add in some exercise to your already busy life. Tell her you appreciate her attention to your overall health. If you don't have an exercise routine already, plan to start one, but start slowly. The key to starting an exercise routine is to find something you enjoy – exercise should be something you look forward to. A recent study found that people doing identical exercise events snack far less afterward if they perceived their exercise as fun or interesting as opposed to work or effort. In particular, look for some activity that both your wife and you enjoy. This might be a sport like golf, tennis or streaking at the football game; it might be agreeing to go for a regular long walk together. If she already has her own exercise routine, look for something you would enjoy independent of her. If she is concerned that you spend time exercising and not enough time with her, talk to her about how much time she thinks is appropriate for you to maintain your good health. A healthier you will be a better partner and less of a potential burden to her later on. As an added benefit, a healthier you will have an improved sex life, with more stamina and better blood flow to all those important areas involved.

3. Taking dietary and workout supplements – The phrase "dietary

supplements" means different things to different people. Many men think about dietary supplements as things that help them gain weight, increase muscle mass, increase their libido or enhance their virility in some other way. These are like Higgs boson pills – they let you gain mass (for any non-physicists out there, be sure to look this one up!). Many women (and men who are not focused on their workouts) might think of supplements as added vitamins, mood elevators or anxiety relievers, or plant extracts designed to improve the function of other bodily systems. Either way, it's important to know that few supplements have science backing up their claims of health benefits. All of them are unregulated in terms of quality and dosage, and many of them are downright dangerous.

If you are taking supplements to enhance your workout or if your wife urges you to take supplements for other health benefits, please do your research about these choices. While the phrase "dietary supplement" seems to suggest that these are as harmless and as well tolerated as food, people take them as if they were unregulated drugs. Some supplements, like fish oil, probably are safe and live up to the benefits claimed (in this case, for heart, muscle, skin and possibly mood); some, like multivitamins, vitamin E and ginseng are probably fairly safe but only provide benefits to the pocketbooks of the companies that manufacture them; while some like kava kava and St. John's wort can be dangerous or deadly if taken for too long or in combinations with certain Western medicines. For the workout minded, creatine and whey protein are probably safe if used carefully, and likely contribute to gains in muscle mass; steroids and supplements designed to increase testosterone should never be used without a doctor's supervision. Do your homework and be good to your body, but don't poison it along the way. Tell your doctor if you're taking something in this category.

4. Sleep – When we were younger, most of us found that getting enough sleep was as easy as spending all our daylight hours in bed. As a teenager that might mean 9 to 12 hours of sleep every night, but most adults do well with about eight hours. These days most of us are sleep deprived as a life style. As Yogi Berra quipped, "If I didn't wake up, I'd still be sleeping." Spending enough hours in bed as an adult becomes a little trickier, especially if you have kids or a demanding work schedule. Even if you spend enough hours in bed, it's important that your sleep be uninterrupted and restful. Not getting

enough sleep leads to poor judgment, lack of impulse control, poor decision-making and exhaustion. It also makes most systems in your body work poorly. If you're having trouble sleeping, take heart – most people experience temporary insomnia at some time in their lives, so you're in good company. Learning a few simple techniques can get you back on track.

Unfortunately, the insomnias have ridiculous names and they can sound misleading and somewhat scary. Having trouble falling asleep is called "primary insomnia" (because the disturbance is in the first part of your sleep cycle); it does not mean that this is a disorder by itself. Frequent waking in the middle of the night is often referred to as "secondary insomnia" (because it happens in the middle portion of your sleep cycle). It does not mean that your wakefulness is due to some other medical issue. Finally (pun intended), problems waking up too early and not going back to sleep are often referred to as "terminal insomnia" (because they occur at the end of your sleep cycle). Yikes! No, this does not mean you will die from this condition. Often, insomnias can be treated with behavioral interventions that improve your "sleep hygiene" but for some people sleep medications are also useful.

If your wife notices you are irritable, distractible or indecisive, she might recommend that you try to get more sleep. Let her know that you recognize she is trying to give you permission to nap instead of asking you to work harder. Taking a nap or going to bed earlier are both fine alternatives. Most often, however, when a wife complains about her husband's sleep habits, it's because he has a tendency to snore, and therefore he keeps her awake. You might sound like a chain saw at night, or like the air is slowly being let out of a pinched balloon, and younger members of your family might already have made Youtube videos of your symphonic variations. Don't make the mistake of assuming this is a humorous trait. Snoring is not only disruptive to your sleep partner, it represents a potential or real health issue because it means that your airway is partly blocked at night. If your snoring isn't temporary (for example, correlated with periods of extreme exhaustion), see your doctor or sleep specialist. You owe it to both you and your wife. You might be surprised at how much credit you get from her for giving away your competitive edge and asking for help.

5. Stress -You know you're too stressed if relatives who have been dead for years come by to visit and suggest that you should get rest. All of us experience stress in our lives, and if we're lucky those periods are few. Stress is more of a problem when it's chronic. This might be caused by ongoing difficult relationships, difficult work environment or hours, a tendency to create a difficult internal environment (chronically beating yourself up with your own thoughts), ongoing medical conditions, etc. We owe it to ourselves to find ways of managing stress because it affects both our happiness and health and that of those around us (yes, stress is contagious). As long as your marriage is healthy, being married can be one of life's great stress reducers. Sometimes someone may present you with a request to reduce your stress by a means you cannot tolerate or accomplish. For example, if your wife might say you need a vacation. If you either have no vacation time accrued or can't afford to take time off work, her suggestion might increase your stress. Your response to her might be this: "For me, taking a vacation is not as effective as other things I practice. I agree that reducing my stress would be a good idea."

According to a recent poll published by the Harvard School of Public Health, many strategies for managing stress are available and used by members of the public. The most frequently used of these is socializing (71% practiced this form of stress management) followed by meditation (57%), time spent outdoors (57%) and healthful eating (55%). The least frequently used stress manager turned out to be time off work (25%). The recommendation to "take a vacation" is the least likely recommendation to be followed. The poll also asked the respondents whether they thought these approaches reduced their stress. The most effective strategies for managing stress turned out to be time spent outdoors (94%) and hobbies (93%), followed by exercise (89%), time with pets (87%), meditation (85%) and socializing (83%). The least effective methods for managing stress appeared to be healthful eating, professional help, and medication. This all suggests that stress management tools are within your grasp and may be things you don't associate with reducing your stress. They may also be effective if you practice them regularly. Don't feel bad if you can't take a vacation; take a hike instead. And if your wife is stressed, take her along (assuming that this doesn't increase her stress or yours).

<u>Her health issues</u>

What if she is the one with the health issue? Hopefully this will stimulate your compassion and your desire to help take care of her or to help her take care of herself. Step one for you is to learn about the issue or condition. There are many physical similarities between males and females (blood, heart, lungs, muscle, etc.), but there are those things that are different (well, you know). Different things may be problematic for women than for men, and even similar health problems may present with different symptoms between the sexes. Women are prone to different cancers than men, to different symptoms of heart attack, to different headaches (women get more migraines, men get more muscle tension headaches), etc. Learn about the issue that your wife is dealing with. If the issue is depression or anxiety, remember that these are serious medical conditions worthy of your respect and are not just "all in her head". Women may not have as much muscular strength as men do, but they are stronger in many ways than men, especially in multi-tasking, resilience and longevity. However they are more prone to wearing out from stress. Learn what you need to know about her health issues.

Step two of your approach is to find out what she needs to do to manage, recover or heal from her condition, and ways you can facilitate that. This might mean you take walks with her because she needs to lose weight; you take her to doctor's visits when needed; or you help watch the kids when she has an appointment or needs to rest. You might not know what she needs from you, so ask her or her doctor.

If her medical issue is hormonal, as in PMS (pre-menstrual syndrome), pregnancy or menopause, then learning about this condition may help prepare you to tolerate the unexpected. She may not always be able to tell you what to expect or why she reacts a certain way when her hormones are in control of her behaviors. Not all women respond similarly to these conditions; for some women the time before or during their period is not very different from any other time. They might only be more tired. For others it can be the difference between a sweet caring partner and an "irritable, cranky witch" to quote a commercial for a medication designed to help with PMS symptoms. The same disparity goes for pregnancy and menopause – each woman responds to these differently.

Some female authors say that PMS really means "Punish My Spouse." While the outcome of having PMS might look like this to the hapless male participant, it's almost never what the woman intends. From this we can derive hints as to your best responses. Don't take her comments personally (See chapter 19 on Dealing with an Angry Wife) because she's showing her internal (hormonal) state. If she has symptoms she can describe, try to empathize with her pains and validate her efforts. She might need to express herself by crying – understand this and don't feel the need to stop her. She might also need more quiet or alone time – ask her about this and make it happen. For anything that is volatile or important, wait a few days before discussing these issues.

Menopause literally means the pausing of menses (a woman's period). Contrary to the way it sounds, it has nothing to do with men. Well, it does if you're the man whose wife is entering menopause. Some women sail right on through menopause while other women have a tougher time. Most of the tips for dealing with PMS apply here too, but the process takes much longer. You will get your partner back, and she will be the same woman she was. Educate yourself about menopause and listen to her talk about her experience of it. Believe what she tells you, even if it sounds strange, because it may seems strange to her too. Stay committed, be supportive and don't take things personally if she takes out her distress on you. Support her health by letting her get enough sleep and by supporting her outside interests. Because menopause may make a woman feel old or unattractive, it will help if you give her extra approval and positive strokes. Because the process takes much longer, there is a possibility she might become depressed along the way and need more significant help, such as therapy or medication. You might need support for yourself as well along the way, so try to know when it's serious. Don't make jokes about your wife in either of these cases unless they are inside jokes between you two and funny to her. Women often feel badly when they are experiencing either PMS or menopause and they don't like to be the butt of jokes at the same time.

Mental health and substance use issues

217

What if the medical issue in your marriage is a mental health one, or one having to do with drug or alcohol abuse? If your wife agrees that there is an issue that needs addressing, then support her in getting treatment for either her or you (or both). Talk to your doctor about referrals to a mental health specialist or an addiction specialist. Educate yourself about her specific condition. Many times with depression or anxiety there are not only things you can do that will be helpful to your wife's recovery, but also many things you must learn not to do that will keep her from getting better. The same will be true with drug or alcohol abuse - it is important that you agree on the approach and are on the same page. If she doesn't agree or doesn't think that there is a problem then you need to get professional help. You will either have to get educated yourself about what constitutes a problem or you will be called upon to set boundaries for the sake of your marriage and your own health. Similarly, if she thinks that YOU have an issue with drugs or alcohol, have a talk with her about her concerns. Remember, her concerns are about her internal state and may not be about your behavior. Listen and try to avoid keeping secrets from one another. Above all be patient, even just a little.

Lessons

1. Your wife has a vested interest in your health, just as you do in hers. Share power with her over these two assets in your joint corporation.

2. Consider her input in areas like your diet, exercise, supplements, sleep and stress management. Most of these can't be objectively judged from the inside.

3. If she has a health issue, learn about it. Many issues of women's health are complete mysteries to men until they seek education.

4. Make sure you're on the same page about mental health and substance abuse.

Example Problem – "I know I should schedule my next physical exam, but I hate going to the doctor. My wife is always nagging me to do it and tells me that my health important to her too. Shouldn't it be my decision?"

John and Celia had only been married for a few years, but it was the second marriage for both. His first marriage ended in divorce after 22 years, and he had two grown children. She had one college graduate and one son still in college from her first marriage, which ended when her husband died at age 48 from colon cancer. They both recognized that her experience with the illness of her first husband left a profound impact on her. She had made it her mission when he was still alive to learn everything she could about colon cancer, its' causes and its' prevention. Knowing it is one of the most preventable cancers around made her all the more determined that everyone she cared about should have regular screenings.

From the time they were first dating, Celia had been after John to get a colonoscopy. He told her he did the regular fecal screens and that since he had no colon cancer in his family he wasn't sure he needed to be "probed by space aliens." Celia was relentless with her insistence that he get "the Full Monte." John felt justified in his desire to make his own health decisions and came to wonder if Celia's pressure was mostly from her earlier cancer trauma. One night he suggested that to her, and her response surprised him.

"I know you think that if my first husband hadn't died from colon cancer I'd be more relaxed about it. It's true that his death made me more aware and more educated about this disease. Now, however, we're married. The more we've entwined our lives the more your health decisions affect me. We love each other and I don't see us ever breaking up our marriage. I just don't want anything else to do that either. I don't want to lose you soon; I want you around to see our grandchildren. I feel much more sure about the future with you in it. This is the biggest thing you could do to make me feel more secure about our future together!"

John then realized that Celia wasn't trying to get him to do what she thought he should do; she was seeking comfort and reassurance about the future. It was a gift he could give to her. He scheduled his screening the following week. It was not quite the same as "getting tubed" was back in his surfing days, but it was worth it because it gave her comfort.

19 - How to respond to an angry wife

Husband to wife: "When I get mad at you, you never fight back. How do you control your anger?"

Wife: "When I'm mad at you, I go clean the toilet bowl."

Husband: "How does that help?"

Wife: "I use your toothbrush."

What if your wife is angry?

"Happy wife, happy life." You may have heard this truism bandied about. Men pay attention to trying to make their women happy. They often feel best about themselves when they succeed (on the other side, they leave women they believe they can't make happy, among other reasons). This is because a women's happiness recharges a man's battery. When she is happy, he feels he's done his job, he feels satisfied and sufficient, and he can now give himself recognition, reward, and even a break. In this way, men are internally motivated.

Unfortunately, women may either not believe that men want to make them happy, or may find that showing happiness comes at the cost of either of being too vulnerable or of risking he will stop trying. In this view, a woman may fear that stating she is happy may be equivalent to her stating that everything is fine now, and that nothing needs to change. However, because of women's diffuse awareness, she is always aware of something that needs to change or improve. She can never use the term "happy" because to her it would mean the end of all required effort (even though to him, it would mean he succeeded in this current endeavor). What a Catch-22! From this perspective, women are more externally motivated. A woman may assume that her criticism is a request for change. Unfortunately, a man receives that same criticism as an indicator he failed in his effort to make her happy.

How should a man respond to a critical, unhappy or even angry wife? I suppose that many of you have started with this chapter because it's one question most often occurring to men. "What can I do other than avoid the problem?" As William Shakespeare said, "Men in rage tend to strike those that wish them best", meaning that angry people often lash out at their families and friends. Are there any good strategies in responding so you can minimize the impact this has on your family? Yes there are. But be warned: the things I will describe are difficult and require a lot of practice to perfect. They won't be easy and they aren't automatic. And at first, they might seem as counter-intuitive as is exposure treatment for anxieties (facing the fear instead of avoiding it). But with rehearsal, these suggestions can help you stay out of the emotional quagmire that angry interactions bring.

So what is anger? As my favorite angry person, Dr. McCoy from the original "Star Trek" series might have said, "Damn it Jim, I'm a doctor, not a linguist!" Even if Dr. McCoy couldn't help define it for us, we need a working definition. Anger is a combination of physical arousal and emotional reactivity (usually strong displeasure or hostility) that results when someone feels a threat or a loss, either real or perceived. As in the case for anxiety, our body's response to threat is to produce adrenaline, a hormone that charges up the body's systems leading to a classic "fight or flight" scenario. This means that high levels of anxiety or frustration most often results in the person getting ready to defend herself against the threat ("fight"), or to run away from the threat ("flight"). Given the two options, a display of anger is usually related to the "fight" result. Some people combine these two responses, yelling at the top of their lungs, "When I get back, you will be in trouble!" as they are running the other way. Common reasons that someone might be angry include: perceived threats to her body, property, values or integrity; a loss of trust or autonomy; feeling guilty about something for which she does not admit guilt; or a situation when her expectations are not met.

Other contributors to anger include "should" statements from one's self or from others since these are usually perceived as criticism ("you should get more exercise instead of watching that TV program"). One other reason for anger is particular to wives. Sometimes they feel their husbands did something (or didn't do something) that resulted in them not feeling cared for, feeling taken for granted, or feeling hurt (sometimes they are just crabby, but you still have to respond in a meaningful way).

We now know that displaying anger in a physical way just begets more anger; it does not, contrary to popular belief, help to diffuse the situation. Screaming, punching a pillow, punching a wall, indulging in rages or tantrums do not purge the anger impulses. They do increase pillow sales however. And they might increase holes in the drywall where the doorknob would hit. Drywall holes are a litmus test for anger in the house. Do you have holes in your drywall? Then you know what I mean. Sometimes people who cannot stand feeling anxious or helpless will express anger instead. Anger may make a person feel powerful instead of weak (or victim-like); anger may make her feel more in control of the situation, whereas anxiety or helplessness may make her feel out of control. All too often the anger takes power away from her because in reality, the emotions are in control. It's important to note however, that verbalizing anger is a wholly different thing, and listening to a woman's expression of her emotions is often a very helpful approach. We just have to listen in a useful way without getting defensive or angry back. Remember that women have a very different relationship with their feelings than men do - be prepared to acknowledge this by telling her you're sorry that her feelings got hurt. They probably did even if you weren't being a jerk.

Like anxiety, anger is a contagious emotion. This means that if your wife is angry around you, and particularly angry AT you, it is difficult not to become angry yourself. In part this is due to the automatic response of defending one's self when one feels attacked. In response to her anger, YOU feel threatened yourself, so you get angry too as a defense against what feels like _her_ attack. (It's like that "Did so!" "Did not!" battle of childhood but for adults, when it's not only permissible but expected to say something like "Oh, what? Now you're getting mad at ME for being mad at YOU?") We are all prone to acting like kids when we fight leading to even more hurt feelings. It's important that you develop ways that protect yourself from being swept up in the emotion. Here are ten suggestions that might help:

1. SEEK FIRST TO UNDERSTAND (and then tell her you understand that her feelings were hurt).

She probably wants you to attend to her so ask what she is really angry about. Listen for hurt feelings, anxiety triggers, perceived loss or threat, or unmet expectation. Clarify with her you really do understand by asking her if your perception of her anger is accurate. "You wanted me to tell you what my plans for the day were, regardless of how I thought they would impact on your day because that's what your girlfriends would do, but I didn't, is that right?" "You wanted me to notice that there were dishes in the sink and put them into the dishwasher and I didn't, is that right?" "You wanted me to pay attention while you showed me an ingrown hair on your leg as I was tiling the kitchen floor, and I didn't stop working, is that right?" Don't assume that you know what she is angry about because as soon as you do, she will actually be angry about something else. Ask her why she's angry, don't try to read her mind. As Steven Covey said in habit #5 of "The Seven Habits Of Highly Effective people," most of us have little experience listening to others. When we listen, we're usually planning a response so we can be understood rather than trying to understand the other. Seek first to understand.

2. NEVER, EVER DEFEND YOURSELF.

It's important not to argue or explain yourself under these conditions. Doing so will entrench her in her own viewpoint, and it will validate her angry approach. After all, when she gets angry enough to verbally attack you, she is taking the "one-up" position relative to you. By defending yourself, you agree that she is in a "one-up" position and that you, in a "one-down" position, need to be defended. Staying equal with her means not entering this competition and refusing to "play." Think about it – the last time your wife got mad at you for accidentally hurting her feelings, and you might have said "But I didn't know it would hurt you!" Did she then stop, calm down right away, and say, "Oh. Well then. Never mind. I was over-reacting"? No, likely she continued the attack with, "Well, why didn't you know!?" or "Well, you should have known!" Defending yourself to an angry wife never works to your advantage and often makes things worse.

There are many useful alternatives to defending yourself as we will discuss. If you can't resist the urge to defend yourself right at the acute moment, you may need to tell her you disagree, that you need a "time-out," and will discuss the issue later. This might be meeting in the kitchen in 15 minutes, or in one hour, depending on how long you each normally take to defuse your own feelings. Then you might need to walk away because at the moment, her logic (or yours) is blocked by anger. It's important that you both do something calming during your time-out (like listening to your favorite music or going for a walk) so you give yourself the time you need to de-escalate. If the situation still seems escalated when you meet up again, call another time-out. I can't stress this strongly enough: NEVER, EVER DEFEND YOURSELF. It's at best a waste of time and at worst will cause her anger to flare up. For instance, she might perceive that you're changing the discussion from something about HER feelings to something about YOUR feelings. Do tell her you're sorry that her feelings got hurt (especially if you were being a jerk).

3. ALL COMMUNICATIONS ARE ABOUT THE SPEAKER.

Remember that no one makes anyone else feel anything. You don't make someone else angry, just like you can't make her happy (even though you try; God knows you try); emotions are always an intra-personal event. A person's thoughts or expectations dictate a person's feelings, much more than do outside events. Because feeling angry is so unpleasant, and because we are so good at projection, we try to find an external cause for our anger. If you listen to her angry statement, it's usually telling you something about her, not something about you. Most of the time, her statement either includes the word "I," or it is implied at the beginning of the sentence (as in "I hate you!"); even "You make me so angry" means "I feel angry;" most importantly here, "You really upset me" often means "I'm really hurt"). This is a communication about the speaker, not about the person she is speaking to.

In fact, all communications are about the speaker. This concept is essential because if you can remember this, you are much less likely to take things like her anger personally. This may seem easier said than done, but may sound easier to do if we say you need to hear that her statement is about <u>her</u> and not about <u>you</u>. This does NOT mean that if she says, "I hate you!" that she really hates herself. What she is telling you about herself is more about how she feels than about what she says. When your wife states something in anger, she is telling you about her own internal state. For example, "You forgot to get milk on your way home like I asked!" means, "I'm disappointed that my expectations weren't met, and my feelings are hurt (possibly because if a woman did what you did, it would mean she didn't care about me)." "You hardly ever touch me any more!" means, "I need to feel desired and I'm hurt that I don't feel desired by you." "I think we need to go to therapy!" means, "I'm frustrated I can't get what I want from you and that you always hog the remote control." That means that these statements are about HER and never about YOU. However, this would probably be a good time to tell her you're sorry that her feelings got hurt.

4. TRY EMPATHIZING WITH HER FEELINGS INSTEAD OF REFUTING HER PERCEPTIONS.

Being able to hear communications as about the speaker means you can empathize with her internal state, rather than argue or refute the "logic" of her anger. Keep in mind that emotions are on a different plane from logic, so feelings are never "logical." Empathizing may mean saying, "I understand that you're angry," and it might mean you agree wherever you can. For instance, if you can put yourself in her shoes for a moment, it might sound like "If I were in your position, I might feel the same way" or "I think many people might feel upset if it felt like someone they loved didn't care back." Really empathizing with someone else's feelings is hard even if you have been in a similar situation to theirs before. It's worth the attempt because it can communicate to your wife that, even if you disagree with her perception of events, you're not rejecting her or her FEELINGS about those events.

However, it does not mean taking responsibility for her feelings. Be careful with the use of the phrase "I'm sorry," even if you normally use that to mean "I have empathy for you" as in "I'm sorry you are frustrated." This phrase can be taken as an apology and ownership of responsibility, and you do not have responsibility for her internal state. Remember that you have no ability to control her feelings. An exception to this rule is that you can always respond with "I'm sorry your feelings got hurt." That might be the single most important phrase for dealing with an angry wife because hurt feelings often equals angry wife. Try to avoid both a power struggle and an escalation. If you cannot avoid escalation, then walk away for a limited time-out.

5. WHEN THE ANGER IS ABOUT SOMEONE ELSE, STAY IN THE AUDIENCE DURING THIS EMOTIONAL PERFORMANCE.

If your wife is upset at other people (like the children, her mother or the policeman who pulled her over earlier), imagine that she is a character in a play or on a movie screen and you are in the audience. If you go to a play or movie, the action might well be in your face, but you understand that this is a performance and you don't have to be involved. The performance is about the performers, and their job is to transmit to you a situation that will create an emotional response. You can watch and even appreciate the intensity of the performance but you need not be involved. You can maintain an emotional distance that allows you not to engage but rather only to observe. This might be what she refers to as "venting" or just telling you about her feelings, and <u>she does not want you to provide solutions</u>. What she <u>does</u> want is to have her emotions understood. This is harder to do if you two are the only ones involved of course (she's actually angry at something you did, rather than at another person). However if her anger is directed at others, you can be a watcher. You might engage in some active listening by responding with "Yes, I hear you," or some other acknowledgement, and not simply remain silent. Yes, you can even have popcorn.

6. BEWARE OF THE VICTIM MENTALITY, AND OFFER TO HELP EMPOWER THE SUFFERER.

When a person is angry because they feel helpless, they often engage in a victim mentality; this thinking style that permits people to believe that "things always happen to me" or "it's just me against the world". This could be temporary or ongoing. This is common in children and teens, partly because they really have little power. However, it can occur in anyone when they feel powerless. One avenue for diffusing her anger is to ask gently if she wants help in determining something <u>she</u> can do, instead of focusing on what she <u>cannot</u> do. This might be refused at the moment of her ire but might be accepted later.

Sometimes she might need you to empathize with her feelings first. She might need to take the perspective that she is a combatant in the war of life and that the enemy will win some of the battles, as opposed to being a helpless victim who <u>always</u> gets trampled on. You might help her strategize how she could set better boundaries, how she could take different actions or change her environment. If your wife feels like a victim, she might resort to anger to express herself. Not engaging in the victim mentality often means she can respond with competitive determination instead of anger. As my grandmother used to say, "Before you get walked on, first you have to lie down on the floor". She meant that we are always participants in situations that leave us feeling like victims, and we can make other choices, even if they are scary or risky. Empathize first, but then don't agree with the victim mindset! Help her figure out how to stand back up and offer your help in fighting the war.

7. LEARN TO AVOID USING OR ANSWERING QUESTIONS THAT ARE ACTUALLY SCOLDINGS.

It will be important for you to avoid questioning unless you can make sure she will not receive it as an attack. Many times we use phrases that sound like questions but are not requesting an answer and are, in fact, scoldings. This includes phrases like "What were you thinking?" or "How could you do that?" or "Didn't you know that if you asked me to stop at the grocery store on my way home from work, I might bump into one of our neighbors and get caught up in a long story about how their vacation at the nudist colony went, and then end up getting home two hours later than usual?"). The primary difference between a question that seeks information and one that is a scolding is often just the tone of voice in which the question is delivered.

These kinds of questions, if they are received as attacks, will escalate her anger rather than help defuse it. If you can use phrases that highlight your request for understanding (perhaps as simple as "Please, help me understand this. What...?"), they will be less likely to be taken as attacks (or worse, as counter-attacks). Questions that are really scoldings only make an angry wife feel blamed and guilty, feelings that result from a perceived attack. Your angry wife will likely feel more attacked, and this will dispose her to defend herself or attack back. That leads to more adrenaline and thus more anger.

It's also important to be aware of these types of questions coming from your angry wife herself. These might sound like, "Haven't I told you not to leave your clothes in the drier too long?" or "How could you let us run out of gas?" Do not try to answer them. Responding to these "questions" by empathizing with her feelings ("It sounds like you're angry") is a much better bet. If she is angry because of something that <u>was</u> your responsibility, own up to your behavior. For instance, if you promised to get more paper towels on the way home from work and you forgot, then admitting your mistake might lessen her anger. "Yes, I did promise and I did forget. I apologize for my part in this. I'll get the paper towels after dinner." You <u>are</u> responsible for your actions, just not for her feelings about them. If she responds with, "No, I need them right now!" you can always respond by setting a boundary like HAL 9000 did: "I'm sorry Dave, I'm afraid I can't do that." Be sure to get the tone of voice correct.

8. AVOID USING "SHOULD" STATEMENTS YOURSELF, AND LEARN TO REFUTE THEM WHEN THEY COME FROM OTHERS.

One specific version of the scoldings mentioned above is the "should statement," a statement that sounds like "You should know that...". These are statements designed to shift the responsibility for your wife's feelings from her to you. For example, she might try to shift her feelings of frustration at not being more explicit onto you by blaming. This might sound like, "You should know that when I say 'please clear the table after dinner,' I really mean put away the food, put the dishes in the dishwasher, wipe down the counters, take out the trash, put on the coffee machine, and let the dog out to pee." But you cannot control another person's feelings, and therefore you cannot have responsibility for them. These statements use a form of cognitive distortion (called "should statements") which implies that your value system is not sufficient, that another value system imported from somewhere else is better. These distortions are often automatic and unless they are observed and refuted, they are likely to cause depression or frustration.

When the statements are ones like "You should pay better attention to me" or "You should learn how to dance better like Marci's husband" or "You have to throw out that old college jacket!" the depression might be yours and not hers. This applies to "should," "have to," "ought to," "must," and even the past tense "should have." Each needs to be refuted by stating something like "There is no 'should' here, it's that you want me to." As Albert Ellis (the founding father of cognitive psychology) might have said, don't let anyone else "should" all over you.

A version of this is the statement that starts with "You need to...." This mostly means, "I need you to...." After all, whose need is it anyway? "You need to pee before we go on our long drive." How do you know I need to pee? You might have a need for me to pee. "You need to wash your hands better than that." Nope, that's not my need. That really means "I need you to wash your hands better than that." Pay attention to whose need it actually is.

9. USE THE "BROKEN RECORD" TECHNIQUE IF YOU NEED TO ASSERT YOURSELF.

If you manage all of these steps and are still maintaining a level head, it's possible that your angry wife will have run out of strategies for directing her anger at you. Although unlikely, there have been instances when, in the midst of a rage outburst, a burst of silence has occurred. At that point, she may try to leave, fulfilling the second part of the "fight or flight" scenario. Let her go but remind her that when she returns, she will need to discuss the situation and deal with it. If she leaves without that reminder, you can always GENTLY ask her later, after the storm, if she is ready to discuss what happened. Don't just ignore it hoping that it will go away because it will more than likely go into her file of minor offenses she carries for life. She may still ask you to give in to something she wants and you object to, or try to blame you for her distress. If you've already tried to negotiate this impasse with her, and she still wants you to give in unilaterally, don't be afraid to use the "broken record" technique of self-assertiveness. Give her your bottom line and refuse to be manipulated by repeating your bottom line whenever she has an argument or counterproposal. It might sound like this:

Her: "You should let my brother and his family stay here when they come to visit again."

You: "You know that you and I talked about this after last time they visited. They made so many demands on us to accommodate them that our lives were turned upside down for two months. We had to leave our old place, change our names and get new bank accounts after that last visit. We agreed then they wouldn't stay in our place again. I understand that you're in a tough situation, but we agreed they can't stay here."

Her: "But you know I've had a hard time with my brother! You're not listening to how hard this is for me. I need you to give in this time!"

You: "I know it makes you frustrated to be in a this situation and how important your family is to you, but we agreed that they can't stay here."

Her: "Obviously you don't care how I feel!"

You: "I do care. But we agreed that they can't stay here."

Notice that there is no use in accusing her of manipulation, something that would undermine your effort. Use the broken record technique if you need to assert yourself but use the other techniques first (like empathizing with her feelings) so you aren't stonewalling her.

10. BREATHING HELPS YOU SLOW THINGS DOWN.

Slowing down the situation is the key to everything. When your wife is angry, she is likely to be less logical than normal, and her emotions are in control; slowing things down will allow the emotions to play a lesser role in the outcome. Slowing down reduces the feelings of urgency that can contribute to her anger and frustration, reducing the apparent threat of the situation. An attorney friend once gave me some advice prior to my appearing in court as a witness: before answering any question from the opposing attorney, take a five-second breath. This action, when repeated with each question, slows down the tempo of the interaction. This is equivalent to a basketball team slowing down the tempo of a game, to deny a "run and gun" offense the opportunity to get the upper hand. Slow things down, take a breath before each response you give, and give yourself (and your wife) time to think instead of just time to react. As Mark Twain said, "When angry, count four. When very angry, swear."

What about humor? This is a double-edged sword. If she can look at the situation with humor then you can join in. But it's best to beware of using your own humor in a situation when your wife is angry, at either you or someone else. The most likely outcome of your attempt is that she will think you are laughing at her, or making fun of her emotions or her situation. She will perceive this as either criticism towards her or belittling of her emotions. In either case it is more likely to result in a counter-attack than in a laughing wife. How many times has this happened to you? You come home from work drunk and three hours late, with the new best friend you just met in the bar (who is an unshaven, equally drunk foreign exchange student smelling of youthful indiscretions, complete with backpack, bedroll and Disneyland maps of the USA) and your wife starts out angrily with "Did you remember that you were supposed to pick up your daughter at school several hours ago!?" without even asking your friend's name first. You try out the humor approach with "Hey babe, it wasn't our primary daughter, right? It was just the auxiliary daughter. OK just don't worry about her for a minute. Let me tell you this great joke that Zoltan and I just made up. Two men and a backpack walk out of a bar..." and she cuts you off in a rage, tossing your friend, his backpack and your dinner out onto the front lawn. See what I mean? The humor approach doesn't work very well. Seriously.

Lessons

1. Seek first to understand.
2. Never, ever defend yourself.
3. All communications are about the speaker.
4. Try empathizing with her feelings instead of refuting her perceptions.
5. When the anger is about someone else, stay in the audience of this emotional performance.

6. Beware of the victim mentality, and offer to help empower the sufferer.

7. Learn to avoid using or answering questions that are actually scoldings.

8. Avoid using "should" statements yourself and learn to refute them when they come from others.

9. Use the "broken record" technique if you need to assert yourself.

10. Breathing helps you slow things down.

11. Be especially careful of using humor with an angry wife.

Example Problem: "During our last three-day weekend I made arrangements to go on a daylong hike with three of my best buddies from college. When I told my wife about it, she got angry at me. She told me I was thoughtless and insensitive and that I must not care about her feelings because she wanted to spend the weekend together. I tried to tell her why she shouldn't feel that way and that I wasn't doing anything other guys didn't do. I even suggested to her that she come with us, but that didn't seem to help. How should I have handled this?"

Ed always thought he was a good husband. He always came home from work on time, helped out around the house, and made sure he remembered both his anniversary and his wife's birthday. When the opportunity came to spend a day with friends he hadn't seen in years, he jumped at the chance. When he told his wife about the new plan, he was completely taken aback by her response. Of course buddies from college are important, and so is exercise, so why wouldn't she be in favor of the hike? Well, it might be that he did something which, if a woman did it, would signify that she didn't care about a friend. Ed made plans for a significant weekend that included neither her nor her input. She got angry because her feelings were hurt. Now, what could he do about it?

First, Ed might ask her what he did that upset her and then make sure he understands <u>why</u> that was upsetting. He shouldn't just try to read her mind but rather ask something like, "What about this situation upset you?" When she tells him she's upset, he could listen to the part of her content about her feelings; she is trying to communicate something about them to him. He could avoid turning it into something about himself by trying to defend himself (the argument that "all the other kids do it" should stay in middle school). Ed could try empathizing with her feelings sincerely by saying something like, "If I wanted to spend time with you and you made plans that didn't include me, I might be hurt too." He should not tell her how she should or shouldn't feel because there is no "should" about feelings (except this "should," of course). Asking her to join them after the fact was probably a non-starter. After all, why on earth would she want to spend the day with you and your smelly buddies working up a sweat and stinking in the sun? (that was a scolding, not a real question - don't answer it). If Ed wanted to plan a hike with his buddies, he could have asked her in advance when a good day to do that might be so she was included in his planning process. Remember she's your life partner, not your mother.

20 - What if I learn best by counter-example? (or

How to be a jerk)

[This chapter is a tongue-in-cheek counter-example to the basic theme of this book. If you really want to keep your wife, do none of the things in this chapter. On the other hand, if you want to get her to leave you, here are some suggestions.]

How to be an insensitive pig (and really irritate your woman)

If you're like most men, you already know that you have the potential to be insensitive to the women in your life. You've been told that you were being insensitive at times in your life, and more than likely, you were surprised to hear it. You had no idea beforehand that what you were doing or saying would be perceived that way. You likely still didn't "get it" after it was explained by the woman in question. Then how can men start out with the best of intentions and end up being "jerks?" Is it just a gift? Is there something in our nature that leads men to do and say insensitive things at the least opportune moment?

It probably isn't either of those. Men do what comes naturally to them, and women perceive men as insensitive based on those automatic behaviors.

Sometimes this situation results from women having expectations that their men will act the way women do. This is not because women intentionally misunderstand men, nor is it because they intend to hurt or disrespect men on purpose. Women want to be happy and to be loved and cherished by the men in their lives. Many women do not understand that their incorrect assumptions about men lead to their own disappointments. Because of this there are many situations, which if applied correctly, will lead you to becoming her Porcine Prince.

This chapter is for those of you who have irritated your women in the past without knowing quite what you were doing. If you follow the following suggestions you'll find a clear and concise path to irritating her. This is based on some gross over-generalizations about men and women. Not all men are the same, nor are all women the same, but these generalizations help to make a point. There are also some things listed at the end of each point to avoid, because those will backfire and lead you instead to pleasing her and convincing her you are, in fact, a gentleman.

1. Forget an event important to her (like her birthday) and then tell her she shouldn't make a fuss about it

The most effective way to remember your wife's birthday is to forget it once.

Women do many things because of how those things make them feel. In particular they desire to feel happy, special and loved. When an event is important to a woman, it's often because that event makes her feel a desirable way. This is so common among women that another woman would understand not only <u>that</u> it makes her feel a certain way, but also <u>why</u> it does.

<u>To really irritate her</u>

As a man, you may not understand why an event makes her feel the way it does. You may however, be able to accept that an event like her birthday might make her feel special, appreciated and unique. Forgetting an event like

236

this one results in the opposite. Actually it results in nearly the opposite situation. Forgetting her birthday will not make her feel less special, but rather it will make her feel you think she is less special. Since any other woman would know this basic fact, she will likely assume that you should know it too. The conclusion she comes to then will be that you forgot her birthday because you don't care. But what does this mean? To a man, "not caring" means "without an opinion or an investment." To a woman, "not caring" means something much more negative. "Not caring" must mean you view her badly, for example, you dislike her, you find her boring and irrelevant, or that she is worthy only of your contempt. This is why having her think that you don't care about her is so devastating to women.

The second part of the "one-two punch" in this example is then to suggest that she is overreacting. Your woman was likely reacting this way because she felt hurt. To her, her reaction is in measure equal to her degree of hurt. Telling her she is overreacting would diminish the importance of her feelings. Now, not only will she believe that she is not important to you, but also that her feelings are unimportant to you. In one fell swoop, you have minimized all she is. Of course, you have become a jerk in the process.

(Make sure you don't do these things because they will actually please her)

Don't go out of your way to learn what dates, events and situations are especially important to her. When you do forget something important (as you inevitably will), don't apologize for it. Don't acknowledge that she has the right to feel whatever way she feels in the present.

2. Belittle her independent activities

Two women friends had gone out for a Girls Night Out and had been decidedly over-enthusiastic on the cocktails. Incredibly drunk, while walking home they realized they both needed to pee.

Being very near a graveyard and one of them suggested they do their business behind a headstone or something. The first woman had nothing to wipe with so she took off her panties, used them and threw them away. Her friend however was wearing an expensive underwear set and didn't want to ruin hers, but was lucky enough to salvage a large ribbon from a wreath on a grave and proceeded to wipe herself with it.

After finishing, they made their way home.

The next day the first woman's husband phones the other husband and said, "These damn girls nights out have got to stop. My wife came home last night without her panties."

"That's nothing," said the other. "Mine came back with a sympathy card stuck between

the cheeks of her butt that said, 'From all of us at the Fire Station, We'll never forget you!'"

Although women prefer being interdependent to being independent, they have a much greater social sphere of influence than do men. This often translates into women having many activities with many friends. This high social conductivity provides many things for women, among them a sense of safety in numbers. The more connected a woman feels, the safer she feels; if one relationship or "lifeline" sours, she still has others to support her. This is one of the many ways that women increase their own sense of safety.

Another way that women facilitate their own sense of safety is to achieve competence in things like providing for themselves, using tools and navigating the environment of goods and services. This is similar to what men do to seek competence. However while men achieve competence both for its own sake and to increase status, women pursue competence to ensure safety (especially in the event that there is no man in her life). Thus, a woman's activities independent of you and outside the home are very important to her sense of safety.

<u>To really irritate her</u>

Remind her that her place is in the home, not out with friends. Tell her that as long as she has you, she shouldn't need lots of outside friends. Remind her that her satisfaction should come from being in the home and raising the family. Show her the "right" way to use a tool and then scold her for not putting it away properly. Remind her you are better at everything than she is and let her know that her efforts are "cute" or "amusing."

(Make sure you don't do these things because they will actually please her).

Don't show interest in her day. Don't ask about her interactions with family or friends and certainly don't wait for her to give you a complete accounting of her thoughts and feelings. Don't encourage her to try things on her own, like classes or new activities. Do not encourage her to do anything "unsupervised" like a girls-only weekend or a mother-daughter road trip.

3. Get mad at her when she doesn't take your advice

My husband said he wanted more space. So I locked him outside.

Women like to collect opinions when they are evaluating something or when they are trying to make a decision. To many women, gathering opinions is like taking a poll. This is different from the way many men understand opinion as men treat "opinion" as identical to "advice." When a woman asks your opinion about something, like "What do you think about this dress?", she is likely comparing your feedback to the chorus of options in her head. She will see this opinion as one of many to consider. She might also hope you will validate an opinion she already holds. The trouble may come when she asks about taking action (for instance, "what do you think I should do about my mother?"). To a man, this might sound like asking for advice. To a woman, however, this may simply be asking for an opinion. The key word here might be "think." If she asks you questions like "do you think...?" or "what do you think...?", these are likely to be requests for an opinion. The only way that you can know she is asking for advice is if she says, "I need your advice about something." Even then, she might well treat your advice as if it were an opinion.

To really irritate her

If you want to frustrate and irritate your gal, you first need to treat all

239

of her requests as if they were requests for advice. Then you need to believe that your advice is the only reasonable thing to do. When she makes a different choice, show your irritation for not following your advice to her. Include phrases like "why do you even bother to ask me?" or "does my opinion even matter at all to you?" Then, as the coup de grace, you might include "don't even bother to ask me next time". She will walk away wondering what she did to upset you, why you're not being helpful to her, and how you could possibly mistake opinion for advice.

(Make sure you don't do these things because they will actually please her)

As she might be looking for validation for a pre-existing opinion of her own, be sure you don't ask her what she is already thinking about the matter. Don't let her know that you don't have to be invested in her decision by saying something like, "This is what I think, but you can make up your own mind."

4. Forget to touch her during the day

How can you tell that soap operas are fictional?
Because in real life, men aren't affectionate out of bed.

Women thrive on connectedness. It's one way they know that they are safe, that they are loved and that they are integrated into the system. Physical touch is a large part of that connectedness, at least for personal or intimate relationships. If she reaches out to touch you during the day by holding your hand, rubbing your shoulders or kissing your cheek, this is her way of telling you she wants to feel connected to you. She is hoping to receive something similar back from you, which will validate her connectedness.

To really irritate her

Not touching her during the day sends a powerful message. Even though you may express your independence by keeping physically to yourself,

240

she will receive this message as one of disconnectedness and disinterest. This might only make her sad or withdrawn unless she has already reached out to touch you and found it not reciprocated (in which case this approach is much more likely to leave her irritated). You don't even need to touch her at all. You just need to know that she is there and she respects you. What is she making all this fuss about anyway?

(Make sure you don't do these things because they will actually please her).

Don't go out to your way to touch her regularly. Don't grab her hand, don't put your arm around her waist for no apparent reason, and don't stroke her hair. Above all, never offer pampering that includes touching, like shoulder massages or foot rubs.

5. Never compliment her outfit

A man told his friend: "My wife only has two complaints: nothing to wear and not enough closet space."

Most women have a voice inside their heads constantly telling them they are not good enough unless they're perfect. This applies to everything about them, but particularly it applies to how they look. Because of that, most women desire validation for their appearance. They hear the lack of validation (meaning no feedback on their appearance at all) as tacitly agreeing with their internal voice. Here, no feedback is as bad as negative feedback.

To really irritate her

Being a jerk in this realm doesn't take much effort at all. In fact, that's exactly what it requires: making no effort at all. Don't notice, attend to or comment on her appearance in any way. Don't give her feedback about her outfit, shoes or jewelry. If she asks you for feedback in a general sense, tell her you just didn't notice. If she asks you for feedback in a specific way, like

"Should I wear these shoes or those shoes?" tell her it just doesn't matter. If she asks you for an overall opinion, as in "Do you like my outfit?" you can always reply with "Sure, it's fine". The voice inside her head will scream out loud, reminding her, "See? No matter what you do, it's not good enough."

<u>(Make sure you don't do these things because they will actually please her)</u>

Make sure you don't accidentally pay her a compliment as she's getting ready. Don't get caught in the trap of choosing something for her. Don't tell her "you look very nice", "all your effort was worth it" or "I like what you did with your hair". Above all, never complement her shoes. They are so far out of the man's normal visual field that, if you notice them, a woman would be convinced that you are paying attention to her.

6. Complain about how long she takes to get ready for an event

The gentleman is standing at the bottom of the stairs, dressed up in his tuxedo, looking at his watch and waiting. And waiting. Finally his wife's voice from upstairs announces, "I'm ready" "Never mind," he replies. "I have to shave again anyway."

The Born Loser

This one is related to the item above. Women often spend more time getting ready to go somewhere than men do, in part because of how important it is to them to look a certain way when they are out in public. When camping, my aunt waited for my uncle to bring her a bowl of hot water in the morning. She didn't want to leave the tent until her face was washed and her hair and makeup were done. It took as long as it took. Your wife might tell you she takes this much time because she wants to look nice for you. This means she wants to be attractive enough that you will notice, compliment her, and refute the voice in her head telling her she isn't good enough.

<u>To really irritate her</u>

Remind her as she's getting ready that she's taking too long. Occasionally re-enter the room where she is getting ready, each time saying, "we'll be late!" Ask her if she can do her makeup in the car. Remind her how little time you take to get ready. Borrowing a line from the old Born Loser comic strip, when she finally is ready, you can tell her you have to shave again anyway.

(Make sure you don't do these things because they will actually please her).

Don't tell her to take all the time she needs to feel satisfied with her appearance. Don't remind her you always like the way she looks. Don't ask her if she wants your input on picking out an outfit or accessories. If she says no, don't go occupy yourself with something interesting enough so you don't notice the passage of time. Don't then tell her how wonderful she looks when she announces she is done.

7. Tell her that she should already know that you love her

A man was invited for dinner at a friend's house. Every time the host needed something, he preceded his request to his wife by calling her "My Love," "Darling," "Sweetheart," etc.

His friend looked at him and said, "That's really nice after all of these years you've been married to keep saying those little pet names."

The host said, "Well, honestly, I've forgotten her name."

In reality, she knows you love her. However, she really needs to hear it all the time. That voice in her head tells her regularly she is not good enough and certainly not lovable if she isn't good enough. Remember, this communication is not just about relaying information to her. Instead, it's her daily rebuttal to that self-critical inner voice. Even though men show their love with actions and by providing, those nonverbal messages will not carry the same weight for woman as the verbal ones she craves.

<u>To really irritate her</u>

When she asks the inevitable question, "do you love me?", reply with a very lukewarm "sure". When she asks, remind her of all the things you do for her. Answer her questions with "I shouldn't have to tell you this all the time." Ask her "how many times do I have to tell you this?"

<u>(Make sure you don't do these things because they will actually please her)</u>.

Don't volunteer those three little words regularly. Don't occasionally embellish that by adding "I love you because...." Don't recognize that, when she's asking, "do you love me?" she's feeling a little insecure; answer with sincerity and enthusiasm.

8. Put work obligations ahead of family ones

A doctor, a lawyer and a manager were discussing the relative merits of having a wife or a mistress. The lawyer says: "For sure a mistress is better. If you have a wife and want a divorce, it causes all sorts of legal problems."

The doctor says: "It's better to have a wife because the sense of security lowers your stress and is good for your health."

The manager says: "You're both wrong. It's best to have both so that when the wife thinks you're with the mistress and the mistress thinks you're with your wife - you can go to the office and do some work."

Most men know how important a work obligation is to them. If the boss asked you to stay late and finish a project, you would never dream of disappointing him. After all, it's your job, right? You would never dream of saying "I just won't go into work today; I don't feel like it". Your productivity defines you. Women feel just as strongly about family. The time you spend at home tells her how important the family is to you. It especially tells her how important she is to you.

Balancing work and family is difficult for most men. Taking care of work not only lets you feel accomplished, it's how you provide for your family. It's relatively easy for men to get overbalanced toward work at the expense of family time. This is something that a woman will notice and misinterpret.

<u>To really irritate her</u>

This one might seem like shooting ducks in a barrel because it's so obvious. Just stay at work late. Ask her to hold dinner for you, or better yet, to separate out a plateful for you and put it in the refrigerator. To really be a jerk, do this on evenings of special importance (like the kids birthdays, or your anniversary), or work on the weekends. You can even consider bringing work home with you to do in the evenings. If she complains, remind her you're "doing this for the good of the family."

<u>(Make sure you don't do these things because they will actually please her)</u>

Don't try to come home at a regular time. Don't give her your schedule for the week ahead of time. Don't set aside special time in the evenings or weekends just for family. Don't delay a work obligation just because a family event came up.

9. Insist on having the house decorated in a functional way

While attending a marriage seminar dealing with communication, Tom and his wife Grace listened to the instructor, "It is essential that husbands and wives know the things important to each other."

He addressed the man. "Can you describe your wife's favorite flower?"

Tom leaned over, touched his wife's arm gently and whispered, "It's self-rising, isn't it?"

The rest of the story gets rather ugly, so I'll stop right here.

Men appoint their houses with functionality in mind. That's why the typical bachelor pad will have something to sit on, something to put one's drink and dinner on, a stand for the television and perhaps an extra chair in the living room. Since items like art, throw rugs, sofa pillows, pictures in frames or small articles for shelves have little function, men see little value in them. In fact, extra items of "decor" might simply end up feeling like clutter to a man. They might get in the way; if an art book or knickknack is on the coffee table when a man wants to put his dinner down there, that extra item might end up on the floor or in a drawer someplace.

Women look at their environment differently from the way men do. Women have a "diffuse awareness" of their environment and are often as engaged with their environment as men are with the problem be solved. She will want the environment to be appointed and decorated so it makes her feel a certain way, either at peace, happy, safe or relaxed. All of her senses will be involved in this, not just her visual sense. Candles to make the area smell a certain way, textures to make it feel just right, and even music to engage her hearing sense will be important to the overall environment. These items, collectively referred to as "a woman's touch," are often beyond the man's senses and are therefore sometimes treated as superfluous.

To really irritate her

To really frustrate your woman, let her know that you don't approve of items in the home that don't have functional value. When she brings home something new, ask her questions like "why do we need that?" and "what does it do for us?" In particular, when she wants to replace the sofa, the bed linen or any other sundry items around the house you already have, remind her that the ones you have "are good enough; they still work." Never, ever let her touch the Lazy Boy chair you still have from college.

(Make sure you don't do these things because they will actually please her)

Don't encourage her to decorate the place based on how she feels. Don't pay attention to the changes in her mood when she brings home an item for the house she likes. Don't try to understand that her appreciation for the environment differs from yours and that the way it makes her feel is very important to her. Above all, don't bother recognizing that if she's happy in her environment your life will be better too.

10. Look at other women when you're out with her

A man approached a very beautiful woman in the large supermarket and said, "I've lost my wife here in the supermarket. Can you talk to me for a couple of minutes?"

The woman looked puzzled. "Why do you want to talk to me?" she asked.

"Because every time I talk to a beautiful woman like you, my wife appears out of nowhere."

A woman loves to feel she is special to the man in her life. The last thing she wants is to feel is that she is just one more woman amid a sea of women in her man's world. A woman competes with other women in the way she dresses, the way she presents herself, and in terms of her social connectedness. The little voice inside every woman's head is continuously telling her she's not good enough unless she's perfect, and she looks to her man (among other places) for validation in this arena. While feeling not good enough is terrible for women, one step worse is to be not as good as another woman. This would indicate that the other woman has achieved what she herself could not.

To really irritate her

When you go out with her, turn your head when another woman passes. If it's an especially attractive woman, take a good long look. Stop whatever you're doing while you look. Whisper the word "wow!" under your breath but loud enough to be heard.

(Make sure you don't do these things because they will actually please her).

247

Don't let her know that she's the only one you have eyes for. Don't look back at your wife instead of noticing another woman. Don't wait for her to remark about the appeal of that other woman. Don't remind her of how beautiful you think she is when you're out together in public.

11. Refuse to state the "obvious"

"Things are more like they are now than they have ever been."
Attributed to Dwight D. Eisenhower, U.S. President

Because men are conservative by nature, they conserve energy and effort. Thus, when something is "obvious" to them, they save time and effort by not stating it or talking about it. However, that same thing might not be obvious to his wife. If she asks for an explanation, it's likely that something wasn't "obvious" to her. Likewise, if she asks a question he thinks is trivial, it might be because what was "obvious" to him was not to her. Women go to great lengths to explain things, often because they don't want to assume that anything is "obvious."

<u>To really irritate her</u>

When you're in a conversation for which she has questions, don't state the "obvious." When she asks a question you think is trivial, tell her "that's obvious; I shouldn't have to say it." Remind her "you should know that already; it's obvious."

<u>(Make sure you don't do these things because they will actually please her)</u>

Don't be patient with her when you're explaining details in a conversation. Don't take her questions about trivial things as her wanting to be sure of her connection with you. Don't tell her you're happy she asks questions because it reminds you she respects your opinion.

12. Tell her to "get to the point" when she's trying to talk with you

I had some words with my wife and she had some paragraphs with me.
Bill Clinton, U.S. President

Women use speech differently from the way men do. Women use words to express feelings and emotions as a form of connecting with another person. This is particularly true when women are speaking with other women. Men use talking as a way of exchanging information, building social status, enhancing productivity or enhancing competition. From a particular point of view, women use language the way men use sport. To a man, it may not matter much what sport he is engaged in as long as he is enjoying himself and competing successfully. To women, the subject of the dialogue may not matter as much as the fact that the dialogue is occurring and is creating a bond. The difficulty often comes when men and women converse with one another. A woman may try to use the language of a story to connect with a man and he may instead try to listen for the relevant information.

To really irritate her

One way to irritate your woman is to keep her from feeling connected when this is what she is attempting to do. If a man requests a briefer communication from a woman, she might hear that as him requesting less of a connection. To do this, just complain that she "beats around the bush." Tell her to "get to the point" when she's telling you a story. Remind her she "takes forever to get to the relevant information" and that you "don't want to waste your time listening to unimportant stuff."

(Make sure you don't do these things because they will actually please her)

Don't sit and wait patiently while she tells you a story. Don't remind yourself silently that the act of telling is how she feels connected to you. Don't carve out time from your day to listen to her. And don't encourage her to "go on, take your time" when she appears to be rushing for your sake.

13. Do something else when she's trying to talk with you

"Cash, check or charge?" I asked after folding items the woman wished to purchase. As she fumbled for her wallet I noticed a remote control for a television set in her purse.

"So, do you always carry your TV remote?" I asked.

"No," she replied, "but my husband refused to stop watching TV while I was telling him where I was going, so I figured this was the most evil legal thing I could do to him."

Remember, when she's talking to you she's trying to connect to you, on many levels. Especially in a new relationship, she'll need your eye contact, facial expressions and other "active listening" responses to judge how connected to you she really is. If you are doing something else at the same time she'll feel much less connected. Women are quite aware that men have a much harder time multitasking than do women; when men focus on one activity, they shut out other outside influences. A woman will know he really isn't listening to her even if a man insists that he is listening while he has the game on TV. From her perspective, that means she is not really connected to him. In later stages of a relationship, after connection has been established, it might be possible for a man to do other activities while listening. Even so these will have to be limited to routine tasks that take little attention (like washing the dishes or gardening).

<u>To really irritate her</u>

Tell her you want to listen to her but you want to watch the game at the same time. Insist that you can do this, let her start telling you a story during the action, then during a break turn to her and ask, "What did you just say?" Then reassert that you actually heard her, but you were just asking for clarification. Or ask her to speak only during commercials and timeouts.

<u>(Make sure you don't do these things because they will actually please her)</u>

Don't give her your full attention when she's trying to connect you. Don't suggest that you go into a different room, free of distractions, so you can attend more fully. Again, this is how she knows that she is connected to you so don't give her the opportunity to feel that.

14. Get defensive (e.g., defend yourself) when she's trying to tell you why she's unhappy

Sometimes women are overly suspicious of their husbands. When Adam stayed out very late for a few nights, Eve became upset.

"I think you're running around with other women," she charged.

"You're being unreasonable," Adam responded. "You're the only woman on earth." *The quarrel continued until Adam fell asleep, only to be awakened by someone poking him in the chest. It was Eve.*

"What do you think you're doing?" Adam demanded.

"Counting your ribs!"

Men in long-term relationships often believe that it's their job to make their female partners happy. Because of the nagging voice inside their heads telling them they are never good enough unless they're perfect, most women would rarely call themselves happy. Part of the way women connect is to relate their feelings with each other. For men, feelings are often experienced like one experiences climate, stable over long periods of time. For women, however, feelings are experienced more like the weather: incidental and changing moment to moment. When a woman expresses her feelings to another woman, she is often expressing how she feels at that moment. When she expresses she is unhappy, it may be momentary or situational, and it might be about a thought she had, an event that just occurred, or even a feeling that came over her. When a man hears that a woman is unhappy, he may feel he is not doing his job in keeping her happy. To rescue himself from that ignominy, he may defend himself, refute the importance of the situation that caused her unhappiness, or even attack her for being sensitive and vulnerable. Some women will interpret this as a man taking her comments and making them about himself, rather than him understanding she was sharing something intimate about herself.

To really irritate her

When she complains to you about being unhappy, respond with "it's not my fault!" before you understand what the communication is about. Tell her that she "shouldn't get so upset about little things." Remind her that she's never happy and should go see a therapist.

(Make sure you don't do these things because they will actually please her)

Don't remind yourself that her commentary about being unhappy is about her, not about you. Don't resist the urge to take things personally. Don't listen with empathy as she shares intimate details about her emotions. Don't recognize this as a very important form of connectivity for her. Don't ask her for more details about her feelings while keeping an open mind.

15. Tell her "but it's not full yet" when she asks you to take out the trash

Q: What do you call an intelligent, good-looking, sensitive man who takes out the trash?

A: A rumor

Men's linear focus on the task at hand allows them to ignore much of their environment, regardless of its state of disorganization. A man uses this trait to enhance productivity and to decrease his distractibility. With her diffuse awareness, a woman finds that her environment calls to her (sometimes even screams at her). He might leave a dish on the sink in the kitchen, believing that he might use it again before it needs to be washed. She will see the same dish and hear it demanding to be put away as it's out of place and the environment is disordered. This gets even worse for the trash. As common and trivial as it might sound to men, the trash has a loud environmental voice to women. Not only does it demand to be taken out but that demand starts when the first foreign item is placed into the trash. That demand to be emptied will not quit while there is trash in the can. A man laboring for a woman reminds her she is worthwhile and cared for (plus, as one woman told me, it saves her from "the ickies"). Thus, taking out the trash is an important gesture to women on many levels.

To really irritate her

To really bother her just refuse to take out the trash by telling her "But it's not full yet!" Tell her "I'll empty it when it's ready." Tell her "I just emptied it last week." Perhaps you can give in to her request, empty the trash and put in a new bag, then throw away a used tissue "just to break it in."

(Make sure you don't do these things because they will actually please her)

Don't show her she's worthwhile by toiling for her. Don't acknowledge that her perception of the environment differs greatly from yours. Don't acknowledge that her efforts at keeping the place tidy make it more livable for you too.

16. Forget to put the toilet seat down

A man takes the opportunity while his wife is away to paint the toilet seat. The wife comes home sooner than expected, sits, and gets the seat stuck to her rear. She is understandably distraught about this and asks her husband to drive her to the doctor. She puts on a large overcoat to cover the stuck seat and they go.

When they get to the doctor's, the man lifts his wife's coat to show their predicament. The man asks, "Doctor, have you ever seen anything like this before?"

"Well, yes," the doctor replies, "but not framed like that."

A case can be made for each person taking responsibility for his or her own activities in the bathroom. This is how boys grow up when sharing a household with their mothers and sisters. Each person must adjust the seat to his or her need as the last person to use the bathroom might have needed something different. As girls grow up, they also need to take responsibility for their bathroom activities. The big difference comes when young adults live alone. In the men's bathroom, the seat is up or down depending on how he intends to use it. In the woman's bathroom, the seat is always down regardless of her intent. Men should think of this gesture as a kindness rather than sticking to the belief that this is her responsibility. There's a small cost to a man of making a mistake by thinking the seat is up when it isn't. The result is simply a "sprinkle when you tinkle." The cost to a woman is much graver: a suddenly wet backside (or even just sitting down on the cold porcelain) would be a rude surprise for anyone.

To really irritate her

This one is easy: always leave the toilet seat up. After all, why should it be your responsibility alone? If she complains, remind her it's her job to check the toilet for herself. When she falls in (and she will), laugh at her and call her "silly." Remember to tease her about falling in at future public events.

Make sure you don't do these things because they will actually please her)

Don't try to put down the toilet seat after you're finished using the bathroom. Don't let her know you're trying to do this. Don't let her know she is important enough for you to make this simple accommodation.

17. Be passive-aggressive with her - say you'll do what she wants you to, and then "forget" to do it

One day at the rest home, an old man and woman are talking. Out of nowhere the woman says, "I can guess your age."

The man doesn't believe her, but tells her to go ahead and try.

"Pull down your pants," she says.

He doesn't understand but does it anyway. She inspects his rear end for a few

minutes and then says, "You're 84 years old."
     "That's amazing," the man says. "How did you know?"
     "You told me yesterday."

In the following advice we will be talking about "forgetting," not really forgetting as in the example above. Because women have a diffuse awareness of their environment, and because they notice things that are missing, women accumulate wished-for changes in their environment. To men, this is the dreaded "honey do" list (meaning, "honey, do this"). Because men are focused on the task at hand, it will seem that a request to do or change something always comes when he is in the middle of something else. To men, this kind of interruption can throw off their sense of purpose and interfere with task completion. These both create great frustration for men.

To really irritate her

To irritate your woman (in this case, that means getting back at her for interrupting you – remember, you're being passive-aggressive), tell her you'll take care of her request when you finish your task. Then continue on with a different task of your own choosing, ignoring hers. If she asks for you to do something while you are relaxing, come up with some creative excuse for not doing it right away. Put it off until you can convincingly claim you "forgot."

(Make sure you don't do these things because they will actually please her).

If you're relaxing don't agree to take care of her request right away. If you're busy with something else, don't schedule a time to accommodate her. Don't agree that her request is important or that you understand she needs your help.

18. Withdraw from her during periods of conflict

A man and his wife were having some problems at home and were giving each other the silent treatment.

Suddenly, the man realized that the next day, he would need his wife to wake him at 5:00 AM for an early morning business flight.

Not wanting to be the first to break the silence (and LOSE), he wrote on a piece of paper,

'Please wake me at 5:00 AM.' He left it where he knew she would find it.

The next morning, the man woke up, only to discover it was 9:00 AM and he had missed his flight. Furious, he was about to go and see why his wife hadn't wakened him, when he noticed a piece of paper by the bed.

The paper said, 'It is 5:00 AM. Wake up.'

Yes, this is another example of passive-aggressive behavior, and to some degree so is withdrawal. Because men grow up with an appreciation (and even a fondness) for competition, they view conflict as a normal part of interaction. Women dislike conflict, at least with people they care about. For them, conflict represents a severing of connectedness. Most women will try to avoid conflict with a loved one if they can. When it cannot be avoided, they will attempt to resolve the conflict (and restore connectedness) as quickly as possible. Withdrawing from your woman under conditions of conflict sends her the message you prefer being disconnected, or at least you do not desire to be reconnected.

To really irritate her

During states of conflict, women are likely to be irritated and frustrated; this may be true for both of you. To escalate that irritation, withdraw from her at the height of the conflict. Tell her that you need some time to "cool off." Overuse the rationale that you're going into your "man cave" and that you will let her know when you're ready to talk again. Then fall asleep in your "cave."

(Make sure you don't do these things because they will actually please her).

Don't tell her it's important to you as well to resolve this conflict. If you do need time to cool off, then at least don't agree to an appointed time at which you two will come together and discuss your resolution. Don't reinforce that being connected to her is important to you too, especially at this vulnerable moment.

Conclusion

Practicing even a few of these tips will forever cement your place in the annals of swine-dom. If your goal is to preserve the male way of life regardless of the impact, these will help. Perhaps you want to strike back at the "Feminazis" (to borrow a phrase from a particular conservative talk show host). Good luck brother - being a pig may come naturally for some, but don't let her see your gentlemanly underbelly. You'll blow your cover, and she will know you are a decent chap in the making!

Notes

1. Lehrer, Tom. "Bright College Days" on the live album "An Evening Wasted With Tom Lehrer", released 1959.

2. Henry Higgins in "My Fair Lady," Lerner and Lowe 1964.

3. Armstrong, A. and Prager, D. The Dennis Prager Show (audio recordings of radio shows, 2009-2012). Safety. The Dennis Prager Store: Tarzana, CA, 2009.

4. ibid, Happy.

5. Tannen, D. You Just Don't Understand: Women and men in conversation. William Morrow and Co: New York, NY, 1990, 74-78.

6. ibid, 76.

7. Hendrix, H. Getting The Love You Want: A guide for couples. Henry Holt and Co., New York, NY, 1988.

8. ibid, 34

9. ibid, 87.

10. Allen, PJ and Harmon, S. Getting To "I Do": The secret to doing relationships right! Avon Books: New York, NY, 1994, 26.

11. ibid, 79

12. Schwalbe, R. Sixty, Sexy and Successful: A guide for aging male baby boomers. Praeger Publishers: Westport CT, 2008, 84.

13. ibid, 125.

14. Gottman, JM and Silver, N. The Seven Principles For Making Marriage Work: A practice guide from the country's foremost relationship expert. Three Rivers Press: New York, NY, 1999.

15. ibid, 130.

16. ibid, 158.

17. ibid, 217.

18. ibid, 100.

19. ibid, 101.

20. ibid, 101.

21. Gray, J. Men Are From Mars, Women Are From Venus: A practical guide for improving communication and getting what you want in your relationship. HarperCollins, New York, NY, 1992, 160.

About The Author

Jim Hatton is an award-winning author, speaker and educator. After spending 13 years as a neuroscientist and 20 years as a marriage and family therapist, he now coaches couples aiming to optimize their relationships. He lives in San Diego with his awesome wife and their two Huskies. In his free time, Jim dabbles in astrophysics and writing science fiction. He hopes to complete his science fiction novel before the sun goes out. You can find him at www.SmartMenSmartWomen.com.